MILDENHALL

BOMBERS, BLACKBIRDS
AND THE BOOM YEARS

Ian Grimes

MILDENHALL

BOMBERS, BLACKBIRDS AND THE BOOM YEARS

MARTIN W. BOWMAN

TEMPUS

Frontispiece: An aerial view of RAF Mildenhall in September 1934. (*Flight*)

First published 2007

Tempus Publishing
Cirencester Road, Chalford,
Stroud, Gloucestershire, GL6 8PE
www.tempus-publishing.com

Tempus Publishing is an imprint of NPI Media Group

British Library Cataloguing in Publication Data.
A catalogue record for this book is available from the British Library.

ISBN 978 0 7524 4292 1

Typesetting and origination by NPI Media Group
Printed in Great Britain

Contents

	Acknowledgements	7
1	'This Way to the Aerodrome'	9
2	'Target for Tonight'	27
3	The 'Blackbirds' and the 'Boom Years'	101
4	The Mildenhall Heritage Trail	139
Appendix 1	RAF Units Stationed at Mildenhall	147
Appendix 2	Permanent US Flying Units at Mildenhall	148
Appendix 3	Rotational Units on Temporary Duty to Mildenhall	149
Appendix 4	USAF Host Units at Mildenhall	150
Appendix 5	US Units 11 July 1950 to Present	151
	Index	155

Acknowledgements

Derek Allen; Ashley Annis; BBMF; Theo Boiten; Bob Collis; Don Clarke MBE; Len Collins; Jim Coman; Fred Coney; Frank Dengate DFC; Frank Diamond DFC; the late Dr Colin Dring; Dan Engle; Dennis Gill; Trevor A. Hampton; Harry Holmes; Captain Jamie Humphries and the staff of the Public Affairs Office, 100th ARW, RAF Mildenhall; Nigel McTeer; Gary Parsons; H.S. Perdue; the late Eric Phillips; Lawrie Reid; Mike Rondot; Lord Sandhurst, The Right Honourable Terence Mansfield; Flight Lieutenant Andy Sell; Frank Tasker; Raymond W. Towler, Airfield Research Group; the late Tom Trower; Gary Wenko.

All pictures are from the author's collection unless otherwise credited.

CHAPTER 1
'This Way to the Aerodrome'

RAF Mildenhall, nineteen miles north-east of Cambridge, is today a massive air base deep in the heart of the Norfolk Breckland but in the years following the First World War there was little indication of what the future would hold. With the Armistice of 1918, the newly created Royal Air Force was the most powerful of its kind in the world. It totalled 22,000 aircraft, of which 3,300 equipped first-line squadrons in the UK and throughout the Empire, and boasted 291,000 officers and men. However, post-war parsimony and disarmament soon followed and by the end of 1919 the RAF's 188 operational squadrons had been reduced to just twelve, of which nine were in the Middle East and just two stationed in southern England to co-operate with Army and Navy units in the area. By March 1920, the RAF had expanded to twenty-five squadrons and by October 1924 it had strength of forty-three squadrons. Fighter stations sprung up around London and westwards from the capital while bomber stations were built in Oxfordshire. In the late 1920s the Government decided to establish an 'East Anglian Bombing Area' to train crews and mount attacks on shipping in the North Sea in the event of war. An inland site was considered much less likely to be bombed than a vulnerable coastal position, and in 1928 the choice narrowed to a site near Beck Row in the extensive Breckland area to the north-east of Mildenhall. For many years the Army had made use of the area for military training. As early as 1912 Army planes had acted as scouts during the annual autumn manoeuvres, and in that year two such planes landed in a field at Worlington where they were seen by John Lankester Parker, then a boy of sixteen. He had already expressed a wish to fly but these were the first aeroplanes that he had actually seen. He joined the Vickers Flying School soon after this encounter, qualified in 1914 and went on to become a test pilot for Short Brothers for nearly thirty years. During the First World War, a Royal Flying Corps aerodrome had operated nearby at Great Snare Hill, just south of Thetford. Aircraft from there used part of Lakenheath Warren, east of present-day RAF Lakenheath, as a bombing practice zone. The RFC was to deter German Zeppelin raids and one Zeppelin bombed a field at West Row, near to the present site of RAF Mildenhall, having probably mistaken the piles of weeds that were being burned in the field for the fires of an Army encampment. There was little flying activity in the district after the war but in October 1929 the decision to begin building an aerodrome at Beck Row to accommodate two twin-engined bomber squadrons was taken.

   Mildenhall was suffering the effects of the agricultural depression and a local writer welcomed the venture as being likely to provide some much-needed employment for a good number of men. Originally, four metal and wood 'Type A Aeroplane Sheds' were to be built. However, during the spring of 1930 plans were revised to include two 'Type A' Sheds, both of which remain and are used as supply warehouses, while provision was made for two of the larger 'Type C' Sheds to be erected. The 'Type A' design had a clear span of 120ft and a length of 250ft with doors at both ends. The doors accommodated an opening 120ft x 25ft high. The 'Type C' design had a span of 150ft x 300ft long and entry/exit doors at each end. Work on the new aerodrome, officially named Beck Row, began in October 1930 when the firm of Fred Hale and Sons of Sutton, Ely, began to construct the first building, a large office for the resident engineer and his staff. The Ministry of Transport laid down concrete roads and in 1931 a London-based building firm took over the main contract. A service road divided the technical site from the living quarters. Entry to the aerodrome was sited where the road from Beck Row swung towards West Row. A 1928-style 'Type G Guard Room' was built facing the

1928-pattern 'Offices and Operations Block' which became the pre-war station headquarters. To the south, on a rectangular area, four of the metal and wood 'Type A Aeroplane Sheds' were erected. North of the public road, the domestic site included, from west to east, the Airmen's Married Quarters, the Barrack Square, four Barrack Blocks, a combined 'Cookhouse and Institute', the Officers' Mess and their Married Quarters. Red bricks for the buildings came from the Midlands and the roofing was of slate. The first phase of construction lasted three years and most of the buildings of this period are still in existence.

The most distinguished building was the Officers' Mess, construction of which started in 1931. Very little has been altered externally and entry still leads into a fine wood-panelled hall. Many local men were employed on the construction works, often as many as 100, some cycling over from Isleham and Soham, could be seen waiting in the road opposite the contractor's office hoping to be given the chance to work. The firm of Redpath Brown, which brought its own specialist workers from Newcastle, erected the steelwork for the hangars. These incomers were regarded as a tough bunch and there was a certain amount of trouble in the village pubs until the locals won the day. Peace then reigned and several of the newcomers later played football for the village teams. The Beck Row team had to move to a new pitch, as the Officers' Mess had been built on its previous pitch. The roof timbers for these first hangars were manhandled into position without the aid of cranes and men working on the roof were paid an extra 2d (1p) an hour. The airfield when finished had three grass runways, the longest being the NE–SW runway at 1,300 yards. During 1933 the station was renamed Mildenhall, although the change was not made official until 1934. Further additions to the layout included a 30,000-gallon, high-level, circular water tower of 1932 design – twin, rectangular water tanks supported by scaffolding were erected in 1940. Increased funding led to discussions about building four 'Type A' hangars but ultimately a decision was taken to retain the two and add three early design 'Type C' steel and brick hangars – in 1940 three 'Type C' hangars were built. The area then covered by the station was much less than today and the perimeter on the Mildenhall side ran from opposite the King's Head in Beck Row across to the West Row side of Mons Wood.

The first aircraft that is known to have landed at Mildenhall touched down at about 11 a.m. on 19 March 1931 and stayed for only a few minutes before taking off again. Another aircraft had been expected the previous month but the visit had been postponed. Three more light aircraft flew in on 1 May 1931 and another visited on 12 August 1932. In her diary, Mrs Annie Bell of Mildenhall recorded the arrival of a 'monstrous aeroplane' on 16 April 1934. This was probably the American Ford Tri-Motor fourteen-seater monoplane that is remembered by Mr Ernie C. Powell of Barton Mills as being the first identified aircraft arrival. This plane was on charter from Croydon, bringing a shooting party to Lord Iveagh's estate at Elveden. No refuelling facilities were then available and Mr Bob Nichols of Mildenhall had to fetch 100 two-gallon cans from Thetford. He remembers passing them up, one by one, to a member of the crew who stood on top of the cabin, emptying them into the fuel tanks through a special leather filter. Soon after this there was a visit made by an Avro 626 trainer, this being the first known RAF aircraft to visit Mildenhall.

In 1934 Britain faced the prospect of not having a suitable entry for the forthcoming Melbourne Centenary Air Race between London and Melbourne. The early 1930s saw widespread unemployment and economic difficulties in Australia and throughout the world, but nevertheless the city of Melbourne decided to pledge its faith in its future by planning celebrations on a grand style to mark the city's centenary. The Lord Mayor conceived the idea of an international air race as a means of focusing world attention on the city and he approached Sir MacPherson Robertson, a millionaire sweets manufacturer. Sir MacPherson agreed to sponsor such an event and gave £15,000 and a gold cup worth not less than £500 as prizes, but he insisted on two conditions for his sponsorship – the race had to be truly international and everything possible should be done to reduce the risk of accidents. During a race from England to Australia in 1919, which was confined to Australian pilots, three of the five aeroplanes that entered crashed with the loss of four lives, and another plane was damaged in a forced landing necessitated by engine failure. The only aircraft to complete the course was a Vickers Vimy flown by Captain Ross Smith, who arrived after a flight lasting twenty-seven days and twenty hours. This record was broken many times over the years and in October 1932 it stood at eight days, twenty hours and forty-seven minutes, the holder being Charles W.A. Scott.

The Royal Aero Club of the UK agreed to supervise the race and Saturday 20 October 1934 was chosen for the start. Many problems arose and for a long time there was uncertainty as to whether the race would be held. It was not until June 1934 that serious consideration was given in choosing a starting point. A shortlist of four aerodromes was drawn up but each one had serious drawbacks. Eventually Mildenhall, which few people had heard of at this time, was considered and an inspection was made. The Race Committee was impressed by the size of the take-off area and by the extent of the hangar accommodation but was put off by the lack of amenities and the remoteness of the area. It was decided to provide temporary hangars at Hatfield, one of the earlier sites considered, but the cost proved prohibitive and so, with some reluctance, Mildenhall was selected.

The competition was divided into two parts: a speed race and a handicap section. Very strict regulations were enforced regarding airworthiness and a complicated handicapping formula was devised. With no British Government funding available, the directors of the de Havilland Co. was prepared to share the cost of entry to the race provided enough orders were received. In January, they decided to design and build their own long-range racing aeroplane and enter it in the speed section of the race, just ten months away. Purchasers were guaranteed a top speed of 200mph. By the end of February, orders for three Comet Racers at a cost of £5,000 each were received. The first order for a Comet Racer was placed by Mr A.O. Edwards, Managing Director of the Grosvenor House Hotel, London, and would be flown by Tom Campbell Black and Charles W.A. Scott. In May, Amy (née Johnson) and Jim Mollinson announced their entry in a Comet Racer, and the third aircraft was entered by the racing driver Bernard Rubin and flown by Owen Cathcart-Jones and Kenneth Waller. Building work on three DH 88s took place at Stag Lane, day and night, amid great secrecy before final assembly and testing at the new factory at Hatfield. The DH 88 was a streamlined low-wing monoplane design with a small frontal area, all of which compensated for the relatively low power of its two 230hp de Havilland Gipsy Six R (Racing) engines. The aircraft had a top speed of 237mph and a range of 2,925 miles. Wooden construction and stressed skin covering not only saved weight, but also speeded up production. Later, these techniques were successfully applied to the Albatross and Mosquito. However, the radical nature of the Comet caused a few technical problems, not least of which were the complicated French Ratier variable pitch propellers, which it was hoped would give better take-off performance in hot climates. The thin wing meant that the fuel tanks would have to be installed in the fuselage and the undercarriage retracted into the lower part of the engine nacelles.

The first DH 88 was flown from Hatfield by Captain Hubert Broad on 8 September, with just six weeks left to the start of the race. A month later, on 8 October, the first Comet attained 235mph at 1,000ft and 225mph at 10,000ft. On 14 October, the aircraft arrived at the start point at Mildenhall, Suffolk. By now all three Comets were painted in distinctive racing colours. Predictably, Rubin's machine was in British Racing Green, with racing number '19'. The Mollinson's black aircraft was registered G-ACSP and named *Black Magic* while *Grosvenor House*, racing number '34', was in gleaming red and white, and registered G-ACSS. Only twenty of the original sixty-four entries from thirteen nations made the starting line.

The Race Committee arrived at Mildenhall on the morning of Sunday 14 October to be met by a scene of utter chaos. Flight Lieutenant Christopher Clarkson, who was acting as Chief Marshal, reported that control of the crowds had broken down and that four competitors were complaining of damage to their aircraft. Local hotel accommodation was grossly inadequate and it was not until the last night before the race that the Air Ministry allowed competitors and ground

A week before the MacRobertson Race began, these thirty-four pilots were portrayed as probable starters. The twenty aircraft which left Mildenhall were crewed by Roscoe Turner; H. Walker (1); John H. Wright (2); Jensen (3); John Polando (4); Flight Lieutenant G. Shaw (6); J.K.L. Baines (7); Squadron Leader Malcolm MacGregor (8); H.K.G. Stodart (9); Amy Mollison (10); James Mollison (11); J. D. Hewett (12); Miss Jacqueline Cochran (13); J.J. Moll (15); M. Hansen (16); Charles W.A. Scott (17); Tom Campbell Black (18); J. Woods (19); K.D. Parmentier (20); H.D. Gilman (21); H.L. Brook (23); K.F.H. Waller (24); C.J. Melrose (25); Clyde Pangborn (26); T. Neville Stack (28); C.L. Hill (29); C.G. Davies (30); C.E. Kay (31); S.L. Turner (32); O. Cathcart Jones (33); D.L. Asjes (34); D.C. Bennett; G.E. Hemsworth; G.J. Geysendorfer; Miss E.M. Lay; R. Parer; S. Wesley Smith and Squadron Leader D.E. Stodart. (*Flight*)

DC-2 PH-AJU *Uiver* ('Stork') of KLM, piloted by K.D. Parmentier and J.J. Moll, with two crew, four passengers and 25,000 letters, reached Melbourne in ninety hours, thirteen minutes and thirty-six seconds to finish second in the speed contest. On the final stages across Australia *Uiver* encountered heavy storms and became bogged during its landings. (KLM)

DH 88 Comet Racer G-ACSS *Grosvenor House* being moved into position at Mildenhall for the 1934 race. (*Flight*)

staff to sleep in the hangars. This caused a certain amount of bitterness. The RAF had not then equipped the station and many essential items were lacking. A rough-and-ready windsock was made from a potato sack but was soon replaced by two pillows sewn together. The Household Brigade Flying Club lent a much more impressive blue and crimson object for use on the actual day. Order was gradually restored but, on Friday 19 October, the organisers were thrown into a further frenzy. It was known that the Prince of Wales intended to make an informal visit but the committee suddenly learned that the King and Queen would also be arriving after lunch that day. The royal party arrived by car and toured the hangars, meeting many of the entrants. When it was his turn to be presented, Colonel Roscoe Turner, the extrovert American and one-time 'barnstormer' who, with Clyde Pangborn, crewed an all-metal Boeing 247D, delighted everyone present by saying 'Hello King'. Turner, who had taken up air racing in 1929, winning both the Thompson and Bendix Trophy races, then enticed the King to climb aboard to inspect the interior of his aircraft. The Queen was unable to contain her delight and finally she turned to Flight Lieutenant Clarkson to say, 'Do you know, His Majesty doesn't really like aeroplanes and I think this is the first time he has ever got inside one.' The visitors then saw an exhibition of low-level aerobatics by John H. Wright in his Lambert Monocoupe *Baby Ruth* before leaving. One expert commented, 'There's a likely winner.' However, the high wing monoplane, which was flown by Wright and fellow pilot John Polando, only got as far as Calcutta.

The night of 19 October will never be forgotten by those at Mildenhall. The race had caught the public imagination and 70,000 turned up to see the start. Thousands bivouacked the night in the fields around the aerodrome until the area resembled a gigantic fair. Dawn revealed every road for miles around choked with cars. Many people abandoned their vehicles to run across the fields to be in time for the start of the race but many others were held up in traffic jams miles from Mildenhall. Several enterprising local farmers opened their fields as car parks for the day. Mr Leonard of Folly Road was somewhat disconcerted when he found that two strangers had charged a large number of drivers 2s 6d, a goodly sum in those days, to park on his land! Henry Skipper, who lived in Beck Row, recalled that 'there was misty, drizzly rain in the morning... We were out there about 5:30 a.m. you can imagine a sleepy village – we'd never seen so many people in all our lives. For about three weeks prior to that, the aircraft were practicing and flying around'. Bill Haylock, a local boy, added:

The Lambert Monocoupe *Baby Ruth* flown by John H. Wright and John Polando, which made it only as far as Calcutta. (*Flight*)

Three of the competitors in the 1934 race. DH 88 Comet G-ACSP *Black Magic* No.63 was flown by Jim and Amy Mollinson. *Black Magic* got as far as Allahabad on 22 October where it was withdrawn after piston trouble caused by unsuitable fuel. DH 88 Comet G-ACSR No.19 was flown by Owen Cathcart-Jones and Kenneth F.H. Waller. This Comet arrived in Melbourne on 25 October and placed fourth in the speed race. No.46 was a Granville R-6H Q.E.D. (NR14307) flown by Miss Jacqueline Cochran and W. Smith. This aircraft got as far as Bucharest on 20 October but was then withdrawn because of a problem with a trailing edge flap. (*Flight*)

Four of the last six aircraft to leave Mildenhall at the start of the 1934 air race. Left to right: Miles Hawk flown by Squadron Leader Malcolm MacGregor and Henry Walker, which set new light aeroplane records to India and Australia; the British Klemm *Eagle*, of Flight Lieutenant G. Shaw, which retired at Bushire with a damaged undercarriage; the Airspeed Courier AS.5 of Squadron Leader D.E. and H.K.G. Stodart, which placed fourth in the handicap race; the DH Puss Moth, of C.J. Melrose, the youngest pilot in the contest and whose solo flight earned him third place and £1,000 in the handicap event. (*Flight*)

Charles W.A. Scott and Tom Campbell-Black who won the 1934 Mildenhall–Melbourne air race. Campbell-Black was killed at Liverpool Aerodrome in 1936 when an incoming plane struck his stationary aircraft. (*Flight*)

Nobody went to school and all the village turned out. The old lads were standing by the gates shouting, 'This way to the aerodrome' and were charging a shilling to get in. The fields had been harvested and I remember distinctly going with my father to the top of the village onto a stubble field and we guided in and parked somewhere between 12 and 20 private little monoplanes. One of them was a triplane and we stood open-mouthed at this thing. But as to the air race itself, the whole village was grid locked. This was a great thing. The whole country knew about it because it was pioneering and they came to see the take off. High society (I don't like the term 'nobility') who had wined and dined in London that evening in their clubs and their smart restaurants came to see the take off in their evening suits. They got out of their chauffeur-driven cars and they stood on the perimeter of the airfield. I prided myself that they didn't have as good a seat as I had because I was up one of the tallest pine trees. All the newspapers had maps showing likely flying paths to Melbourne and we would stick pins in each day. But of course aircraft were falling by the wayside and some fellas lost their lives doing it. The air race was really something.

The sun came up from a bank of rosy cloud and a few minutes later a rainbow hung over the take-off, forming an arch through which every aeroplane was to pass. The race was started at 6.30 a.m. by Sir Alfred Bower, the Acting Lord Mayor of London. First to take off was G-ACSP *Black Magic* flown by Amy and Jim Mollinson, who had married in August 1932. Two years earlier, Amy, a twenty-six-year-old Hull-born typist, had become the first woman to fly solo from Britain to Australia when on 5 May 1932 she piloted *Jason*, a de Havilland DH 60G Gipsy Moth from Croydon and arrived in Darwin on the 24th of the same month. In 1931, Jim Mollinson had flown his own Moth from Australia to England in just under nine days. On 18–19 August 1932 he had made the first solo east-west crossing of the Atlantic, flying a special long-range de Havilland Puss Moth from Southern Ireland to New Brunswick. He also became the first man to fly from England to South America, the first to fly solo across the South Atlantic from east to west and the first to cross both the North and South Atlantic in 1933. The other competitors followed at forty-five-second intervals. The crowd was astonished when the Airspeed Viceroy flown by Stack and Turner circled to land immediately after taking off. They had officially started but were returning to pick up newsreel film for Australia. By 6.45 a.m. all the planes had left and the crowd began to melt away. All the competitors had to follow the same route, which was by way of five main control points at Baghdad, 2,530 miles from Mildenhall, Allahabad (4,830 miles), Singapore (7,040 miles), Darwin (9,124 miles) and Charleville (10,513 miles) with several intermediate checkpoints in France, Italy, Greece, Asia and Sumatra. The Mollinsons arrived at Baghdad first after flying the leg non-stop in twelve hours and forty minutes. The other two Comets and PH-AJU *Uiver* ('Stork'), a Douglas DC-2 airliner of KLM, and the Boeing 247D, crewed by Colonel Roscoe Turner and Clyde Pangborn, followed. The DC-2 was piloted by two Dutchmen, K.D. Parmentier and J.J. Moll, and carried two crew, Prins and Brugge, as navigator and flight mechanic respectively, four fare-paying passengers and mailbags containing 25,000 letters, thus proving that an air service to Australia was possible.

The Mollinsons retired from the race at Allahabad with piston trouble caused by unsuitable fuel.[1] The race was marred by one fatal accident, when the Fairey Fox I, flown by the New Zealanders Flying Officer H.D. Gilman and J.K.C. Baines, burst into flames when making a forced landing near Foggia in southern Italy on 22 October. Scott and Black in *Grosvenor House* pressed on and completed the 11,300 miles to the Flemington Racecourse in Melbourne with an elapsed time of seventy hours, fifty-four minutes and eighteen seconds, at an average flying speed of 176.8mph to win the speed race. It was not known for some days that they had also won the handicap section. Scott and Black were awarded the £10,000 speed prize and the £650 gold trophy but, as each competitor could win just one prize, the handicap prize went to Parmentier and Moll in the DC-2. Turner and Pangborn were third in the Boeing 247D, and Jones and Waller's Comet finished fourth (and third in the speed section). Seven more competitors were to arrive before the race officially ended on 5 November but the last valiant straggler, a Fairey Fox flown by G.E. Hemsworth and R.J.P. Parer, did not finally limp in until

13 January 1935. The Centenary Celebrations had long since finished but Sir MacPherson Robertson presented them both with gold medals. Scott and Black returned to England by sea, taking a month to complete the journey, to face a blaze of publicity. Scott was killed in an accident at Speke Airport near Liverpool in October 1936 whilst preparing for another air race, and Black committed suicide in April 1946 after both his marriages had ended in divorce. In 1938, two more DH 88 Comet Racers were built, the first being F-ANPZ for the French government and the second for Cyril Nicholson, named *Boomerang* for long distance record-breaking flights. Two of the three original Comet Racers later served in Europe and Africa with Belgian, French and Portuguese operators, but G-ACSS returned to Britain, narrowly avoiding being turned into scrap following a landing accident, was renamed and went on to take part in further air races. In 1938 it fell into deep neglect, but it was restored in 1943 and took part in the Festival of Britain in 1951. The aircraft was put on display until October 1965, when it was donated to the Shuttleworth Trust. Fully restored to airworthy condition, *Grosvenor House* returned to Mildenhall for the US Air Fête in May 1987 – fifty-three years after leaving the airfield for the memorable flight to Australia, since when, after another crash-landing, at Hatfield, it was again rebuilt. Mildenhall's cinema, when it opened in 1935, was named the 'Comet' as a permanent local memorial to the historic events of the preceding year.[2]

Meanwhile, on 19 July 1934, Prime Minister Stanley Baldwin announced that in view of German re-armament, the RAF was to be increased in size from eighty-seven to 128 squadrons over the next five years. An advance party of the Royal Air Force under the command of Flight Lieutenant H.B.S. Ballantine arrived at Mildenhall on 15 August 1934. On 16 October, Mildenhall was still incomplete when the Station Headquarters opened under the command of Wing Commander F.J. Linnell OBE. The official opening of RAF Mildenhall was reported in *Flight* magazine, where it was stated that the station had been placed under the command of the AOC Western Area, within the command of the AOC-in-C Air Defence of Great Britain. 99 (Bomber) Squadron, which was to come under the command of the AOC Western Area with effect from 14 November 1934, was expected to arrive on 14 November but the airfield was shrouded by fog. This lifted a little the next day and the squadron's eleven Handley Page Heyford biplane bombers, under the command of Squadron Leader J.B.S. Candy MC, flew in at 3.30 p.m. These heavy biplane bombers were the pride of the RAF at the time but had a top speed of only 142mph at 12,500ft. In her diary, Mrs Annie Bell recorded that night flying started on 17 January 1935 and that about forty aircraft arrived on 21 March 1935, leaving again at 2 p.m. At least 195 planes flew in on 15 May and 150 arrived on 5 June. Work was progressing slowly on the airfield buildings. The steelwork for hangars 2, 3 and 4 was erected early in 1935 but the construction programme did not get fully under way again until 1936, when Fosters, a firm of building contractors from Hitchin, took over the contract.

On Saturday 6 July 1935, HM King George V and the royal party visited RAF Mildenhall for the first full review of the Royal Air Force since its creation as a service in its own right on 1 April 1918. The review was held in honour of the Royal Silver Jubilee and the date chosen happened also to be the King's forty-second wedding anniversary. Thirty-eight squadrons comprising 356 aircraft were on parade. The roads around Mildenhall were once again packed, as 26,000 visitors converged on the airfield. Henry Skipper recalls:

> The Royal party included the Prince of Wales, who became King Edward VIII and the Duke of York, who became King George VI so, we actually had three kings of England at Mildenhall at the same time. I was at school then and we were taken up as a class to see this happen. There was a RAF Band and that type of thing. At the time, the airfield was mostly tents and some of the aircraft were lumbering open cockpit biplanes and open gun position Handley Page Heyfords. They could reach speeds of 120 mph – with a tail wind. The airfield became part of the village. Because it was RAF, the children and the dependants all intermingled. There were married quarters but a lot of the families lived off base as a lot of the Americans do now. They attended local schools and boosted the shopkeepers' incomes and just about all the ancillary trades' incomes. Of course, it was novel for us

children to go to school one morning and find in the desk next to us was someone talking with a totally different accent. They were the sons or daughters of serving airmen. It made quite a difference for the choice the village girls had in a boyfriend – which wasn't much help to us really. Just about every male in the village was a farm hand because the demands on the farms were great. So along comes the military base and a lot of the males became batmen and waiters in the Officer's Mess. Let's not forget the dustmen and the stokers. These were the fellas who kept the solid fuel fired central heating system going. These were jobs that were sought after because many of them were sheltered. You're not working in the field in the middle of November – you're indoors.

The royal party arrived by car at 11.20 a.m. and received a tremendous chorus of cheers as they entered by the old main gate. They were received by the Lord Lieutenant of Suffolk, resplendent in his dress uniform of black and silver and complete with cocked hat. The Royal Salute was given and a Guard of Honour, formed by recruits from the RAF depot at Uxbridge, was first inspected. The royal party and the attending officials then mounted a cavalcade of open cars to begin the main inspection. The King was in the first car, an apple-green Rolls-Royce tourer that had been lent by its private owner for the occasion. The 356 aircraft were drawn up in eight ranks in a great arc. The officers stood in front of their formations, and the aircrews, dressed in spotless white flying overalls, stood by their machines whilst the ground staff was drawn up in lines in the centre of the rows of aircraft. The King drove slowly through the parade, stopping five times for officers and airmen to be presented and to examine equipment, and after fifty minutes returned to the reception area where he presented decorations to three of the officers responsible for the organisation of the day's events. Three years later, in August 1938, the Right Honourable Sir Kingsley Wood MP, the then Secretary of State for Air, unveiled a memorial tablet outside the Station Headquarters (now Building 562, Wing HQ) to mark the site of this historic event.

Three hearty cheers were given and the royal party then left by road for Duxford to be joined by the Queen and the Duchess of York for lunch in the Officers' Mess. Furious activity then began at Mildenhall. Twenty of the squadrons on parade were to take part in a fly-past over Duxford and the airfield had to be cleared to allow these 182 assorted aircraft to take off. Taxiing lanes appeared as if by magic and airmen bearing yellow flags showed the way for the squadrons. The heavy bombers took off singly to be followed by the fighters taking off in squadrons. There was not a single engine failure as all went off without a hitch. Once in the air the squadrons flew off to mark time in their appointed areas before assuming formation for the fly-past over Duxford, twenty-five miles to the south-west. Given the differing speeds of the aircraft, taking part in the fly-past was a masterpiece of organisation but it was criticised at the time as being a somewhat tame spectacle. However, it was simply a fly-past and not a flying display. 99 Squadron at Mildenhall had the privilege of leading the fly-past. The squadrons that took part in the Royal Jubilee Review included eleven fighter squadrons equipped with Bulldogs, Demons, Furies, Gauntlets and Harts, six light bomber squadrons, a medium bomber squadron, five heavy bomber squadrons equipped with Gordons, Harts, Hinaidis, Overstrands, Sidestrands, Virginias, Wallaces and Wapiti and two Army Co-operation squadrons flying Audaxes. While this great display of biplane type produced a very impressive spectacle, the lack of modern monoplane aircraft showed how ill-prepared the RAF was for war.

There had been tremendous organisation behind the one-day review. The squadrons had all flown in on 1 July, some coming almost directly from the RAF display at Hendon. A 'tent city' had to be provided at the edge of the airfield to accommodate 400 officers and almost 4,000 airmen. The aircraft made a most impressive spectacle, when for reasons of security they were illuminated at night by searchlights. To overcome the problems of so many aircraft navigating independently to Duxford it was decided that the route should be marked by a series of smoke flares. Disaster threatened during the preliminary rehearsals, as there were so many agricultural bonfires that many of the squadrons became hopelessly lost. Some failed to find Duxford, but there was no truth in the rumour that one squadron had landed at Manchester. Using

HM King George V inspects Handley Page Heyford bomber crews during the 1935 RAF Silver Jubilee Review at Mildenhall on 6 July 1935. Heyfords were among the 356 aircraft that took part in the review, and at Mildenhall they equipped both 99 and 38 Squadron. The latter was equipped with the Heyford from September 1935 to November 1936 when conversion to the Fairey Hendon took place, and on 5 May 1937 the squadron moved to Marham. (MoD)

Hawker Nimrods led by an Osprey over the massed ranks of biplane fighters at the RAF Silver Jubilee Review at Mildenhall in 1935. (MoD)

Part of the huge crowd during the RAF Silver Jubilee Review in 1935 as HM King George V inspects the Honour Guard. (MoD)

special red flares solved the problem and the first full dress rehearsal was so successful that the second was held in skeleton form only. Many of the aircrews were free to attend a dance in Mildenhall town hall on the eve of the review. The climax of the evening's activities came when a game of rugby started in the centre of the floor, ending in a pile of bodies at least ten deep.

In September 1935, 38 Squadron was re-formed at Mildenhall under the command of Squadron Leader S.M. Park from 'B' flight of 99 Squadron and equipped with Heyfords. 38 Squadron had originally been formed in April 1916 for home defence against Zeppelins but moved to France in May 1918 for night-bombing duties, being disbanded on its return to England in 1919. Prominent among the squadron's early commanding officers was Captain Arthur T. Harris (14 July–14 September 1916), who was later to gain a place in history as C-in-C Bomber Command from 1942 to 1945. In November 1936, 38 Squadron became the first and only unit to receive the RAF's first all-metal low-wing monoplane bomber, the Fairey Hendon, which proved to be an under-powered anachronism. 38 Squadron remained at Mildenhall until 5 May 1937 when it moved to RAF Marham, where it stayed until it transferred in November 1940 to the Middle East for the remainder of the war.

The first of the Empire Day Air Shows was held on 23 May 1936 when 6,000 visitors attended, to be entertained by flying displays and exhibitions of technical equipment. These displays were held annually until 1939, being replaced after the war by the Battle of Britain Open Days. The Open Day in 1938 was visited by the Under Secretary of State for Air but bad weather curtailed the flying programme that year. Over 10,000 people attended the 1939 event, reflecting the greatly increased public awareness of the importance of the Air Forces, as war clouds loomed. There was another royal visit on 8 July 1936 when King Edward VIII and the Duke of York arrived by air at 2.55 p.m. for an inspection. The AOC No.3 (Bomber) Group received them and they then proceeded to inspect the resident 99 and 38 Squadrons, and also 40 Squadron, which had flown in from Abingdon for the occasion. The visit ended with a tour of the airmen's barrack blocks. 99 Squadron had only just returned from taking part in the Air Display at RAF Hendon.

The RAF was at last being expanded and streamlined in preparation for a possible war. No.3 (Bomber) Group was formed at Andover in May 1936 but moved its headquarters to RAF Mildenhall on 13 January 1937. No.4 (Bomber) Group was formed on 1 April 1937 with its headquarters at Mildenhall but moved to Linton-on-Ouse, Yorkshire, on 29 June 1937. This Group's first AOC was Air Commodore Arthur Harris. No.5 (Bomber) Group was formed at Mildenhall on 1 September 1937 but moved its headquarters to Grantham, Lincolnshire, the following month. A number of other units were also formed at Mildenhall in the same year. 73 Squadron was formed on 15 March 1937 and it was initially equipped with Hawker Furies but changed to Gloster Gladiators when it moved to RAF Debden in June. 211 Squadron was reformed at Mildenhall on 14 June 1937 and moved to Grantham in August, leaving, however, a detachment at Mildenhall until September. This squadron was at first equipped with Hawker Audaxes but began to re-equip with Hawker Hinds only two months later. A small party assembled at Mildenhall on a cold and windy day on 1 February 1938 to travel to Stradishall, to open the new airfield there. The only aircraft then on the strength of RAF Stradishall was a Miles Magister trainer, intended for the use of the Station Commander.

In March 1937, aircraft from Mildenhall joined in a large-scale search operation for the Duchess of Bedford who had taken off from Woburn in a Gipsy Moth biplane on 22 March but the seventy-one-year-old had been driven off course by a sudden snowstorm. Despite strenuous efforts, no trace was found of her aircraft until wreckage was washed ashore at Great Yarmouth ten days later. She had been a notable figure in British aviation, even though she had not flown solo until she was sixty-one, and she had not obtained her pilot's licence until the age of sixty-eight. The Duke of Bedford donated £1,000 to the RAF Benevolent Fund as a token of appreciation for the RAF's eight-day fruitless search.

In April 1937 149 Squadron was formed at Mildenhall from part of 99 Squadron and was equipped initially with Handley Page Heyford bombers. The first commercial airliner to make use of RAF Mildenhall touched down on 10 June 1937 when a Dutch aircraft had been diverted to Mildenhall because of thunderstorms over Croydon Airport. The passengers were sent on to their original destination by bus. A top-level German Air Force mission, which included General Erhard Milch, the architect of the Luftwaffe, visited RAF Mildenhall on 19 October 1937. The party arrived by road at 11.45 a.m. and first inspected the Heyfords of 99 and 149 Squadrons. The Germans then inspected new types of aircraft and equipment before watching a fly-past of new medium and heavy bombers. The visitors lunched in the Officers' Mess before leaving by air for Cranwell, where they spent the night. The same year saw two more official visits. The Under Secretary of State for Air inspected the station on 12 November and the AOC-in-C, Air Chief Marshal Sir Edgar Ludlow-Hewitt, presented the Unit Badge to 99 Squadron on 21 December.

A Centralised Maintenance Flight was formed in April 1938 to take responsibility for the 120-hour major inspections of the aircraft of the two resident bomber squadrons. The station's engineer officer took command of this flight. The period 26 September to 4 October 1938 saw considerable activity at Mildenhall as a result of the Munich crisis when Prime Minister Neville Chamberlain flew to Munich to try to persuade Adolf Hitler to call off his threatened invasion of Czechoslovakia. The station defences, started earlier in the year, were hurriedly completed. It was not planned to fully mobilise Nos 99 and 149 Squadrons at this time and so large numbers of the personnel of these squadrons were suddenly posted elsewhere. All married families were warned to be ready to evacuate their quarters but, in spite of the tense situation, complete calm prevailed and not one family chose to leave voluntarily. Britain and France gave in to Hitler's demands and Chamberlain returned triumphant to Britain declaring 'Peace in our Time'.

Handley Page Heyford I 'R' of 99 Squadron at Mildenhall in 1934. Designated a heavy bomber, the Heyford carried 2,500lb of bombs as its normal load but could carry up to 3,500lb. Note the ingenious retractable 'dustbin' rotating gun turret protruding from under the fuselage. (*Flight*)

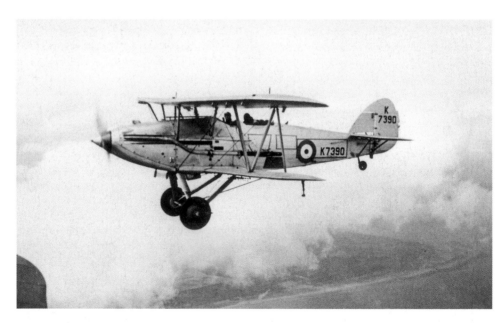

Hawker Audax in flight. This type, the Army Co-Operation version of the Hart, equipped 211 (B) Squadron at Mildenhall from June to September 1937. (Wing Commander G.C.C. Bartlett)

Fairey Hendon II K5085 of 38 Squadron, the only unit to be completely equipped with the type during its short career with the RAF. 38 Squadron operated from Mildenhall from September 1935 to May 1937. (Fairey Aviation)

Engine fitters working on one of the two 600hp Rolls-Royce Kestrel VI engines powering the Fairey Hendon night bomber. The Hendon was the first all-metal low-wing cantilever monoplane to enter squadron service with the RAF. It began equipping the only squadron in November 1936 when 38 Squadron began working up on the type at Mildenhall. (Wing Commander G.C.C. Bartlett)

The only known photograph of L4215, the first Wellington I to enter RAF service, seen here circling Mildenhall on 10 October 1938 for acceptance by 99 Squadron. (via Dr Colin Dring)

A Wellington I overhead the hangars at Mildenhall. (via Dr Colin Dring)

Chamberlain clung to this delusion, and as late as 10 March 1939 he pronounced the international situation as 'satisfactory'. Five days later the German Army, which had occupied the Sudetenland after Munich, marched in to occupy Prague. Ever since Munich, Britain had embarked upon a period of intensive training and re-armament in preparation for war that was to follow. On 10 October 1938, No.3 Group had begun to re-arm with Wellington I twin-engined medium bombers. The first of these aircraft went to 99 Squadron, which in November transferred its obsolete Heyfords to 148 Squadron at Stradishall. After January 149 Squadron began to receive its new aircraft and both squadrons were fully equipped by June 1939. An intensive flying programme familiarised the aircrews with their new aircraft. Long-distance training flights were frequently made to France and formations of the two squadrons' Wellingtons 'showed the flag' over Paris on Bastille Day, 14 July 1939. No.2 (Bomber) Group staged a mock attack on RAF Mildenhall in January 1939, releasing tear gas over the station. Decontamination trials were carried out on Wellingtons and it was found that by using mechanical sprayers, it was possible to fully decontaminate an aircraft in fifteen minutes. It was clear to all by the summer of 1939 that war was probable, if not inevitable, and so the two squadrons at Mildenhall continued their training in earnest.

Notes

1   Amy Mollinson (*née* Johnson) made several record flights, including those to Cape Town and back in 1936, before she met her death as an Air Transport Auxiliary (ATA) pilot in January 1941 while ferrying an Airspeed Oxford in bad weather from Prestwick in Scotland. HMS *Hazlemere*, patrolling off Herne Bay, spotted a parachute coming out of the clouds and dropping into the sea. The CO jumped overboard and tried to reach her but both were drowned and Amy's body was never recovered. Jim Mollinson, who also served in the ATA, remained convinced right to the end of his life that she had been shot down.

2   One of the few remaining DC-2s was shipped over from the USA to Holland in the livery of the KLM Royal Dutch Airlines DC-2 PH-AJU for the fiftieth anniversary of the London to Melbourne Air Race. It stopped off at Mildenhall on 22 December 1983 to refuel and begin its re-enactment of the original route flown by the 1934 DC-2 to Australia. On its return journey it suffered an engine problem and the Douglas Historical Foundation responded by flying out a spare engine.

CHAPTER 2
'Target for Tonight'

Throughout Britain, partial mobilisation was ordered on 1 August 1939 and on the following day RAF Mildenhall received orders to assume a state of readiness for war. The next week saw a flurry of activity, including simulated gas and bombing attacks on the base. The final preparations were made and the blackout system was brought into operation. Fuel storage tanks were filled to capacity, emergency rations were brought up to war strength and identity discs and field dressings were issued to all personnel. During the evening of Wednesday 23 August 1939, RAF units in Great Britain and abroad were secretly placed on a war footing and mobilisation of the Auxiliary Air Force, and 3,000 members of the Volunteer Reserve began. Fifty-five squadrons strong in the last month of peace, the overall strength of Bomber Command by the end of September was thirty-three home-based first-line squadrons (of which ten were sent to France as the Advanced Air Striking Force) or 480 aircraft. These consisted of six squadrons of Bristol Blenheim IV light bombers of 2 Group and six squadrons of Wellington Is and IAs of 3 Group (with 214 and 215 Squadrons in reserve) stationed in East Anglia. The rest of the force comprised five squadrons of Whitleys of 4 Group based in Yorkshire and six squadrons of Handley Page Hampdens of 5 Group in Lincolnshire. Wellingtons were first-line equipment for 9 Squadron at Honington, Suffolk, 37 Squadron at Feltwell, Norfolk, 99 and 149 Squadrons at Mildenhall, and 38 and 115 Squadrons at Marham, Norfolk, while 214 and 215 (at Methwold) were similarly equipped in reserve. On 1 June 1939, No.1 RNZAF Unit had begun forming at Marham to fly Wellingtons. A decision had been taken early in 1937 that the New Zealanders would have a complement of thirty Wellingtons, six of which would be ready to leave for the antipodes in August 1939. When war clouds gathered, the New Zealanders were put at the disposal of the RAF and the unit moved to RAF Harwell, where it became 15 OTU.

Under the RAF Bomber Command 'Scatter' plan, the majority of bomber squadrons were immediately dispersed to satellite bases. Wellingtons of 115 Squadron were sent to the satellite airfield at Barton Bendish and by 2 September all of 99 Squadron's Wellingtons had been moved to the Rowley Mile racecourse on Newmarket Heath. The famous racecourse had been used as a landing ground for aircraft in the First World War. HRH The Prince of Wales landed at the strip in 1935 before travelling by road to attend the Jubilee Review at Mildenhall. The Rowley Mile course in about 300 acres north of the Beacon Course and Cambridge Hill offered one of the largest grass landing and take-off runs – 2,500 yards – in an east–west direction. A Wellington IA filled with 1,500lb of bombs and 720 gallons of fuel required a 1,080-yard run to become airborne, which left little margin for error. The Rowley Mile strip was the longest of its kind in Britain where a Wellington IA could operate carrying 2,000lb of bombs. Although long and flat, crews had to remember to hurdle the 20ft-high Devil's Dyke running along one boundary. Accommodation for air and ground crews was in the racecourse administration buildings, the grandstand and requisitioned housing locally until new huts could be built. 99 Squadron operated from Newmarket Heath under the control of RAF Mildenhall, for the first eighteen months of the war.

It was a sombre Neville Chamberlain, the British Prime Minister, who announced his country's declaration of war over the air on the BBC, on the morning of 3 September. His resigned tones had barely vanished into the ether, when reconnaissance revealed German warships leaving Wilhelmshaven. At 5 p.m. an order was sent to RAF Mildenhall for twelve

Wellingtons of 99 Squadron to be made ready to attack them. No Wellingtons could be airborne until 6.30 p.m. and then only three aircraft were operational. They took off, but bad weather and oncoming darkness forced them to abort. They returned to Suffolk after jettisoning their bomb loads in the North Sea.

The only way to carry the war to Germany was to make attacks on German capital ships in the Heligoland Bight. However, British War Cabinet policy decreed that no civilian casualties were to be caused as a direct result of the bombing. The RAF Bomber Command could strike at ships at sea or underway, but vessels moored in harbours were not to be bombed for fear of injuring 'innocent' civilians. Plans were laid for the first RAF raid of the war to take place during the afternoon of 4 September. While fifteen unescorted Blenheims took off for a strike on the *Admiral von Scheer* at Wilhelmshaven, eight Wellingtons of 9 Squadron and six Wellingtons of 149 Squadron, also without escort, flew on over the North Sea towards Brunsbüttel. Their targets were the battle cruisers *Scharnhorst* and *Gneisenau,* which had earlier been spotted by a Blenheim reconnaissance aircraft from RAF Wyton. Squadron Leader Paul Harris was leading 149 Squadron this day. En route, Harris ordered his gunners to test fire their Brownings. He was startled to discover that not one gun was in working order! However, not wishing to miss the first action of the war, he decided to press on to the target. Unfortunately, bad weather added to the problems beset by the crews and five of his squadron were forced to return early. Harris lost sight of the two remaining aircraft in thick cloud. As he flew over Tonning, his Wellington took a direct flak hit. Harris' bomb aimer aimed his bombs at a bridge over the Eder and turned for home. Harris nursed the ailing aircraft the 300 miles back to England and landed at Mildenhall six and a quarter hours after taking off. 9 Squadron had fared little better.

A combination of bad weather and the lack of suitable targets as dictated by War Cabinet policy delayed squadrons from using their new Wellington IAs and during the next few weeks on several occasions aircraft took part in sweeps over the North Sea. Otherwise, they were mainly occupied in bombing and firing practice and formation exercises, some of them in co-operation with fighter squadrons. 99 Squadron's first operation of the war came on the night of 8 September when three of its Wellingtons were sent to drop propaganda leaflets over Hanover. One aircraft had to turn back but the other two successfully completed their mission. Meanwhile, 149 Squadron was chosen to feature in the popular propaganda film *The Lion Has Wings*, starring Ralph Richardson and Merle Oberon, and the whole squadron was marched down to the Comet cinema in November to see a preview of the film. King George VI made a surprise visit to RAF Mildenhall on 2 November and inspected crews of 149 Squadron. Later that month a detachment of 99 Squadron moved to Lossiemouth on loan to Coastal Command but returned the following month.

The Air Ministry planners were still of the opinion that close-knit formations of Wellingtons, with their healthy defensive armament, could survive everything the enemy could throw at them and penetrate heavily defended targets. Recent heavy losses in British merchant shipping and pressure from Winston Churchill, the First Lord of the Admiralty, in particular, prompted the War Cabinet to order Bomber Command to mount, as soon as possible, 'a major operation with the object of destroying an enemy battle-cruiser or pocket battleship'. However, the directive added, 'no bombs are to be aimed at warships in dock or berthed alongside the quays'. The War Cabinet wanted no German civilian casualties.

During the late afternoon of 2 December 1939, 115 and 149 Squadrons at Marham and Mildenhall were alerted that a strike would be mounted against two German cruisers moored off Heligoland. Immediately, twenty-four Wellington IAs were bombed up with four 500lb SAP (Semi Armour Piercing) bombs and 620 gallons of fuel, ready for a strike early the following morning. Leading the attack would be thirty-four-year-old Wing Commander Richard Kellett AFC, a distinguished pre-war aviator, now Commanding Officer of 149 Squadron. On the morning of 3 December, the weather had improved and at 9 a.m. Kellett led his twelve Wellingtons off in four flights of three. He rendezvoused with three Wellingtons of 38 Squadron and nine of 115 Squadron from Marham, and the force flew out over the North Sea towards Heligoland in four 'battle formations' of six 'Wimpys' each.[1] At the head of the bomber force, Kellett positioned his section well out in front. Following some distance behind and leading the remainder was Squadron Leader Paul Harris. Off to his right and a little way behind, and leading the remainder flew the third section led by a young Canadian, Flight Lieutenant J.B. Stewart. The fourth section, led by Flight Lieutenant A.G. Duguid, flew directly behind Stewart. Two cruisers were spotted at anchor in the roads between the two tiny rock outcrops that are Heligoland in the German Bight. Kellett prepared to attack from up sun. As a result of the early losses, the bombing altitude had been raised to 7,000ft (considered 'high level' bombing altitude at this time). Harris claimed hits on one of the warships and Stewart attacked a large merchantman anchored outside the harbour but a cloud obscured the targets and results were unconfirmed.

On 13 December, the loss of five Wellingtons in 99 Squadron was so disastrous that Air Vice-Marshal J.E.A. 'Jackie' Baldwin, AOC 3 Group, was compelled to compare it to the *Charge of the Light Brigade*. Despite the losses, Bomber Command opined that the Wellingtons had survived repeated fighter attacks and faith in the old adage that 'the bomber will always get through' seemed as unshakable as ever. On the evening of 17 December, Wing Commander Kellett and Squadron Leader Paul Harris of 149 Squadron were summoned to Group Headquarters at Mildenhall, along with the squadron commanders and section leaders of 9 and 37 Squadrons, for a briefing on another raid on Wilhelmshaven the following morning. Unfortunately, there would be little cloud cover, for the weather forecast for 18 December predicted clear conditions. Harris was informed that Peter Grant would be flying with him, together with three of 9 Squadron's aircraft. This was the first time they had ever flown together and, as they strolled away from the briefing, Harris put his hand on Grant's shoulder and said, 'Stay close to me whatever happens'.

No.9 Squadron was airborne from Honington at 9 a.m. At 10 a.m. nine Wellingtons of 149 Squadron led by Wing Commander Kellett took off from Newmarket Heath and rendezvoused over King's Lynn with the nine Wellingtons of 9 Squadron. The six Wellingtons of 37 Squadron took off from Feltwell and flew straight across north Norfolk, falling in behind the rear elements of the formation while over the North Sea. The formation flew a dog leg course over the North Sea and at 12.30 p.m. Kellett sighted Sylt about fifty miles ahead. The formation was still at 15,000 feet and there was not a cloud in the sky. It was an open invitation for enemy fighters. As the Wellingtons approached the German coast near Cuxhaven, Bf 109 and Bf 110 fighters of *Jagdgeschwader 1*, guided by radar plots of the incoming formation made by the experimental *Freya* early warning radar installation at Wangerooge and directed by ground control, were waiting. Kellett led the formation through the flak-stained sky over Wilhelmshaven and each bomb aimer prepared to drop his three bombs on the ships below. Suddenly, Kellett gave the order not to bomb. All the battleships and cruisers were berthed alongside quays and harbour walls. Kellett's orders were precise – he was not to risk German civilian casualties. Bomb doors were opened, but no bombs fell. Moored in the middle of the harbour were four large ships that appeared to be merchantmen. Heavy anti-aircraft fire was coming from them. It was all the encouragement Paul Harris needed. They appeared to be fleet auxiliaries, so he dropped his bomb load on them. Another Wellington in his section did the same but the results were obscured by cloud. Kellett's formation had become strung out and disjointed. 9 and 37 Squadrons had become detached and fanned out in the face of heavy barrage. The Wellingtons were easy pickings, and the RAF crews were caught cold as the cunning German fighter pilots made beam attacks from above. For almost half an hour forty-four Luftwaffe fighters tore into the Wellingtons. 9 Squadron, which had despatched nine Wellingtons, lost five aircraft shot down, including Squadron Leader Archibald Guthrie, one of the flight commanders. Fighter attacks continued until the bombers were only eighty miles from home. Kellett remembered Paul Harris' suggestion after 3 December raid and 'flew a little slower' to allow the stragglers to keep up. Off to his right Peter Grant obediently stuck rigidly to Harris' Wellington. The tightly knit formation of ten aircraft of 149 Squadron fought their way through. *B-Beer*, piloted by Flying Officer J.H.C. Spiers, was shot down during a beam attack by a Bf 110. There were no survivors. *P-Peter*, piloted by Flying Officer M.F. Briden, ditched near Cromer Knoll. All of Briden's crew perished before they could be rescued. Squadron Leader Harris circled the scene of the crash and attempted to drop a dinghy to the stricken crew but its attached rope snagged the tail of his Wellington, and Harris was forced to land at the fighter airfield at Coltishall, near Norwich, which was still under construction. The one survivor from 37 Squadron, Flying Officer 'Cheese' Lemon, crash-landed at RAF Feltwell, where the Wellington was destroyed.

The RAF post-mortem into the disastrous raid on Wilhelmshaven had concluded that its Wellingtons could no longer cross German territory in daylight and expect to survive against Luftwaffe opposition. The losses seemed to shake the War Cabinet out of its chivalrous attitude towards the German civilian population, but it would not be until March 1940 that the so-called 'niceties' of war were dispensed with and Bomber Command was allowed to bomb land targets for the first time. Unfortunately, the darkness was to prove no greater ally than daylight had been.

In very cold weather, 149 Squadron mounted its first night sorties on 18/19 January 1940 when Wing Commander Kellett and Flying Officer A.F. Riddlesworth set out to drop propaganda leaflets over Hamburg and Bremen. The next night operation followed on 1/2 March when Sergeant Jack Goad set off for Hamburg and Flying Officer L.R. Field followed in Wellington N2984, intending to drop leaflets over Bremen. They were airborne for barely eleven minutes. During his take-off, Field's starboard engine failed to give the necessary power and suddenly his port engine cut out. Field attempted to pull the Wimpy off but the aircraft plunged into the ground 500 yards north of Poplar Farm, Mildenhall, about two miles north-west of the airfield. All the crew perished in the crash. On 3 March, Wellington IA N3006 of 99 Squadron, flown by Flying Officer E.G. Scott, who had set off from Newmarket on a *Nickel* sortie to Hamburg and was recalled because of bad weather, crashed at Chalk Hill, Barton Mills, killing all six crew.

On 3 March the first Wellington ICs were issued to 149 Squadron, quickly followed by 99 Squadron. The Mk IC had re-designed hydraulics and a 24-volt electrical system, which permitted the use of the new directional radio compass. Crews, ever mindful of the beam attacks made by the Luftwaffe, soon installed hand-held machine-guns in the long narrow side windows. Mk ICs were first used on 20 March during an uneventful sweep over the North Sea. The next day, Wellington ICs of 149 Squadron made a night reconnaissance over Germany. P9224 became the first IC to venture over Germany. On 23 March a crew captained by Flying Officer F.W.S. Turner, in P9225, overflew the river Elbe and Hamburg. They lost their way and encountered heavy AA fire while flying low over Dunkirk. With low fuel, they had little choice but to abandon their aircraft and luckily they reached the safety of Allied lines. They were back at RAF Mildenhall three days later.

On 7 April, Wellington crews were brought to a state of readiness when many German ships were sighted in the North Sea heading north. During the afternoon Blenheims attacked but their bombs missed and another attempt by two squadrons of Wellingtons was thwarted by bad visibility. Two days later news broke that the German ships were part of the invasion force attacking Norway. Most of the country was out of range of RAF aircraft and only 3 Group's Wellingtons could reach the southern areas of Norway. On 12 April, six Wellingtons of 149 Squadron took off from Mildenhall and followed in trail behind six Wellingtons of 38 Squadron from Marham. They were ordered to head for the Norwegian coast near Stavanger and search for German warships. No warships had been sighted when the Wellingtons were intercepted by a group of Messerschmitt Bf 110s. The second 149 Squadron section pulled ahead of the first, which had come under such severe attack that two Wellingtons that had turned inland were not seen again, although two German fighters were claimed. Then more Bf 110s arrived and started beam attacks causing the bombers to dive almost to sea level to escape. On returning to RAF Mildenhall, the reports again said that no enemy warships had been attacked.

A wide range of flying gear is in evidence in this photograph of 149 Squadron crew as they prepare for a night raid at Mildenhall in 1940. (via Dr Colin Dring)

Bombing up a Wellington of 149 Squadron at Mildenhall. (via Wally Gaul)

A pilot climbs from the cockpit of a Gloster Gladiator of the Mildenhall Met Flight in the summer of 1940. The Met Flight had arrived from Duxford in April 1939, and in November 1940 became 401 Flight and moved to Bircham Newton, Norfolk, on 29 October 1941. In November 1942, 1403 (Met) Flight was reformed at Mildenhall before being posted overseas. (RAF Museum)

149 Squadron Wellington ICs and their crew at Mildenhall. (via Dr Colin Dring)

The 4,000lb high-capacity (HC) light-case bomb, commonly called a 'Cookie' bomb, was first dropped in anger on 31 March/1 April 1941 when two of 149 Squadron's Mk II Wellingtons were despatched carrying the 'Cookies'. The first aircraft, OJ-X W5439 *X-X-ray*, piloted by Pilot Officer J.H. Franks (seen here, centre, with moustache, on 1 May 1941), and a 9 Squadron Wellington successfully completed the operation. (RAF Museum)

Late on 25 April, six Wellingtons took off in formation for a night attack on Stavanger airfield in Norway before the squadron once more attempted North Sea sweeps and night patrols over Sylt to prevent mine-laying seaplanes from operating. An attempt on Aalborg Airfield in Denmark where the Germans had established a major base for support of their Norwegian campaign was also attempted. On 10 May 1940, the German *Blitzkrieg* in the West began and the following night six Wellingtons bombed Waalhaven in the Netherlands. Then on the night of 14/15 May the most significant RAF Mildenhall operation to date took place when nine Wellingtons of 149 Squadron were sent to attack a target in Germany for the first time when Aachen was the destination. The following day the War Cabinet authorised Bomber Command to attack east of the Rhine and on 15/16 May Bomber Command began its strategic air offensive against Germany when ninety-nine bombers, thirty-nine of them Wellingtons, bombed oil and steel plants and railway centres in the Ruhr. Throughout May 1940 during ten nights, 149 Squadron operated with limited success against tactical targets on railways and roads in Northern France and Belgium in an attempt to halt the advancing German armies. Then, as the Allied armies were being evacuated from Dunkirk, attacks were made on enemy troop formations to prevent them reaching the beaches. On 4 June, as 149 Squadron raided Monheim, German bombers dropped twenty-three high-explosive bombs on the Mildenhall area but they exploded well wide of the station.

Italy's decision, at midnight on 10 June, to declare war on Britain and France caused Bomber Command to re-direct its bombing strategy. Benito Mussolini, the Italian Dictator's intentions had already been anticipated and it was agreed that as soon as Italy joined the war, Wellingtons and longer range Whitleys would bomb her heavy industry in the north of the country. Accordingly, on 3 June, preparations were begun to transform Salon in the Marseilles area into a refuelling and operational base. At 3.30 p.m. on 11 June, Wellingtons of 99 Squadron flew in from England and landed at the forward base. Behind the scenes chaos reigned as first one order to bomb Italy was given, then countermanded by the French. Finally, an exasperated Group Captain R.M. Field, the CO of *Haddock* force at Salon, ordered the Wellingtons off (a force of Whitleys, having refuelled in the Channel Islands, was already en route to Turin and Genoa). The Wellingtons were prevented from taking off when at the last moment a procession of French lorries were driven directly into their path and left there! When the political shenanigans had been sorted out, more Wellingtons made the seven-hour flight from England to Salon. On 15 June, two Wellingtons of 99 Squadron and six of 149 Squadron took off from Salon for a raid on Genoa. Violent thunderstorms en route prevented all but one of the Wellington crews from finding their targets and seven bombers were forced to return to Salon with their bomb loads intact. On the night of 16/17 June, nine Wellingtons made another attempt to bomb Italy but only five crews were able to find and attack the Caproni works at Milan. Crews returned to Salon to discover that the French had sued for an armistice and effectively all future operations were brought to an end. 149 Squadron was joined on its return to Mildenhall by 218 (Gold Coast) Squadron, which had been evacuated from France where it had been operating since the outbreak of war. This squadron was posted in July to RAF Oakington and there exchanged its battered Fairey Battles for Blenheim Mk IVs.

During July 1940 the Wellingtons of 3 Group carried out attacks on west and north-west Germany, with the occasional raid on targets in Denmark. The two Mildenhall squadrons then began a series of raids that were to take them regularly deep into the heart of Germany. The industrial area of the Ruhr and the ports of Hamburg and Bremen were, together with many other towns, visited and revisited by bombers of No.3 Group. Each of the two Mildenhall squadrons sent up a dozen aircraft on twelve to fourteen raids every month. On 23/24 July, the Wellington crews made a deeper penetration to Gotha. On 11/12 August, 149 Squadron became one of the few squadrons in Bomber Command to drop *Razzle*, an incendiary device consisting of a wad of wet phosphorous placed between two pieces of celluloid, which ignited to produce an 8in flame when the phosphorus dried. A biscuit tin was used to carry up to 500 examples and it was envisaged that a campaign could be waged against dry German crops with each Wellington carrying fifty tins. For fear of retaliation, however, British Prime Minister Winston Churchill ordered the scheme to be halted.

On the night of 25/26 August, 149 Squadron made its first attempt to bomb Berlin. They flew a repeat of the eight-hour flights on 30/31 August. On 7 September the Luftwaffe retaliated with heavy raids on London. Berlin then became 149 Squadron's main target. By the end of the year, ten raids consisting of seventy-three sorties had been despatched to the 'Big City'. In September 1940 the Wellingtons carried out eight night attacks on barges massed in the channel ports for the intended German invasion of England. The weather proved a difficult obstacle and fog frequently blanketed the East Anglian airfields. On the night of 8/9 September 1940, 133 bombers were despatched to bomb ports at Hamburg, Bremen and Emden, as well as Ostend and barges at Boulogne. Two Wellingtons were lost. One of these, Wellington IC P9245 OJ-W of 149 Squadron, ran into a severe electrical storm near its target at Boulogne. Squadron Leader L.V. Andrews climbed to get above the storm but ran into even more turbulent conditions, which made the 'Wimpy' uncontrollable for a few seconds. Ice quickly formed on the surfaces of the aircraft, obscuring the pilot's view and forcing him to lose height. With his compass hopelessly defective, the pilot turned for home but within minutes the port engine failed and burst into flames. Eventually, the crew was forced to bale out but they opened their parachutes while they were still miles out to sea off Clacton. Only the second pilot, Pilot Officer C.W. Parish, survived from the crew of six, after he swam about seven miles in full flying kit whilst battling cramp and seasickness. Parish was killed two and half years later on his fifty-fourth operation of the war.

German intruders posed another hazard. During the early evening of 27 November 1940, seventeen Dorniers made concentrated attacks on four East Anglian bomber aerodromes and thirty-three bombs fell on RAF Mildenhall. A hangar was damaged and a barrack block received a direct hit. Casualties amounted to two killed, two seriously wounded and three slightly injured. The Newmarket satellite was also attacked that day.

A deep penetration to Munich was carried out on the night of 8/9 November. On the night of 16/17 November, 127 bombers, the largest number yet despatched, raided Hamburg. On 4 December 1940 came the first raid from England into Italy when an attack was made on Turin, a distance of 1,350 miles, there and back. January 1941 saw the start of 'the milk run' to Brest, the French dockyard where large German warships sheltered from the Royal Navy until February 1942. The ability to fly in bad weather was essential to the night bombing campaign. Between March and July 1939 Squadron Leader R.S. Buckle AFC had trained pilots to use blind approach equipment, using an Anson at RAF Mildenhall. Eventually, over fifty special Blind Approach Training Flights were formed. No.3 Blind Approach Training Flight was formed at Mildenhall in January 1941 and operated first Wellingtons and then Airspeed Oxfords.

Nine Wellingtons raided Venice on 12/13 January. HQ Bomber Command sent messages of congratulations to the squadrons involved after the more successful of these missions and both 99 and 149 Squadrons received many such messages. HM King George VI congratulated crews when he visited RAF Mildenhall on 18 January 1941 to decorate a large number of officers and airmen. The King decorated Wing Commander (later Group Captain) J.A. Powell OBE DSO the 149 Squadron CO who, while flying N2769 very low, with his crew raked Padua airfield with machine-gun fire after aiming their bombs at an industrial target. King George VI and Queen Mary inspected the operations room and the photographic section and made a tour of the aerodrome, lunching in the Officers' Mess. When visiting the Airmen's Mess, the King and Queen saw that the men were being entertained by a string orchestra as they ate – one wonders if this was part of the normal routine! An enemy aircraft appeared overhead and was engaged by the station defences whilst the royal party was still at the station. No bombs were dropped.

Night-bombing raids continued and included attacks on Düsseldorf on 22/23 January, the first concentrated attack on Hanover on 10/11 February and Bremen on 17/18 March. The raid on Hanover, which fell during the February new moon, saw a total of 222 aircraft sent to bomb oil targets. The previous highest Bomber Command sortie rate was 135, to Gelsenkirchen in the January 1941 moon period. HQ No.3 Group described the raid on Hanover when over 100 Wellingtons, including nine of 149 Squadron took part, as 'by far the most ambitious as yet undertaken' by the group. Clouds caused the bombing to drift off target. The next night, when Hanover and Bremen were the targets, airfields in East Anglia became enveloped in dense fog and twenty-two aircraft, including eleven Wellingtons – two of them from 149 Squadron – were lost in crashes. Eight Whitleys were temporarily attached to RAF Mildenhall in February. Admiral of the Fleet, Sir Roger Keyes, made a visit on 6 February and on the following day the Whitleys took off for a special operation to Malta.

Meanwhile, Mildenhall and other airfields in East Anglia had become regular targets for German intruders. A Dornier Do 215 made exceptionally low-level attacks on 30 January 1941 and again two days later on 1/2 February, causing considerable damage to aircraft and buildings. A Dornier returned on 2 February, dropping ten bombs in a shallow dive, but no serious damage was done. A Dornier Do 17 flying at 2,500ft attacked the Newmarket satellite again on 3 February. Ten bombs were dropped and two aircraft were damaged, in addition to several buildings. Mildenhall's anti-aircraft guns engaged an intruder on 18 February. No bombs were dropped and the gunners claimed a direct hit. Enemy action later that day caused a breakdown in communications between RAF Mildenhall and HQ No.3 Group and the Newmarket satellite. An additional bombing raid was carried out on 24 February and then on 27 February three separate attacks were made by a single Dornier Do 215. No bombs were dropped on the first two approaches but eleven were dropped on the third, causing only crater damage. The Mildenhall 'K' site at Cavenham was also attacked on 27 February. 'K' sites were dummy airfields designed to lure enemy aircraft away from their true targets, the flares on the landing paths being positioned closer than usual to give an illusion of greater height. At first, obsolete or unserviceable aircraft were left on these fields as decoys but later realistic dummies were specially made for this purpose at the Shepperton Film Studios. The 'K' site at Euston was so realistic that Wellington *U for Uncle* of 149 Squadron once landed there, on a totally unprepared field, when returning short of fuel from a raid. Such sites had served their purpose by 1942 and were then either abandoned or converted to genuine operational stations. The Cavenham site was abandoned but a new airfield, RAF Tuddenham, was opened in 1943 only a few hundred yards from the original dummy site.

In February 1941 Trevor A. 'Happy' Hampton's trained bomber crew were posted to 149 Squadron at Mildenhall. He recalls:

This was the squadron that featured in the well-known wartime film *Target For Tonight* and for a short time our station was like a film set. After a few days in the Officers' Mess I seemed to detect a subtle sort of deference being bestowed upon me by other junior officers. Nothing was said but everyone was so 'very nice'. At first I thought it might be that I had arrived as a fully-fledged flying officer, with 600 flying hours in my logbook, rather than the more usual humble pilot officer straight from training school. For a day or two I basked in my fool's paradise. We had been assigned a brand new Wellington IC [R1474], which should have made me a little suspicious. My ground crew painted on it our squadron letters 'OJ' and our identification letter 'M'. For radio telephony purposes, each letter of the alphabet has an associated word and the code in those days was '*A-Apple*', '*B-Baker*' and for 'M' it was 'Mother'. Secretly, I was delighted. I had a good mother and she would look after me - it was an omen.

Apart from myself, my own crew consisted of a front gunner, second pilot, navigator, radio operator and I had arranged for an old friend to be my rear gunner Sergeant George Gray but to me he was 'Junior', as he was so very young. 'Junior' had been a commissioned pilot. He was an excellent officer, much better than I, knew his King's Regulations – but as a pilot he was accident prone. He also clashed with his flight commander, who did not rest until 'Junior' had lost his commission. I was there and saw it all, and it was most unfair. But these things happen in the services and the RAF nearly lost a good man – but not so. 'Junior' promptly rejoined in the ranks as an aircrew gunner and didn't put up his pilot's wings, which he was fully entitled to but '*M-Mother*' finished up with three qualified pilots in the crew.

I began to notice that my crew, also, were being treated with a touching courtesy quite alien to the wartime RAF. I mentioned the phenomenon to 'Junior'. He looked at me incredulously. 'Don't you know Skipper? There have been eleven "*M-Mothers*" since Christmas!'

I was a bit shaken but I soon consoled myself – I still had faith in mother. Out of our squadron of eighteen aircraft, they must have been losing one '*M-Mother*' every week.

It was usual to do several trips as a second pilot before getting a command, but in view of my flying experience, although mostly on fighter types and my seniority, I had been given command immediately. However, just to show me the ropes and to see how 'easy' it was (his words), my flight commander, Squadron Leader Sawry Cookson, decided to accompany us on our first trip. He naturally assumed command and we left my second pilot behind.

The first trip was, more or less, a 'blitz' on Cologne. The Germans had a go at Coventry in November 1940, which I had seen burning from my own aircraft, so I didn't feel too badly about it – but really at heart, I was no bomber pilot.

With an inferno below we steamed over the city at 140 knots, at 8,000ft, the ceiling for a Wellington with a bomb load. Having done two runs over the target area, we were chased off by ground fire and searchlights, diving into the protective cloak of darkness clear of the city and leveling out at 2,000ft. Cooky let me take over and he went aft for a word with the crew. When he returned to the cockpit I was climbing but he stopped me – 2,000ft would be OK.

We cruised along quietly and eventually came across an enemy airfield, all lit up for night flying. 'Go down and stir them up a bit,' said Cooky. So down we went. Once round the circuit, they realised there was a cat among the pigeons and let us have some flak and light tracer fire. I looked at Cooky and he nodded towards home. I set course and started to climb but again he told me to stay at 2,000ft. It didn't seem right to me – but he should know.

We stooged along for some time and I was beginning to feel confident. I noticed that when I looked straight down immediately beneath I could see intermittent flickering lights beneath the aircraft. So much for blackout precautions – I was looking straight down the chimneys of a large city, probably Rotterdam but I didn't get the chance to confirm with the navigator, Sergeant Cymbalist. At that moment there was a blinding flash and 'M-Mother' was on the instant the focal point of countless searchlights and we seemed to be trapped in a cage of golden rods. I was petrified into immobility but it did slowly dawn on me that the air was composed of vicious tracer shells and bullets. The crack of exploding shells could be heard above the noise of our engines. That meant they were close and then a much louder one rocked the aircraft. The starboard wing went down, followed by the nose. I had the stick right back and the wheel hard over to port but 'M-Mother' was diving out of the sky and I was quite helpless. The altimeter was unwinding like a mad thing, I watched it go past 500ft in numb despair and I knew we were 'going in' – this was it and on our first trip. 'Oh, Mother!'

Under such circumstances imminent death brings with it no acute agony of mind, as one would expect, but a hopeless numb realisation of the end. I knew it was no good struggling anymore and I was just about to let go of the controls and cover my face for the final blinding crash when Cooky's voice came over the intercom, 'Come on, hold it!' We might have been on a training exercise. I hung on, with Cooky leaning across me, helping to take some of the weight and we eventually leveled off at 200ft, the searchlights and flak losing us as we dived earthwards.

Our speed was down to eighty-five knots and we were flying in a semi-stalled condition, tail down and nose up. Our two Bristol Pegasus engines were at full boost but we couldn't gain speed or height, and I dared not let our nose or wing go down the slightest degree. We staggered home across the North Sea, every moment expecting the aircraft to drop a wing and spin in but as we burnt up our fuel, inch by inch we made a little height and crossed the English coast at 500ft. Cooky could see that I was exhausted and he managed to slide underneath me into the pilot's seat. Cooky saved 'M-Mother' that night. He was a remarkable person who just did not acknowledge danger and was quite fearless. This was proved time and time again, and some of the stories of his exploits made me decide to be on my own, thank you. He was awarded a DSO later and he had a DFC. What became of him, I do not know. I hope he made it – but I doubt it. I felt I had the edge on him as a 'safe' pilot but who wanted 'safe' pilots in 1941? We could not possibly have made the usual circuit round the airfield but luckily, with the light of dawn, we managed to make a straight approach from the east, right on to the grass runway. I expected Cooky to make a full power approach and do a wheel landing, but too late, I realised he was holding off to do a 'three pointer'. The starboard wing naturally stalled first, a great chunk of it was missing and down we came into Mildenhall, a shaken crew.

At dawn the ground crew pushed off for breakfast, having written us off as one more M-Mother. However, they were soon out on 'M site' again and seemed genuinely pleased to see us back, although it meant the fitting of a new wing.

I was rather looking forward to the interrogation by our Intelligence Officer, John Cobb, of water and land speed record fame. 'Everything OK?' asks John. 'Yes, bombs on target,' says Cooky. 'Come on, let's get some breakfast.' I was learning fast.

After some sleep, to my surprise, I found that the night's experience had improved my morale and my faith in 'M-Mother' had been justified. My crew was not convinced and Junior privately expressed the hope that he would be re-commissioned before he got the 'chop'.

A new wing was fitted and I carried out an air test. On reporting the aircraft serviceable again, Cooky informed me that he was ending my 'M-Mother' to 'A' Flight for the coming night's operation. I could stand down with all my crew, except for my second pilot, Sergeant Evan Roy Cooke, who they wanted to borrow.

During the afternoon of 17 March, Sergeant Ronald Warren, the captain of the unserviceable 'A' Flight aircraft, sought me out in the 'B' Flight crew room.[2] He was in a dreadful state and made little effort to hide it. 'I'm told I have to take your aircraft tonight, Sir – and it's '*M-Mother*'.' I said, 'Yes, look after her; she's flying nicely with the new wing.'

The poor boy was nearly speechless but in a rambling disjointed manner he told me he had done twenty-eight operations, had only two more to do of his present tour and now fate had dealt him '*M-Mother*'. (In 1941 twenty-eight ops was really something, for in those days we didn't make one dive for the target, let everything go and then race for home – no. We were instructed to drop half our bomb load, fly away and then make a second attack, having stirred up a hornet's nest and let the rest go. The idea I presume, being to let the enemy think we had twice the number of aircraft. And we did it one at a time, not hundreds at a time as they did later, to keep them up all night.) In 149 Squadron she really was the 'end'. I felt a little piqued. I didn't like to think of my aircraft as a leper. In truth, there was little expressed sympathy wasted in the wartime RAF and none was expected. This expression of fear to an officer he hadn't even spoken to before was unprecedented in my experience. It was more than just a premonition to the boy. He had made up his mind they were for the 'chop'. Instead of trying to laugh him out of it, I found myself comforting him and my last words were, 'I guarantee "*M-Mother*" will bring you right back.'

I lived out of camp in a caravan at Barton Mills, deep in the woods and I was woken up by the sound of firing. The following morning, 18 March, driving along the road from Barton Mills to the airfield, I saw the tail end of a Wellington bomber sticking up out of the roof of a house. Just clear of the slates, I read 'M-OJ'[3].

A new Wellington [R1587] was towed out to 'M' site and yet another '*M-Mother*' was prepared for operations. In this one, we completed a few operations and to everyone's surprise, returned intact. One night, intent on blasting Hitler's three pocket battleships lying in Brest harbour, we were being shaken up by the combined defensive fire of the three battleships and all the Brest Peninsular flak. The navigator was chanting over his bombsight for my benefit, 'Left. Left. Steady. Right. Steady', when I heard Junior shout something about a fighter. Without any conscious intention on my part, I had '*M-Mother*' in a vertical diving turn to starboard. The navigator shouted, 'Bombs gone' but added that he didn't know where and from the rear turret Junior howled, 'Hell, Skipper. What are you doing? You frightened the daylights out of the Jerry fighter. You turned right across his bows.'

It wasn't only the Jerry who was shaken.

Back at base Junior got me on one side; the others had delegated him. 'Skip, you really must see Doc about your ears.' I did and was grounded for further examination. To my surprise the news caused consternation in the crew. Squadron Leader Anthony W.J. Clark, just posted to the squadron, took over 'B' Flight from Cooky, who was promoted to Squadron Commander. Clark also took over '*M-Mother*' and my crew for the time being and decided on a daylight training flight to get to know the aircraft and the boys. He had only been on the camp a few hours and could not have known '*M-Mother*'s' reputation. Being a senior officer and on such short acquaintance, my crew wouldn't have presumed to mention such a subject and I didn't say anything; what good could it have done?

I watched '*M-Mother*' climb away with mixed feelings on 17 May. It is not nice being grounded, even temporarily, and I had a guilty sense of having let my crew down. I wandered into the crew room, wondering what I should do until their return but hearing the commotion of the fire engine and the ambulance getting underway, I went outside to see what was up. Someone shouted across to me, 'Your aircraft has gone in. A Hurricane flew smack through her.' I jumped into my car and headed for the distant column of black oily smoke that marked the end of one more '*M-Mother*'.

In the of a potato field I stumbled amongst the still smoldering remains of my aeroplane and friends, until the station doctor walked me away. 'You shouldn't be here. You can't do any good.' It was of course bad for morale, my morale. One of the fire crew came up and told me that the tail gunner and rear gun turret were in the next field, unburnt. My unspoken question was answered before I dare ask it. 'The rear gunner didn't have time to get out. They were only at 2,000ft.' I walked over to a stretcher on, which was the only body they had recovered. From beneath army blankets protruded two beautifully polished boots. It was the last I was to see of 'junior' – the 'tail end' captain of '*M-Mother*'.

To the others around, it might have seemed that I was staring morbidly at my dead friend but they didn't know I was trying to get a final message through top him and the intercom was worse that usual. 'You very nearly made it Junior – your commission had been approved.'[4]

I had a talk with Cooky, who laughed at me at first but once he realised I was dead serious he agreed to drop '*M-Mother*' from the squadron aircraft board and replace it with '*P-Peter*'. I was posted away for training as a test pilot and lost touch with Bomber Command friends but I hope the trick worked. However, '*M-Mother*' had looked after me. I felt she would – I had a good mother.

In March 1941 meanwhile, significant changes occurred at RAF Mildenhall. The headquarters of No.3 (Bomber) Group moved to Harraton House at Exning, near Newmarket, not to return to Mildenhall again until January 1947. By the end of 1941, No.3 Group's strength had increased to more than 200 bombers and fourteen squadrons, all of which were equipped with the Short Stirling four-engined heavy bombers. On 18 March the operational control of the Newmarket satellite was passed to RAF Stradishall. No.99 (Madras Presidency) Squadron was then posted to RAF Waterbeach to be part of No.5 Group and early the following year moved to India to operate against the Japanese in Burma. The squadron's two tours of duty in India are reflected in its official title of 99 Squadron. This left 149 Squadron as the only bomber squadron now under the control of RAF Mildenhall. On 30/31 March, 109 aircraft, including fifty Wellingtons – eight from 149 Squadron – were ordered to attack the two German battle cruisers *Scharnhorst* and *Gneisenau* lying in dock at Brest on the French coast. 149 Squadron dropped sixty-four 500lb bombs on this operation, bringing the total so far dropped by the squadron to 1,000 tons. Repeated attacks were made on the two cruisers – known to the RAF crews as 'Salmon and Glukstein' (a famous London department store) and on German ports and Ruhr towns throughout April.

On 3 March, 149 Squadron had received two of the new Wellington Mk II bombers which, with their powerful Rolls-Royce Merlin engines, were capable of carrying a 4,000lb high-capacity (HC) light-case bomb, commonly called a 'Cookie' that was being brought into service. This bomb was first dropped in anger on 31 March/1 April 1941 when six Wimpys were despatched on the raid on Emden, while twenty-eight Wellingtons attacked Bremen. Two of 149 Squadron's aircraft acted as cover for the Mk II Wellingtons carrying the 'Cookies'. The first aircraft, OJ-X W5439 *X-X-ray*, piloted by Pilot Officer J.H. Franks, successfully completed the operation. The second, coded OJ-Q, failed to get airborne and slid to a halt in a barley field at the edge of Mr Norman's small-holding at West Row – the 'Wizard of Oz' painted on the bomber had failed to work its magic. OJ-H R1229 flown by Sergeant G.J.P. Morhen landed heavily on return, stalled and crashed. One gunner died of his injuries later. A second 'Cookie' was dropped by a 9 Squadron Wellington. These 'high capacity' bombs soon came to be called 'Luftminen' by the Germans.

From Batavia, Dutch East Indies came ironically 4,000lb of tea for delivery to the occupied Netherlands. Placed in 2/3oz packets, it was passed to 3 Group stations whose Wellingtons delivered thirty packets at a time. The packets were small to avoid bursting upon ground impact.

Throughout spring, summer and autumn, 149 Squadron operated mainly against Bremen, Cologne, Kiel, Munster and Mannheim. On 18/19 June 1941, when fifty-seven Wellingtons and eight Stirlings went to Brest, Pilot Officer Forman had to nurse T2898 back with the hydraulics badly damaged. He then decided to circle until daylight. When fuel was low, he decided to land but two other aircraft turned onto approach ahead of him. He had to belly land at RAF Lakenheath, which was not yet in operation. Another less fortunate crew, hopelessly lost in sea fog near Ilfracombe, were killed in the ensuing crash. Sergeant Hanlon was on his bomb run to Münster when R1802 *F for Freddie*'s port engine became troublesome. He had almost reached base when the propeller began to wobble, and then fell off.

A bomb train for a Wellington of 149 Squadron at Mildenhall on 10 May 1941 for the operation to Hamburg, when 119 aircraft attacked the city and another twenty-three bombers raided Berlin. Seven aircraft, including one 149 Squadron Wellington, failed to return. (IWM via Dr. Colin Dring)

Wellington IC OJ-R of 149 Squadron. (RAF Museum)

Engineering personnel working on a Wellington.

A Wellington of 149 Squadron at Mildenhall in 1941. (IWM via Dr Colin Dring)

Wellingtons of 149 Squadron at Mildenhall with OJ-N nearest the camera. (IWM)

No.149 Squadron continued to play a full part in the bombing campaign throughout 1941 and it was also chosen to participate in the making of *Target for Tonight*, by Harry Watts, which was filmed by the Crown Film Unit. It featured the Wellington *F for Freddie* flown by Flight Lieutenant Percy C. Pickard, who took the 'leading roles' and for a short time Mildenhall was like a film set.[5] The *F for Freddie* that appeared in the film had never actually taken part in an operation against the enemy. The original Wimpy had been wrecked when it ran into the earth bank of the bomb dump at Mildenhall, upon returning from a raid. On 14 July, Sergeant D.A. 'Tony' Gee of 149 Squadron brought *N-Nuts* home to Mildenhall after being coned in the searchlights at 8,000ft over Bremen and fired on by accurate flak. Gee finally escaped but he was down to 2,000ft. His navigator-bomb aimer, The Right Honourable Terence Mansfield, who was flying his eleventh operation, recalls.

> No-one was wounded but, as daylight came we found lots of it coming in everywhere. Our wireless was not working so we could not tell base that, although we were a long way behind schedule, we were still coming. By the time we got back to Mildenhall we were classed as overdue. Someone classified the damage to R1593 as not repairable and '*N-Nuts*' was taken away in pieces.[6]

On 24 July 1941, Wellingtons, Hampdens and Fortresses made daylight attacks on the *Gneisenau* and *Prinz Eugen* at Brest, while Halifaxes attacked the *Scharnhorst* at La Pallice. Sixteen bombers failed to return and two other aircraft were lost when they ditched on the way home. In August, Mr Bayliss, an American who until recently had been attached to the American Embassy in Berlin, gave a lecture on the effects of the bombing campaign as seen by an observer at the receiving end. On 18/19 August 1941, during the raid on Duisburg, Wellington IC X9746 OJ-A of 149 Squadron flown by Pilot Officer Gregory was coned by searchlights near Venlo and then attacked by a Ju 88 and severely damaged. The rear of the Wimpy caught fire but Sergeant Billington, the rear gunner, extinguished the flames with his hands. Gregory brought his aircraft back safely despite the elevators being put out of action and with large areas of fabric missing. Gregory was awarded the DFC and Sergeant Billington, the DFM.

On 7/8 September 1941, 197 bombers went to three aiming points in Berlin while another fifty-one bombers headed for Kiel. The Berlin force comprised 103 Wellingtons, forty-three Hampdens, thirty-one Whitleys, six Halifaxes and four Manchesters – 137 crews claimed to have bombed their allotted targets in Berlin. Fifteen bombers were MIA and at least ten are thought to have been shot down by nightfighters. One by one the returning bombers landed back at their stations in eastern England. Pilot Officer Mike Evans and crew of a 149 Squadron Wellington returned to Mildenhall after what was an eventful trip, as Sergeant Jim Coman, the WO, recalls:

All went fairly well until we were making our bombing run, straight and level, when we were coned in searchlights and received numerous hits by flak. After releasing the bombs at 9,500ft we took evasive action but were unable to get out of the searchlights so we dived to roof top level and moved out of the target area as quickly as possible. The AA gunners were actually shooting bits off their own buildings trying to hit us. We gained height as soon as possible to regain our bearings and arrived back at the Dutch coast short of fuel. All the main tanks were empty so we had approximately twenty minutes flying time on the engine nacelle tanks. We were attacked by a Ju 88 over the Dutch coast south of the Friesian Islands and north of Rotterdam, which our rear gunner engaged and the fighter broke off trailing smoke from one of its engines. We made an emergency landing at the nearest airfield on the English coast, at Martlesham Heath, a fighter drome. As we landed the engines cut out. They had been running for nine hours after take off. We counted 150 holes in the aircraft before we left for Mildenhall but we failed to spot the most serious damage, which must have happened over the target when a shell must have penetrated the main spar when the bomb doors were open.

In September 1941, the Wellingtons were flying further afield, as Terence Mansfield, of 149 Squadron, recalls: 'On 26 September, while en route to Genoa, we had been recalled over France due to forecast bad weather at base.' Three days later the Wellingtons went all the way. Mansfield continues:

We had a lovely view of the Alps but Genoa was mostly covered by cloud so bombing was on estimated position using the coast. After leaving Genoa our wireless blew up and cloud developed solidly below 10,000ft so navigation was solely on astro fixes. Fortunately, we hit the Mildenhall Lorenz beam almost on ETA. Duggie Fox, my pilot, turned on to it and descended in the low cloud. Honington had been alerted and they fired a massive assortment of pyrotechnics as we approached and we crawled in under a cloud base of, at most, 20ft.

On 30 September the Wellingtons carried a new weapon, as Terence Mansfield recalls:

We carried a new 65-lb incendiary for marking purposes. This horrid weapon was very light case, rather like a large oblong tin, the contents of which were spontaneously combustible on contact with air. The resulting fire was very visible but it was a menace, as a leak brought fire.

On 12 October we again carried 65-lb incendiaries to Nurnberg. We had orders to drop only on visual. It was totally dark and although we flew around the area for forty minutes, we could see no ground detail. Then bombing started but it was not Nurnberg. Anyhow, we went over to investigate at just over 4,000ft and I was confident that I could make out a small town. Since the fires were well established, we added to them and sent a signal back that we had bombed a secondary target. Further astro fixes on the return trip confirmed my calculated positions. On landing, we were told that we were the only crew not to find the target but our photograph proved that we were right and that almost the entire attack had been against the wrong place. We got our haloes back!

On 7/8 November, [when Berlin was the target for 169 aircraft] my last [trip] with Duggie Fox and 149, we carried the 65-lb incendiary again. All the outward route was appalling, with high cloud, very bad icing, turbulence and rattling hail. Using the occasional breaks in the tops, I managed to get a series of astro fixes, so that at least we thought we were almost on track. Total cloud cover at the target meant that we could not drop our bombs and we brought them all the way back! That we crossed the Suffolk coast almost on track and only five minutes late on ETA proved the value of my sextant. We saw no signs of any defensive action and felt sure that the high losses [twenty-one], were due solely to the weather.[7]

In the closing days of 1941, 149 Squadron at Mildenhall began exchanging its Wellington IIs for the Short Stirling. No.3 Group, since it operated Bristol-engined bombers, had, in August 1941, been selected for re-equipment with the huge four-engined bomber but deliveries were slow. On 12 October, N6093 and W7448 arrived at Mildenhall. By the end of the month, 149 Squadron had eight Stirlings and conversion was underway. The new aircraft could carry a 14,000lb bomb load over short ranges but it was slow and with a load could reach only about 16,00ft. With evasive action over occupied territory, it was at around 12,000ft over a Ruhr city. At that height, it was also vulnerable from above if a Lancaster at 20,000ft released bombs. Bombing times were set to prevent this but not every crew kept to its time slot. The first of the four-engined bombers, the Stirling's wingspan was 9ft less than the original design. This was by special request to Short Brothers, the makers, to allow it to pass through the doors of the standard RAF hangar! This was an important requirement if it were to be serviced away from the elements but this fundamental change caused problems. It had to have a huge undercarriage, which meant that the cockpit window was 20ft from the ground. The Stirling was slower and had a much lower ceiling than the Lancaster or the Halifax, both of which came later and replaced the Stirling towards the end of 1943.

On 7/8 November, 149 Squadron sent eight Wellingtons to Berlin. Only one reached the target while twenty-one aircraft were lost from the 169 bombers despatched. On 26 November the squadron became the third to operate the Stirling when N6099 operated from RAF Mildenhall, when the target for sixteen Wellingtons and two Stirlings was Ostend. Only seven aircraft bombed, and there were no losses. On 30 November, N6099 sortied to Bremerhaven with five of the squadron's Wellingtons. The heavy four-engined bomber was unsuitable for the grass runways at Mildenhall, which was soon badly damaged and both squadrons moved to the satellite airfield at Lakenheath, which had concrete runways. On 10 January four crews took off at 4.15 a.m. One Stirling attacked Brest, returning with a badly holed fuel tank, which emptied itself. Another Stirling was hit by flak and had to force land at Weston Zoyland with a seriously wounded rear gunner. On 28 January 1942, four of 149 Squadron's crews were ordered to Lossiemouth for Operation *Oiled*. On the night of 29/30 January, two of the Stirlings along with five others and nine Halifaxes were detailed to attack the German battleship *Tirpitz* but extremely bad weather prevented all, except two aircraft, from reaching the Norwegian coast and bomb ships seen there. One Stirling was lost and *T-Tommy* of 149 Squadron piloted by Flight Lieutenant R.W.A. Turtle ran off the icy runway on landing and was written off.

No.419 Squadron RCAF meanwhile, had been formed at Mildenhall on 15 December 1941. This was the third Canadian squadron to be operational overseas and it was equipped with Wellington ICs coded VR. The Wellington IC was fitted with Type 423 gear for carrying 4,000lb bombs. Because there were so few Canadians, the squadron recruited RAF personnel as ground crews. The first aircraft arrived on 4 January 1942 and 419 Squadron made its operational debut in RAF Bomber Command on 11/12 January when the Canadian squadron despatched two Wellingtons to Brest where the German battle cruisers *Scharnhorst* and *Gneisenau* were bottled up by the Royal Navy. The first German target was Hamburg on 15/16 January. Then, amid general expectation that the German battle cruisers *Scharnhorst* and *Gneisenau* and the lighter cruiser *Prinz Eugen* must soon leave Brest, the bombers stood by. When, on 12 February, they finally made their dash for their home ports, the RAF and Royal Navy were found wanting. In the late afternoon, when all else had failed, three Wellingtons and two Stirlings from RAF Mildenhall were despatched to attack the German ships. However, they failed to find them in poor weather and two of the Wellingtons failed to return. Almost immediately the squadron was declared non-operational again, when its Wellington ICs were replaced with the Hercules-engined Wellington III. On 21 February the Canadians stood down while conversion took place, and the squadron first operated them on 9/10 March when RAF Bomber Command bombed Essen.

Meanwhile, on 22 February, having been recalled from the USA where he was head of the RAF Delegation, Air Marshal Arthur T. Harris arrived at High Wycombe, Buckinghamshire,

Wellington IC R1593 *N-Nuts* of 149 Squadron being bombed up at Mons Wood, Mildenhall in 1941. The odd drawing beneath the pilot's window is of a drunken firefly and represented, variously, the wireless operator (antennae), the pilot (wings), the tail-gunner (scorpion sting) and the eyes for the half-blind navigator. The whole portrayed a crew that flew by night and was supposedly drunk by day. On 14 July 1941, following a raid on Bremen, R1593 was taken away in pieces, damaged beyond the possibility of local repair. (Lord Sandhurst)

An early infrared camera captures the aircrew of 149 Squadron being driven to dispersal for a raid on Kiel Docks on the night of 11/12 March 1941. Left to right: Wing Commander (later Group Captain) Powell OBE DSO, squadron CO; Sergeant R.A. Petter (killed 17 May 1941), WOP of Wellington *M-Mother*; Pilot Officer Coryat; Squadron Navigation Officer. Standing: Flying Officer Trevor A. 'Happy' Hampton. Seated: Sergeant D. George 'Junior' Gray (killed 17 May 1941). Twenty-seven Wellingtons claimed many hits on the shipyards at Kiel and no aircraft were lost. (T.A. Hampton)

The crew of *M-Mother* in 149 Squadron. Left to right: Sergeant D. 'George' Gray, rear gunner; two members of the ground crew; Flying Officer T.A. Hampton, skipper; Sergeant Cymbalist, navigator; Sergeant Redmond, front gunner; Sergeant R.A. Petter (killed 17 May 1941), wireless operator. (T.A. Hampton)

The last unlucky *M-Mother* had its letter changed to 'P'. (T. A. Hampton)

Above: The crew of Wellington *N for Nuts* in 149 Squadron in early 1942. Left to right: Sergeant (later Warrant Officer) Len Collins RAAF; Dick Gallagher; Bill Phillips; Bill Barnes; Doug Baker; Ron Cook. Collins was shot down flying with Squadron Leader G.W. Alexander in a Stirling on 29/30 June 1942 and was taken prisoner. He was the crew's only survivor. (Len Collins via Theo Boiten)

Right: Wing Commander J. 'Moose' Fulton DSO DFC AFC who was from Kamloops, Canada, and Flight Sergeant Alexander stand beside the splintered port prop blade of their Wellington following an encounter with a Bf 110 on the night of 28/29 April 1942 after bombing Kiel. Flight Lieutenant Bob O'Callaghan, Gunnery Leader, was wounded. The hydraulic system was damaged, and the undercarriage and bomb doors stuck in the down position. Fulton failed to return from a raid on Hamburg on 28/29 July 1942 and 419 adopted his nickname in his memory. (via Dr Colin Dring)

to take charge of RAF Bomber Command from AVM J.E.A. 'Jackie' Baldwin. Harris's concept was to break the German spirit by the use of area rather than precision bombing and the targets would be civilian, not just military. Such a concept two years before would have been unthinkable but Harris saw the need to deprive the German factories of its workers and therefore its ability to manufacture weapons for war. Mass raids would be the order of the day, or rather the night, with little attention paid to precision raids on military targets. However, Bomber Command did not possess the numbers of aircraft necessary for immediate mass raids. On taking up his position Harris found that only 380 aircraft were serviceable. Only sixty-eight of these were heavy bombers, while 257 were medium bombers.

On 3/4 March, ten of the new Stirling bombers took part in the raid on the Renault factory at Billancourt near Paris, which had been earmarked for attack for some time. It was the first target selected by Air Marshal Arthur T. Harris. A full moon was predicted, so Harris decided to send a mixed force of 235 aircraft, led by the most experienced crews in Bomber Command to bomb the French factory in three waves. The first wave was manned by fully trained crews, a second wave of medium bombers and a third wave of Manchesters, Halifaxes and Wellingtons, equipped for 4,000lb bombs. All aircraft were to carry as many flares as their bomb loads allowed. The first wave was to light up the target, then bomb, and then drop its remaining flares to windward. The second wave was to do the same so that the target would be well lit the entire time. Two separate groups of buildings were to be bombed with the aircraft of No.3 Group aiming at the works on an island in the Seine and the rest at the main factory on the riverbank.

It was calculated that approximately 121 aircraft an hour had been concentrated over the factory, which was devastated and all except twelve aircraft claimed to have bombed. It was reported that 300 bombs fell on the factory destroying 40 per cent of the buildings. Production was halted for four weeks and final repairs were not completed for several months. A post-war American estimate said that the production loss was almost 2,300 vehicles. Just one aircraft (a Wellington) was lost but 367 French people were killed, 341 were badly injured and 9,250 people lost their homes. Later that same month, on 28/29 March, a raid on Lübeck destroyed a huge accumulation of stores that had been intended for use in the Russian campaign.

In April, 149 Squadron began mine-laying operations around the Friesian Islands and these continued on a regular basis over the following months. Although still under the control of Mildenhall, 149 Squadron now operated almost exclusively from Lakenheath. On the night of 6/7 April 1942 157 bombers went to Essen but the crews encountered severe storms and icing and there was complete cloud cover at the target. Only forty-nine aircraft claimed to have reached the target area and there was virtually no damage to Essen. Five aircraft were lost and a 149 Squadron Wellington crew[8] had a narrow escape, as Sergeant Jim Coman, WOP/AG, recalls:

> We were returning from Essen when we were attacked by a Messerschmitt 110 over the Dutch coast just south of the Friesian Islands at about 18,000ft. The 110 hit us in our port wing, holing one petrol tank and causing us to lose about 400 gallons of fuel. The gunners returned fire and it broke off the attack and dived back through the clouds trailing smoke. Before landing at base we lowered the undercarriage to examine the port wheel for damage but nothing appeared amiss. However, the pilot decided to keep the weight off the wheel for as long as possible and landed port wing up but on reaching stalling speed and the wheel touching the ground, it collapsed. The wing hit the ground and swung us round 180 degrees and the wing broke across one of the fuel tanks. We all evacuated the aircraft quickly, as we could hear the engine sizzling in the petrol spillage. Fortunately, it did not catch fire.

On 24/25 March, 149 Squadron laid mines for the first time when a dozen were dropped off the Isle de Groix on the approach to Lorient. Air Vice-Marshal Edwards, chief of the air staff of the RCAF, inspected 419 Squadron at Mildenhall on 23 April. In April, 149 Squadron moved to RAF Lakenheath, which for some time remained under RAF Mildenhall's control.

On 29 May 1942, it was apparent that something out of the ordinary was about to happen. Top level consultations between Harris and his subordinate commanders had revealed that the raids on Rostock achieved total disruption. Whole areas of the city had been wiped out and 100,000 people had been forced to evacuate the city. The capacity of its workers to produce war materials had therefore been severely diminished. Harris had for some time nurtured the desire to send 1,000 bombers to a German city and reproduce the same results with incendiaries. Although RAF losses would be on a large scale, Churchill approved the plan. Harris (now Sir Arthur), gave the order 'Operation *Plan Cologne*' to his group commanders just after midday on 30 May so that 1,000 bombers would be unleashed on the 770,000 inhabitants. Some 599 Wellingtons, including four of Flying Training Command, made up the bulk of the attacking force, which also included eighty-eight Stirlings, 131 Halifaxes and seventy-three Lancasters. The rest of the force was made up of Whitleys, Hampdens and Manchesters. All bomber bases throughout England were at a high state of readiness to get all available aircraft airborne for the raid. At Mildenhall 419 Squadron RCAF had eighteen first line Wellingtons ready, together with seventeen Stirlings of 149 Squadron. A quarter of the 1,046 aircraft despatched came from 3 Group, which operated in a fire-raising capacity, carrying loads of 4lb incendiary canisters. 419 Squadron sent eighteen Wellingtons, mostly carrying 810 4lb incendiaries. Flight Lieutenant, The Honourable Terence Mansfield, 419 Squadron Bombing Leader recalls:

> 419 were wholly equipped with Wellington IIIs and there were crews for every aircraft. 'Moose'[9] was not one to take over someone else's aircraft so he borrowed an elderly IC from the Blind Approach Training Flight. This normally spent its time flying along our Lorenz-beam training pilots to use it. We took off at 2325 hours. Although 419 were in the first wave, we were not. At approximately 50-mph slower than the IIIs, our IC was also handicapped by trying to get to the briefed height of 18,000ft, 4,000ft higher than I had ever been before in a Wellington. We made visual identification on arrival at Cologne and made one circuit of the city before our attack. We then flew round the target again as Moose had a pair of night binoculars, which were remarkably effective but I made no notes of what I could see. I think I must have been more interested in looking down from what seemed such a great height; this being the occasion on which I had dropped bombs from over 10,000ft. Our attack was made as ordered: Height 17,500ft; Night photograph taken and later plotted within 800yds of the aiming point. The weather over the target was remarkably clear and not as we had come to expect from the Ruhr area.

For ninety-eight minutes a procession of bombers passed over Cologne. Stick after stick of incendiaries rained down from the bomb bays of the Wellingtons, adding to the conflagration. Almost all aircraft bombed their aiming point as briefed. The defences, because of the attacking forces size, were relatively ineffective and flak was described variously as 'sporadic' and 'spasmodic'. Flight Lieutenant Pattison, who piloted a 419 Squadron RCAF Wellington, wrote:

> When I bombed there was a huge fire on the east bank of the Rhine and another just starting on the west bank. When I left the target area both sides were getting it thick and fast and eventually, large concentrations of fires were spread practically across the length and breadth of the entire built-up area.

Of the forty-three RAF losses, it is estimated that thirty were shot down by nightfighters. In all, 898 crews claimed to have hit their targets. Post-bombing reconnaissance certainly showed that more than 600 acres of Cologne had been razed to the ground. The fires burned for days and almost 60,000 people had been made homeless.

No.419 Squadron put up nineteen aircraft for the second 'Thousand Bomber' raid on Essen on 1/2 June when a force of 956 aircraft was ready. Again some bombers returned with mechanical and engine problems. Although seemingly lacking the concentration of the earlier raid on Cologne, the bombing was nevertheless effective enough to saturate the defences. One skipper went as far as to say that the fires were more impressive than those of Cologne were. A belt of fires extended across the city's entire length, from the western edge to the eastern suburbs. Many fires were also spread over other parts of the Ruhr.

Both 149 and 419 Squadrons participated in the third 'Thousand Bomber Raid' on Bremen on the night of 25/26 June, when 419 Squadron put up seventeen aircraft as part of the force of 1,006 aircraft, which included 102 Wellingtons of Coastal Command. At least two crews from 425 'Alouette' French Canadian Squadron, which was still in the process of forming at Dishforth on the Wellington III. The CO, Squadron Leader 'Joe' St Pierre and his flight commander, Flight Lieutenant Logan Savard, captained their own crews and flew in 419 Squadron's formation led by Wing Commander J. 'Moose' Fulton DSO DFC AFC, this time in a Wellington III. Terence Mansfield, Fulton's navigator-bomb aimer, who was on the thirtieth and final operation of his tour, recalls:

> We took off at 23:25 hours. Although briefed for a greater height, we found the target area completely 'covered by cloud and came down to 12,000 feet in the hope of getting' some visual identification from which we could start a timed run. We ended up doing what others did, namely bombing what we thought was the most likely place. Not very satisfactory and nor were the results.

Crews were given the opportunity of bombing the red glow of the fires, using *Gee* as a check, or proceeding to a secondary target in the vicinity of Bremen. The cloud conditions prevailed at many of the targets of opportunity and many crews, unable to bomb, brought their lethal cargoes home. The risk of collision and enemy fighter activity proved a constant threat and crews had to be ever watchful. Squadron Leader Wolfe's 419 Squadron Wellington was involved in an engagement with a Bf 110 nightfighter, north of Borkum at 4,200ft over the North Sea. Sergeant D.R. Morrison opened fire and the enemy fighter's port engine was seen to burst into flames, which almost at once engulfed the entire wing. It dived into the sea, leaving a large circle of fire around the point of impact. 'Moose' Fulton and Terence Mansfield landed back at Mildenhall at 4.45 a.m. without incident. Mansfield had completed his tour and later became Bombing Leader on a squadron of Lancasters. Bremen was the third and final 1,000-bomber raid in the series of five major saturation attacks on German cities. The German High Command was shaken, while on the home front, morale soared.

King George VI paid another visit to Mildenhall on 12 June, the date of two crews' attempts at a cloud-cover day raid, which they had to abandon when cover ran out. Four night's later Flight Sergeant Swanson's aircraft was hit repeatedly by flak near Essen. The crew fought a rear fuselage fire while a night fighter chased X3699 and the Wellington suddenly stalled and fell 200ft with its bomb doors hanging open and the undercarriage dangling. The second pilot and the front gunner had been wounded. Miraculously, Swanson force landed his aircraft at Finchingfield without further injury to the crew.

When on the night of 29/30 June, Bomber Command despatched 253 aircraft to Bremen, eleven aircraft failed to return. Warrant Officer Len Collins RAAF, a Stirling gunner in 149 Squadron who had completed his tour and was awaiting a posting to an EFTS to train as a pilot, volunteered for an extra op. He stood in for the mid-upper gunner, who was ill, on the crew of Squadron Leader G.W. Alexander, who would be flying N6082. It would be Collins' thirty-third trip. He recalls:

> Other than the second pilot, Flying Officer W.G. Barnes, on his first trip to gain experience, remainders of the crew were on their thirtieth. All were RAF. I was the only Aussie. The trip to Bremen was uneventful. Conversing with the squadron leader I found that he was most interested with the pyrotechnic display from the *Flak* and the colours of the searchlights as we crossed the

enemy coast. I predicted we were in for trouble when a blue one slid off our wing tip. However, either our doctored *IFF* did not work or the Germans were given a tip-off. Over Bremen we received a direct hit from flak on our inner starboard engine, killing Alexander and Pilot Officer C.W. Dellow, observer and injuring the WOp D.S. Hickley. The bombs were dropped live, a photo taken and we headed for home on three engines. Over the Zuider Zee a night fighter appeared.[10] I can still recall the flash of his windscreen in the darkness as he opened fire. As I was speaking to the rear gunner, Sergeant R. Gallagher, he was blown out of his turret. I was ringed with cannon shells and injured in the leg by shrapnel. Owing to the electrical cut out which protected the tail of the aircraft from the mid-upper guns, I was unable to fire on the fighter attacking us. Fortunately, the turret became jammed in the rear position, allowing me to vacate it. Forward, the aircraft was burning like a torch. I could not contact any crewmember. The position was hopeless. I felt I had no option but to leave the aircraft. My parachute was not in its storage holder. I found it under the legs of the mid-upper turret with a cannon shell burn in it. I removed the rear escape hatch, clipped on the parachute and sat on the edge of the hatch. I pulled the ripcord and tumbled out. The parachute, having several holes from the shell burn, 'candlesticked' (twirled) as I descended and I landed in a canal. I was apprehended the following day and was taken to Leeuwarden airfield for interrogation. Here I met the pilot of the Messerschmitt 110 who claimed to have shot us down. I abused him in good Australian. He understood, having spent three years at Oxford University.[11]

During 1942 many VIPs visited RAF Mildenhall. The King and Queen visited again on 12 June, Mr W.J. Jordan, the High Commissioner for New Zealand on 8 October and Prince Bertil of Sweden on 12 October. On 28 July, the Duke of Kent and the Honourable Vincent Massey, Governor-General of Canada and the High Commissioner for Canada visited RAF Mildenhall to watch 419 Squadron leave for Hamburg on the night of 28/29 July 1942. News was later received that X3488 carrying Wing Commander J. 'Moose' Fulton DSO DFC AFC, the squadron commander, had been shot down off the Friesians. Fulton's nickname was incorporated in the official title of the unit.

On 14 August, 419 Squadron's seventeen Wellingtons left RAF Mildenhall for Leeming in Yorkshire. The Canadians were renowned throughout the Mildenhall area for their high spirits and they would be greatly missed – the squadron moved twice more before being posted in November 1942 to RAF Middleton St George from where it was to operate, as part of No.6 (RCAF) Group for the remainder of the war. Two new Ventura squadrons, 464 RAAF and 487 RNZAF, arrived at RAF Feltwell and 75 (New Zealand) Squadron moved temporarily to Mildenhall. On 25 September, 115 Squadron's Wellington IIIs joined them from RAF Marham, which had been placed in 2 Group, pending the arrival of two Mosquito squadrons. There were other administrative changes at this time, in that 1503 BAT (Blind Approach Training) Flight, which had been operating from Mildenhall throughout the summer, was replaced on 5 September by 1505 BAT Flight, which was equipped with Oxfords. The unit moved to Upper Heyford on 17 December 1942. 75 Squadron resumed operations almost immediately with three raiding Osnabrück on the night of 17/18 August. On 28/29 August, ten crews were part of the force of 159 aircraft that set out on the seven-hour journey to Nuremberg. Twenty-three aircraft were lost. Frightening moments still abounded, as when Sergeant Blinkers was flying BJ790 to Essen on 16/17 September. Flak battered the starboard mainplane and tore a hole in the fuselage making a turn to port impossible. Coming home, a nightfighter raked the Wellington, injuring the wireless operator. Even with the hydraulics out of use, Blinkers still managed a safe belly landing.

Attacks on industry in North Italy were resumed in October and on the night of 28/29 November 1942, 228 aircraft, including 117 Lancasters and forty-seven Stirlings raided the Fiat Works at Turin. Flight Sergeant Rawdon Hume Middleton RAAF of 149 Squadron piloted one of the Stirlings (BF372). The aircraft met unexpectedly high headwinds over the Alps and had used so much fuel that many had to turn back. Middleton decided to press on and he went down to 2,000ft in order to establish the exact position of the target.

Three Wellingtons of 149 Squadron fly low over the hangars at RAF Mildenhall. Behind is a Type A hangar. (IWM)

The west end of the hangar line with the original Mildenhall to Littleport road in the foreground on 8 July 1942. (IWM)

On 28 July 1942, Group Captain the Duke of Kent (seen here inspecting members of 419 Squadron RCAF) and the Honourable Vincent Massey, Governor-General of Canada visited RAF Mildenhall to watch 419 Squadron leave for Hamburg on the night of 28/29 July. News was later received that X3488 carrying Wing Commander J. 'Moose' Fulton DSO DFC AFC, the squadron commander, had been shot down off the Friesians. The duke, who was killed in a Sunderland flying boat a month after this photograph was taken, had visited Mildenhall on 25 June 1941 to inspect 149 Squadron. (IWM)

Wellington III VR-Q Z1572 of 419 'Moose' Squadron RCAF in the summer of 1942. (IWM)

New Zealand High Commissioner Mr W.J. Jordan shakes hands with Warrant Officer Bernet DFM during a visit to 75 (New Zealand) Squadron at Mildenhall on 8 October 1942. (via Dr Colin Dring)

Short Stirling I OJ-G of 149 'East India' Squadron in 3 Group at RAF Mildenhall in 1942. (via Theo Boiten)

Late in 1942 Mildenhall continued to control its three squadrons, even though none were now at the parent airfield because of reconstruction. 115 Squadron was at East Wretham, 149 Squadron continued to fly from the Lakenheath satellite while 75 Squadron, converted now to Stirlings (pictured), was at this time stationed at Newmarket. (TAMM)

Flight Sergeant Rawdon Hume Middleton RAAF of 149 Squadron received a posthumous VC for his actions on 28/29 November 1942 when, mortally wounded, he flew Stirling BF372 back to England after a raid on the Fiat Works at Turin, Italy. Five of his crew baled out to safety but when BF372 ran out of fuel it crashed into the English Channel, and Middleton and his flight engineer and front gunner, who had remained aboard to help their captain, drowned. 149 Squadron flew 2,628 Stirling sorties on 244 bombing and 160 minelaying raids, losing eighty-seven aircraft before converting to the Lancaster in August 1944. (IWM)

The Australian's Stirling was caught by anti-aircraft fire as he made his first approach, but despite this, he made two more runs over the city and on the last the Stirling was hit repeatedly. The windscreen was shattered and Middleton's right eye was completely destroyed. He was also badly wounded in the body, but despite his fearsome wounds, he kept his aircraft on target until all the bombs had been dropped. Flight Sergeant Leslie Hyder, the second pilot, recovered consciousness from a head wound and struggled with Middleton to keep the crippled bomber airborne as they flew away from the immediate danger zone. When Middleton saw how badly Hyder was injured, he ordered him to go back into the fuselage to receive first aid but, just as Hyder was doing this, Middleton suddenly lost consciousness and slumped over the controls. 6,000ft were lost and the Stirling was down to only 800ft before the wounded Hyder could muster sufficient strength to check the descent and put the aircraft into a slow climb back on the homeward track. In the fuselage the wireless operator, Pilot Officer Norman Skinner, and a wounded gunner, Sergeant Harold Gough, received first aid from the uninjured crew members but both insisted on returning to their posts. The aircraft was badly damaged and fuel was short. Hyder assumed temporary command and ordered everything possible to be jettisoned. Even the guns were thrown out, leaving the Stirling completely defenceless. Middleton, conscious again but practically blind, called the crew around him to discuss the alternatives. They decided to stay with the aircraft and to try to make the English coast. For almost four hours Middleton kept the Stirling on track, taking evasive action as searchlights caught them over France. He must have suffered agony as the biting wind rushed through the shattered windscreen on to his hideously mutilated face. Fuel was running out as they were over the English Channel and Middleton gave the order to bale out. Sergeant John Mackie half carried the wounded Hyder to the escape hatch, placed the second pilot's hand on his parachute release and pushed him out. Gough, who was flying his thirty-third operation, Flight Sergeant Douglas Cameron and Flying Officer George Royde jumped next, followed by the wounded Skinner. As they floated down, they saw the Stirling turn back over the sea with Middleton, Jeffery and Mackie still on board. The bodies of Sergeant James Jeffery and Mackie, who was on his thirty-first operation having volunteered, like Gough, to fly until his skipper had completed his tour, were washed ashore the next day. Middleton's body was not recovered for three months after he was washed ashore on Shakespeare Beach, Dover, on 1 February.

On 13 January 1943, Flight Sergeant Middleton was posthumously awarded the Victoria Cross, the highest award for gallantry. The official citation stated in part: 'His devotion to duty in the face of overwhelming odds is unsurpassed in the annals of the Royal Air Force'. On 5 February Middleton was buried with full military honours in the Military Cemetery in the churchyard of St John's Church in Beck Row. He was buried with the rank of Pilot Officer. News of his commission had not reached him before his death.[12]

No.115 Squadron arrived on 24 September 1942. Since 18 September, 75 (New Zealand) Squadron had been busily mining and 115 Squadron began the same on 25/26 September. Two days later on 28 September, three crews tried cloud-cover daylight raids on Lingen on the Dortmund-Ems Canal but again cover ran out. Only one aircraft bombed ships, but missed. A pair of Wellingtons was successful on 22 October with a cloud base at 700ft, when twenty-two Wimpys were sent to bomb Essen, the Ruhr and the Dortmund-Ems Canal. The two Wellingtons reached Lingen and bombed from a very low level. 115 Squadron also took part, sending out eight aircraft. One was attacked by a fighter near Nienham and the wireless operator was killed. Another bombed Essen through cloud cover and two attacked Lingen from 400ft causing considerable damage to its rail installations. One of the Wellingtons came down low and machine gunned a train near Lingen, setting one of the carriages alight. No aircraft were lost.

On 29 October, six Wellingtons of 115 Squadron were given a 'roving commission' of the Ruhr and a repeat raid on Essen resulted in the loss of three of their aircraft. On 1 November, 75 Squadron moved to Newmarket, leaving 115 Squadron on 8/9 November to operate the last Wellingtons on mining raids from Mildenhall before moving to the satellite at East Wretham.

Right: Flight Sergeant Leslie Hyder of 149 Squadron, the second pilot of Stirling BF372 on the night of 28/29 November 1942, seen here recovering from wounds received on the raid. Hyder, Sergeant Cameron and Sergeant Gough were awarded the DFM for their actions on the operation. (IWM)

Below: Bombing up Stirlings *N-Nuts* and OJ-T of 149 Squadron on the end of the south-east runway near the Mildenhall to Thistley Green road on the south side of the airfield on 10 March 1942, when the target that night was Essen. (IWM)

A Lancaster illuminated by fires and pyrotechnics during the raid on Hamburg on 30/31 January 1943. (IWM)

Mildenhall closed so that McAlpines could begin construction of three concrete runways and bring the airfield up to 'Class A' standard. The longest runway involved realignment of the Beck Row to West Row road. For some time the old line taken into part of the perimeter track remained. When completed, the main runway was 2,000 yards long and the two intersecting runways, both 1,400 yards long. A hard-surfaced perimeter track and aircraft dispersal points had been constructed piecemeal during the early war years and further construction brought the total up to thirty-six dispersals. A consignment of 600 Canadian-built Ford trucks was received while the runway work was in progress. These were intended for distribution throughout Norfolk and Suffolk but no spares were available and drivers raided other vehicles for the parts that they needed. Several ground units used RAF Mildenhall at this period, including No.1 Engine Control Demonstration Unit from April 1942. 1403 Meteorological Flight formed in November 1942 before moving to Gibraltar and No.3 Group Servicing Unit resident from December 1942 to November 1943. The 1503 Beam Approach Training Flight's Oxfords, which had been at Mildenhall since early September 1942, left for RAF Upper Heyford in mid-December.

RAF Mildenhall continued to control its three squadrons, even though none were now at the parent airfield. 149 Squadron, by now one of the only three squadrons in Bomber Command to have been trained for gas bombing, continued to fly from the Lakenheath satellite while 75 Squadron, converted now to Stirlings, was at this time stationed at Newmarket. 115 Squadron was dispersed to East Wretham and in March 1943 it began converting from Wellingtons to Lancasters.[13] On 4 March 1943, No.3 Group had on strength six Stirling squadrons (15, 75, 90, 149, 214 and 218), which were gradually converted to the Lancaster. Three Special Duty Squadrons operated a variety of aircraft.

On 5/6 March, the night that has gone into history as the starting point of the Battle of the Ruhr, Nos 149, 115 and 75 Squadrons took part in a raid on Essen and the Krupp steelworks. Fourteen out of 442 aircraft despatched failed to return. On 9/10 March, 264 aircraft of Bomber Command attacked Munich for the loss of eight aircraft. At the end of March 1943, RAF Mildenhall ceased being responsible for its satellite airfields. 149 Squadron continued to fly from Lakenheath, now an operational station in its own right, and as the war continued became increasingly involved in specialised mining techniques – Lakenheath remained operational until May 1944 when it closed for expansion and improvement. It re-opened in April 1947 and has since grown to become the largest USAF-operated airbase in Great Britain.

Meanwhile, Mildenhall, now fully equipped with concrete runways, Drem approach lighting and a new control tower, re-opened in April 1943 as part of a new organisation of airfields known as 32 Base (3 Group Base, clutch item 2). 15 Squadron, which was equipped with three flights of Stirlings IIIs, arrived from Bourn in Cambridgeshire on 15 April when two Airspeed Horsa gliders, towed by Whitley Vs, were used to move personnel and equipment to the new station. The squadron flew its first operation from Mildenhall on 16/17 April 1943 when eighteen Stirlings took part in the raid on Mannheim. Stirling BK659 crash-landed on its return and caused many other aircraft to be diverted to other airfields. BF474 LS-H flown by Pilot Officer J.L. Shiells DFM and his seven-man crew were killed when they were shot down by a night-fighter at St-Erme-Outre-Et-Ramecourt (Aisne). BK691 LS-F was shot down at Hetzerath, Germany, killing Flight Lieutenant D.H. Haycock DFM and six of his crew. One man survived to be taken prisoner.

On the night of 4/5 May, 596 aircraft of Bomber Command carried out a heavy raid on Dortmund. Ninety Stirlings were part of the Dortmund force and thirty-one aircraft or 5.2 per cent of the bombing force was lost – another seven bombers crashed in England in bad weather. Stirling III BK658 of 15 Squadron, flown by Sergeant W.M. McLeod RNZAF, fell victim to Unteroffizier Karl-Georg Pfeiffer of 10./NJG 1 for his third victory.[14]

One of the Stirling crew members on 15 Squadron was Sergeant Frank Diamond, who was the navigator in Sergeant Hugh 'Wendell' Wilkie's crew. Frank Diamond recalls:

> Wilkie was a very competent 20-year-old New Zealander. He was a year younger than I was and all the others except our wireless operator who was old at thirty-two. We were all sergeants. The bomb aimer was 'Curly' Palmer and the wireless operator was Bill Mudge. Jock Palmer was the tail gunner. The mid-upper gunner was John Ledgerwood, a nicely spoken Englishman with something of a wry smile and we had a Welsh flight engineer. The crews were usually seven. The earlier practice of carrying a co-pilot had been discontinued purely on the grounds of waste of manpower. The bomb aimer stood in that capacity to give the normal assistance with takeoff and landing controls. Should a pilot be killed or injured, the crew would look to him to fly the machine if it were possible to do so rather than the ultimate of abandoning it and relying on a parachute. We were all young and short on experience. I have no idea how many hours flying the others had but I had 180.
>
> The flight engineer's main function was to monitor the engines and, as the Stirling had fourteen fuel tanks, he had to ensure that fuel was fed to them and taken in the correct order to maintain the optimum balance of the aircraft. Our wireless operator's most important function was to listen out to base in case there should be a recall signal. To miss it could not only mean flying on to the target when everyone else had gone home but result in failure to be alerted to adverse weather conditions. It was rare indeed for him to transmit as a transmission could show our position.
>
> Our tail gunner and our mid-upper gunner each sat in a power operated turret which could be turned to a limited degree in a sideways arc and their guns could be raised and lowered through about 60 degrees. They searched the sky continuously for the dark shape of hostile aircraft. It was the tail gunner's responsibility to give the pilot instructions as to the turns that should be made when a fighter attacked from the rear to ensure that the attacker could not bring his guns to bear on our aircraft.

At Mildenhall the Reaper stood beside us. A tour of operations was thirty and we soon found that it was difficult to find tour-expired people. The loss rate was especially high among Stirling crews. The decision to operate under cover of darkness was a direct result of catastrophic and unsustainable losses in daylight attacks in the first years of the war. The German fighter aircraft outmanoeuvred our slow and lightly armed aircraft and they had weapons of higher calibre and range. Our techniques were very different from those of the US daylight formations, which relied both for navigation, and the release of bombs on the leading aircraft in each formation. Their arrival over the correct target depended on the skill and the survival of the lead navigator and the lead bombardier gave the signal for bombs to be dropped. I believe it was only the pilot and these two key members of a crew who always flew together. The crew of each RAF aircraft operated separately and lost contact with the other aircraft in their squadron as they climbed away from their base into a dark sky each aircraft without navigation lights, the navigator's chart table illuminated by a small orange lamp and he surrounded by a curtain. The engine exhausts were masked as far as was practical. Care was taken in every way to avoid detection. Each member was responsible to the other crewmembers to give of his best in his particular function, as the lives of the others were dependent upon it. The bond within crews illustrated just how strong this was and to have another man fly with you as a replacement because of a regular crewman's sickness was regarded as a bad omen indeed. The fear of disaster on such operations was there right up to the point of a safe return.

It was usual for crews to keep to the same aircraft. Pilots preferred it that way and it was their responsibility to air test the machine in the afternoon prior to a night operation and liaise with our ground crew to ensure that every function was as good as it could be. The support we had from those who worked in all weathers to give us a safe and reliable aircraft was great and the erks, as we sometimes called them, were never given sufficient praise. (It was for them in particular that Bomber Harris fought for a Bomber Campaign medal to recognise their loyalty and even refused a peerage because they were not given the honour he considered to be their due).

Navigation was my function. Each operation started with the preparation of my chart; drawing the route, measuring the distances, and calculating the courses to fly by using the forecast winds the weather man had given us. It would be a continuing task in the air to fix the aircraft's position. Air navigation at that time was so very different from anything that came later. We did have maps with some surface detail and colouring for daylight flying but not for high level night flying. We used charts with a scale of 1:1,000,000 so this gave us the eastern side of England and much of Europe. It was plain black and white and the black was there just to show coastline, major rivers and inlets lakes and large cities. We had room for plenty of pencil work. It was fixed to the navigation table and was the focus of constant endeavour. As a Mercator projection, lines of longitude were shown as parallel and vertical lines on which a protractor could be placed in order to draw compass lines, a fundamental requirement if one was to determine a course to fly and transfer it to the pilot's compass. Further, the degrees of latitude shown on each side of the chart each divided into sixty minutes and with one minute equivalent to one nautical mile. (Distances were measured in nautical miles and sped was expressed in knots). From 1942 when the Pathfinder Force was formed the less experienced crews were given guidance by the use of pyrotechnics particularly for target marking, and electronic aids for positioning became available to all crews. Nevertheless, the basic method still relied on the ingenuity of each navigator in splendid isolation to bring his aircraft to complete its task and return to base this being written with all deference to the vital functions performed throughout by the pilot and others in the crew.

Prior to an operation there was a navigation briefing at which pilots, bomb aimers and navigators were shown the route, heavily defended areas and other problems, which might arise. The fuel and bomb loads, both of which would be influenced by the target and its distance from base, and, most important for Stirling crews, the time to be over the target. The Lancaster and Halifax crews flew up to 10,000ft higher than we did but if both their timing and ours were as planned all was well. However, I know of one instance when an incendiary dropped from above was caught in the wing of a Stirling and the pilot of that aircraft had it for many years. He used it as a doorstop in his house.

Take-off was always an anxious time. We had confidence in Hugh Wilkie but there was always the possibility of a failure outside his control. Engine failure with a full load had only one outcome.

It was lonely when the last dimmed lights of our base were left behind. Those of the crew, who had a view, both the wireless operator and I being excluded, would be scanning the sky for other aircraft. Collisions were surprisingly rare but with several hundred aircraft flying the same route we did feel the occasional disturbance as we crossed someone else's slipstream and were reminded that darkness had its dangers in other ways.

New navigation aids and a target marking device code named 'Oboe15' were coming into use early in 1943 but the effective range for both was limited. With the new aids and the approach of shorter nights, as well as the requirement that we should attack the industrial cities, the bomber offensive was directed towards the Ruhr. Our tour started in March as this began.

My first training flight had been in a flying boat of Pan American Airways in Florida on 11 March 1942. It was on 11 March 1943 that we completed our first operation. Our task was to lay mines in the waters off the Dutch coast. We did three of these relatively easy trips and were fortunate not to meet any opposition but there was still the grim reality of flying at night with no contact at all with our base and against an enemy out to destroy us. The Ruhr was well defended. The twinkling display of shell bursts as we approached the target area was intimidating to say the least. German night fighters had airborne radar to find us on the blackest of nights. And we were unaware of a new and deadly tactic by which, having found us, the fighter could with stealth come close and fly in the blind spot beneath us and deliver fire with upward-firing guns. They soon learnt to direct their fire at the wings instead of the fuselage. An exploding bomb load could bring the destruction of the fighter as well as its victim.

I did not keep a diary, a source of great regret, and with hindsight I suppose I was not mature enough to think of writing for posterity and for that matter we thought more of survival. The nights we did not fly were cheerful occasions when the odd glass of beer helped all of us to relax and get a good night's sleep.

It was quite early in our tour when on 20/21 April our squadron was included in an attack on the Baltic port of Rostock.[16] My record just gives a start time of one hour before midnight, that it was low level and took eight hours – the longest we ever did. Our departure point on leaving home territory was Southwold on the coast of Suffolk. We were instructed to fly on a course from there to a point on the coast of Denmark. By flying at 2,000ft we were told that we would escape radar detection and the presence of a full moon would not cause problems. It was unusual to fly close to the sea and I am sure that those who did not have the curtained area, which was mine, enjoyed the scenery. However, my pleasure came in a different way. I had always been interested in the way that Pan American Airways had put emphasis on astro navigation which had been so very important to them in the pioneering days of the 1930s when they circled the globe with their passenger routes. This came through whilst I was at their school in Miami, Florida during my time there in 1942. So, here was my opportunity. To be successful with a bubble sextant it is vital to have a steady platform. The short explanation is that the instrument is held in both hands and with one eye at the eyepiece a small bubble in the liquid contained in a chamber at that point is illuminated to give a circle. When the star, or in this instance the moon, is brought into the centre of this by adjusting the sighting mechanism its altitude can be read on the sextant's scale. An unsteady platform will cause the light circle to move and make an accurate and useful measurement impossible. At that point we were flying on automatic pilot, George as we called it, so the machine was more stable than if it were being flown manually.

The moon was at about 40° above the horizon and on the nose of the aircraft – a near perfect position. I suppose we were over that part of the North Sea for about two hours.

During the last forty minutes or so I took several shots of the moon and the calculations gave position lines at right angles to our track. These were most valuable as we converged on the coastline and ensured that we crossed it at the correct point. To cross too far south would have put us in danger. A Stirling of another squadron, which crossed to the south, was shot down over Esbjerg airfield. The flak gunners could hardly miss an aircraft at that height.

After the coast we were over the Kattegat and turned south and through the islands to the Baltic. It was here that we had our first experience of light tracer from flak ships. Quite disturbing to watch. You see it leave its source and snake up towards the aircraft gradually twisting closer then seeming to accelerate to a point where we must be hit, only to see it move away and eventually be out of range. Others were having the same treatment, but the gunners seemed to have no successes. We continued to Rostock where our industrial targets included an aircraft factory. As always we carried out our instructions and were glad to return without any problems. Only four days before we had been hit by flak over Mannheim.

In May we went to three cities in the Ruhr. The defences there were quite fearful. The Mosquito marker aircraft using the very accurate *Oboe* system had to face their particular share of flak. These Mosquito crews flew at 25,000ft along a radio beam and released their pyrotechnic marker on the appropriate signal from the controller in England. And the marker fell within yards of the intended point. To do this the aircraft had to be flown with precision and the flak gunners soon found the release point so up went every available shell and those crews had to keep straight on into them. These target markers were to make our attacks more effective but ultimately it still depended upon the skill of the individual bomb aimers to place the bombs on the industrial targets which we were sent to destroy. This was the only accessible part of Germany during the short nights. The press called the concentration on these cities 'The Battle of the Ruhr'. Anti-aircraft guns were moved there from other areas and I believe there were in the region of 40,000 there at that time. Fighters were still a menace on the fringes of the area. My logbook has a note that on 29 May our rear gunner fired at what he thought was a Me 109.

However, our near demise came on the night of 11/12 June in Stirling III BF470 *G-George*. I have never been at all superstitious but it was our thirteenth and it could have been a Friday![17] We were over Düsseldorf and fortunately we no longer had our bomb load. We were turning away for home when the port outer motor was hit. The engine was very quickly an inextinguishable fire and the propeller turned ever faster. The engine noise was terrifying. I had a window in the fuselage to give me a full view of the engine as I sat at my table. John Ledgerwood, the mid-upper gunner, had the best view and his was the first voice over the intercom. He was very calm. We all were. Hugh said very little. He was working hard to handle a crippled aircraft but he was quiet and efficient and like the rest of us he was never one to use bad language and curse if matters did not go as planned. John Ledgerwood's voice was calm and his comment to Hugh was that the propeller was likely to leave the engine and he suggested that a gradual dive and climb movement would ensure that when it did come off it would go over or under the aircraft. Little was said by anyone and Hugh proceeded as suggested.

Meanwhile, the noise from the runaway engine became louder and the propeller boss glowed red hot and then white hot. That noise and my clear view of the engine were scary but John's calm voice and Hugh's silence kept us all in a shaken but hopeful mood it seems. The situation was under control to a degree, but the outcome was still in doubt until another comment from John, who was best able to monitor the situation that the propeller had come off and had spun over his turret. He was greatly relieved that his turret had not been damaged and with hindsight we were pleased that the tail of the aircraft had not been hit.

Our height over the target area had been 12,00ft . We were now at 8,000ft. The weather was not entirely against us. Above we had a clear sky, almost no moon and the blackness made the canopy of stars brilliant. Below us a sheet of cloud with the top a few thousand feet below. How lucky we were to have remained above the cloud whilst disposing of our propeller! Hugh's task would have been infinitely more difficult if he had been battling to cope with our problems in cloud. In fact it could have been impossible.

We now had problems in my department. The violent movements of the aircraft, which occurred, had caused the gyro of our master compass to topple. This can be corrected but it takes time during, which there is no steady pointer to steer by. However, I could see the North Star – Polaris – very clearly. And, with Polaris on the right, to starboard, I knew we were flying a westerly course. The engine we no longer had was the one which operated the generator for our navigational equipment so fixing the aircraft's position had to be by other means. The cloud prevented recognition of ground features, but we had no maps for that purpose and it is very difficult on a dark night to identify even large landmarks. Radio fixes were not available except near or over England and to transmit a signal for that purpose is to invite any enemy station to also take a fix. We were much slower now as well as low in the sky. An easy target for a fighter pilot who could increase his tally with very little effort. The only way to fix our position would be in the manner of the pioneers! To fly straight and level over enemy territory at 8,000ft was not a popular suggestion at all, but essential as I have described previously. From the technical viewpoint it was a nigh perfect position as I stood under the perspex blister we called the astrodome. Brilliant stars all round so that I could choose three for each fix and have them positioned nicely through the circle. Apart from the time required to identify and select the stars to be used, the sextant had an averaging, wind-up mechanism, which whirred away and took sixty readings over a minute to produce an average. Directly after noting the read-out it was vital to note the time, and to the second. Our watches were always checked against Greenwich before departure. To the minimum five minutes needed to take these observations it took more than another five before three lines could be drawn on the chart to mark our position, as it had been ten minutes or earlier! After correcting the sight readings for dome refraction, as the sighting was taken beneath a curved surface, and for the effect of the earth's rotation on the bubble, calculations were then made using the tabulations printed in the Air Almanac. It is clear that we were a very worried crew but in the light of this, and the fact that I fixed our position three times in this way, is some testimony to the way we handled our near calamity. It was important that we should know that we were not only tracking to the west and homeward but that we were to break cloud near to Mildenhall, our base. The cloud sheet over the Ruhr extended far in to England. We had a base beacon, placed at a distance from the airfield and repositioned daily. It was indeed a relief when we saw it flashing. For two hours or more Hugh had flown the aircraft on three engines and, much to everyone's relief he had put it down safely at our home base. *G-George* was repaired and we flew it again eight days later to Le Creusot.

We operated over the Ruhr on seven more nights in June. Our rear gunner exchanged fire with a Junkers 88 on the 19th and on the 28/29th; our return from Cologne was on three engines. There were other life threatening incidents and one was blissfully ignorant of the near misses but when we began to lose hope of reaching the stand down figure of thirty for no one we knew had done so, there came sudden and totally unexpected relief. Our commanders did recognise our plight.

My last two operations were in the last week of July. We were on the first of the heavy series of raids against Hamburg which caused such catastrophic damage that Albert Speer invited Hitler to see it for himself and reported that a few more such attacks would make it impossible to continue the war. It was beyond our capabilities at that time too. The raid on 24 July was the first time that 'Window' was first used. This radar countermeasure was basically to shower these defences with narrow aluminium strips about 6 inches long, each backed with blackened paper. These reflected the radar beams and created a mush of false signals on the defender's receivers. The force that night was 791, of which twelve aircraft were lost. The losses on well defended cities at that time where normally 6 per cent so this could be compared with fifty aircraft. 'Window' could be said to have saved the lives of 300 air crew. Just 125 of the vulnerable Stirlings were there; perhaps another near miss for us?[18]

At the start of the Battle of the Ruhr, 'Bomber' Harris had been able to call upon almost 600 heavies for Main Force operations and at the pinnacle of the battle, near the end of May, more than 800 aircraft took part. Innovations, such as Pathfinders, to find and mark targets with their TIs (target indicators) and wizardry, such as *Oboe*, which enabled crews to find them, were instrumental in the mounting levels of death and destruction. Little it seemed could be done to assuage the bomber losses, which by the end of the campaign had reached high proportions. There was however, a simple but brilliant device, which at a stroke could render German radar defences almost ineffective. On 24/25 July, when Harris launched the first of four raids, code-named *Gomorrah*, on the port of Hamburg, Bomber Command was at last allowed to use 'Window'. Although 'Window' had been devised in 1942 its use had been forbidden until now, for fear that the Luftwaffe would use it in a new Blitz on Great Britain. These strips of black paper with aluminium foil stuck to one side and cut to a length, 30cm x 1.5cm, were equivalent to half the wavelength of the *Würzburg* ground and *Lichtenstein* airborne interception radar. When dropped by aircraft in bundles of a thousand at a time, at one-minute intervals, 'Window' reflected the radar waves and 'snowed' the tubes. 'Window' was carried in the 791 aircraft, which set out for Hamburg. Led by *H2S* PFF aircraft, 728 bombers rained down 2,284 tons of HE and incendiaries in fifty minutes on the dockyards and city districts of Hamburg, creating a firestorm, which rose to a height of two and a half miles. Only twelve bombers, just 1.5 per cent of the force, were lost. Frank Diamond continues:

> On the following night, the 25/26th, it was a four-hour flight to Essen. This compared with six to Hamburg. Nothing exceptional to record in the logbook but I am sure we had a lively reception and it was probably the weather which brought about the change of target. If we had known that Essen was our last one there would have been great jubilation, but it was only Hugh's twenty sixth 'op' so we were still fearful as to the outcome of the last four the rest of us had. But we did anticipate a stand down after his thirtieth. I had just twenty-two ops and I could have been required to fly with another crew. However, my guardian angel saved me.
>
> Our next op, early in August, we were taken right up to the wire, so to speak, by the normal daytime air-testing of our machine, attending briefing and having the usual meal in the Mess. It was then when we were thinking of boarding the aircrew bus for the aircraft with some unspoken foreboding, for we never talked about survival in any negative way, the message came that our tour was finished and we were 'tour expired'. A person pardoned on the scaffold could not feel greater relief! Two months later my squadron converted to Lancasters and the Stirlings ended their time as tugs for gliders and general transport aircraft. The crew broke up and we each went to training units to pass on our experience to others. Sadly and within six months, in April 1944, our pilot Hugh Wilkie was killed in an accident at night in a Stirling at Stradishall.

Eric Phillips, a Stirling rear gunner in 15 Squadron at Mildenhall, recalls:

> The governor, Bomber Harris, addressed us. He said, 'I feel sure that a further two or three raids on Hamburg, then probably a further six raids on Berlin and the war will finish. Well done lads. You have flattened the Ruhr so you will be pleased to know you will not have to return there again.' But we did return to the Ruhr – the next night in fact. Because of bad weather over north Germany we went to Essen. There was full cloud over the target so pathfinders dropped a flare outside the target and the navigator gave the pilot a course on a timed run from the flare and dropped the bombs through cloud. The navigator asked me to watch out for the flare. Within seconds the flare was dropped and just as I reported this, a Ju 88 came in from the port quarter firing two cannons. My rear turret and the starboard outer engine were hit and set on fire. The pilot, thinking the starboard wing was also on fire, ordered bale out. Then the engine fell away from the aircraft and the order to bale out was cancelled. The Stirling lost height from 18,000 down to 8000. The bombs were dropped at this height in the Essen area and the aircraft then made a safe journey home with me keeping watch from the astrodome, as the rear turret was unserviceable.[19]

On 10 August 1943, 15 Squadron detached 'C' Flight and its seven Stirlings to form 622 Squadron whose first operation took place the following night, 10/11 August, when it despatched five Stirlings as part of the force of 653 aircraft that bombed Nuremberg. The Stirling was the oldest and least effective of the four-engined bombers and so the two resident squadrons were used increasingly on mine-laying operations for the remainder of the year.

Above: 1 Squadron Leader Smithers and his crew of Stirling W7455 OJ–B of 149 Squadron at Mildenhall on 15 January 1942. (IWM)

Left: 2 The 6ft x 5ft oil painting by Laura Knight, entitled 'Take Off, Interior of a Bomber Aircraft', of a 15 Squadron Stirling crew at Mildenhall, was completed in 1944.

Flight Lieutenant Ray F. Escreet DFM, a wireless operator in 15 Squadron who features prominently in the painting, was killed in March 1945 on an abortive SOE (Special Operations Executive) operation when the Hudson aircraft he was flying in was shot down. When Laura Knight heard of Escreet's death, she was concerned that his mother should receive a photograph of the painting. It hung in the Royal Academy in 1944 and is now in the Imperial War Museum. (IWM)

3 Jet Provost T.Mk 5 of 1 FTS at Air Fête 1981.

4 Buccaneer S.Mk 2A of 237 OCU at RAF Honington at Air Fête 1981.

5 Royal
Netherlands
Air Force
'Grasshoppers'
Alloutte III
helicopter display
team at Air Fête
1983.

6 Avro Vulcan
B.Mk 2 XH558
landing during Air
Fête 1986.

7 KC-135A with
boom extended at
Air Fête 1988.

8 Ohio ANG LTV A-7D *Scrappy* at Air Fête 1989.

9 *Les Patrouilles de France* aerobatic display team at Air Fête 1989.

Opposite above: 10 Avro Vulcan B.Mk 2 XH558 at Air Fête 1990.

Opposite middle: 11 PANAVIA GR.1 Tornado of 16 Squadron at Air Fête 1990.

Opposite below: 12 Phantom XV582 of 'Treble One' Squadron at Air Fête 1990.

13 Avro Shackleton AEW2 of 8 Squadron at Air Fête 1990.

14 48th TFW F-111Fs at Air Fête 1991. 74-0177 was one of twelve aircraft that bombed Libyan targets in Operation *El Dorado Canyon* in 1986.

15 McDonnell Douglas Phantom F-4J (UK) F.Mk 3s of 74 'Tiger' Squadron at Air Fête 1992.

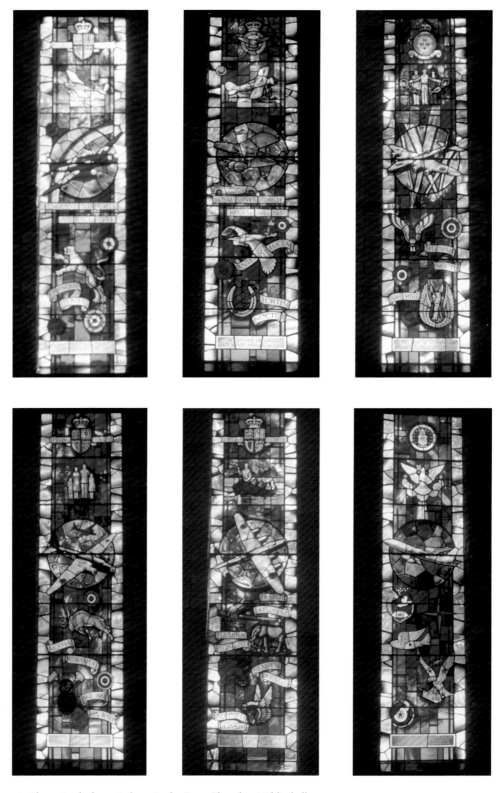

16 The stained-glass windows in the Base Chapel at Mildenhall.

17 C-130K XV292 celebrating twenty-five years of the Hercules in RAF service at Air Fête 1992.

18 BAe Hawk T.1A at Air Fête 1992.

19 Harrier GR.Mk 3 of 233 OCU at Air Fête 1992.

20 KC-10A Extender of 22 AREFW based at March AFB at Air Fête 1992.

21 F/A-18D Hornet of VMFA 224 at Air Fête 1994.

22 USAF Thunderbirds.

23 BBMF Lancaster *Mickey the Moocher* in formation with Spitfire XIX PS915.

24 View from the Lancaster cockpit.

25 BBMF Lancaster cockpit.

26 BBMF Lancaster landing at Air Fête 1990.

27 BAC Canberra T.Mk 17A WD955 ECM at Air Fête 1994.

28 Rockwell B-1B Lancer *The Reluctant Dragon* at Air Fête 1994.

29 Belgian Air Force Alpha Jet E of 7 Escadrille/Smaldeel at Air Fête 1995.

30 HC-130N 69-5826 of the 67th SOS, 352nd Special Operations Group.

31 BBMF formation passing the B-2 *Spirit* at Air Fête 2000.

32 Red Arrows taxiing at Air Fête 2000.

33 Royal Netherlands Air Force F-16A J-016 at Air Fête 2001.

In the daylight reconnaissance, twelve hours after the Peenemünde attack on 17/18 August 1943, photographs revealed twenty-seven buildings in the northern manufacturing area destroyed and forty huts in the living and sleeping quarters, completely flattened. The foreign labour camp to the south suffered worst of all and 500–600 foreign workers, mostly Polish, were killed. The whole target area was covered in craters. The raid is adjudged to have set back the V-2 experimental program by at least two months and to have reduced the scale of the eventual rocket attack on Britain. (Australian National Archives)

Flying Officer Frank Diamond in 1943 proudly wearing his 1939–43 Star. Altogether, he flew twenty-two ops on Stirlings, fifty more on Mosquitoes on his second tour, and he was promoted to flight lieutenant and also awarded the DFC. (Frank Diamond)

Both squadrons usually flew against the same targets and as two-flight squadrons with nominal strength of thirty-two Stirlings and eight reserves. On 17/18 August, only six Stirlings of 15 Squadron took part in the famous raid by 596 heavies of Bomber Command on the V-2 rocket site at Peenemünde. In all, fifty-four Stirlings were despatched and two were among the forty aircraft that failed to return.

Towards the end of 1943 the Stirling era was coming to an end and there were some who wished to commemorate its passing, as 'Archie' Hall a WAAF, recalls:

> We had many famous and interesting visitors to the station during those years. In November 1943, Dame Laura Knight came for a lengthy stay, appointed official war artist to paint a RAF picture. I was made her guide in her search for a subject – a very happy association. She wasn't the least interested in inanimate subjects, obviously. She wanted life and drama, so one evening I did a very 'not done' thing, and took her into an aircraft being prepared for take-off. The startled crew quickly responded to her excited outburst – 'Oh, here's my picture – don't show me anything else!' So from then on she settled down to her picture entitled 'Take-Off', with different crews only too willing to sit for her during their precious free time. She won all hearts during her stay with us and painted some beautiful crests on several of the aircraft. I very much treasure a small, signed, pen and ink copy she did for me of the wireless operator in her picture.[20]

Laura Knight reportedly chose a Stirling at Mildenhall because the type was soon to be phased out by 15 Squadron and replaced by the Lancaster. A spare Stirling bomber was put at her disposal for her to study and make preparatory sketches before she made her final painting. She painted a large pierrot on the nose of this aircraft beneath the pilot's window, with the legend 'Midgley's Flying Circus' above; a reference to Flight Lieutenant D. Midgley DFC who was a pilot on 15 Squadron at the time. The 6ft x 5ft oil painting entitled 'Take Off, Interior of a Bomber Aircraft', was completed in 1944. Flight Lieutenant Ray F. Escreet DFM, a wireless operator on 15 Squadron, who features prominently in the painting, was killed in March 1945 on an abortive SOE (Special Operations Executive) operation when the Hudson aircraft he was flying in was shot down.[21] When Laura Knight heard of Escreet's death, she was concerned that his mother should receive a photograph of the painting. It hung at the Royal Academy in 1944 and is now in the Imperial War Museum.

When a single crew in 15 Squadron flew on the operation to Berlin on 26/27 November, they were making the squadron's last Stirling bombing raid, pending the Mildenhall squadrons' conversion to the Lancaster. The Lancaster could carry widely assorted bomb loads, whereas the Stirling's narrow bomb cells restricted its versatility. It also flew faster and higher than was possible in Stirlings, although losses remained fairly high. The final Stirling mining operation by 15 Squadron took place off Cherbourg on 22 December 1943. 622 Squadron flew its last Stirling operation on 20 December when twenty-three Stirlings carried out mine-laying in the Friesians. A week later, 15 Squadron's last Stirling left Mildenhall. By this time the squadron had flown Stirlings operationally for longer than any other squadron. 622 Squadron bade their last Stirling farewell on 11 February 1944. 15 and 622 Squadrons flew their initial, combined operation on 14/15 January 1944 when 496 Lancasters and two Halifaxes carried out the first major raid of the war on Brunswick. Thirty-eight Lancasters were lost – 7.6 per cent of the force. Both squadrons later sent twenty-six aircraft to take part in the 800-bomber attack on Berlin on 24/25 March. In March 1944, 15 and 622 Squadrons flew 198 operational sorties. Among 622 Squadron's Lancasters was L7576, an aged machine, which flew many more sorties. 15 Squadron had eleven Lancasters operating, one crew claiming a Ju 88 nightfighter. Both squadrons subsequently fought furiously during the Battle of Berlin[22] and took part in gigantic attacks on German cities.

Frank Hercules 'Herks' Dengate from Tamworth, New South Wales, was a twenty-two-year-old Australian pilot on 15 Squadron from March to August 1944, after having trained on Wellingtons and the Stirling. The crew had come together in the usual manner, as Dengate recalls:

'Crewing up' had no basis at all, you just picked. You had to try and pick a navigator you thought was a reliable sort of a bloke. Then you'd finish up probably getting a wireless operator or bomb aimer. You certainly didn't have nay chance of looking over their record to see whether they were reasonable sort of blokes or what they were. The navigator got airsick and he coped with it, but it got worse when he got into the Wellington and he was sitting at the table in the little enclosure. This made him sick every time. He still did his job. We even did a trip to France in a Wellington and he was quite satisfactory but it was the first trip we did into enemy territory. The medical people decided that as he got airsick all the time he shouldn't fly. He eventually went into the *Oboe* marking system. His replacement was Flying Officer Art Cantrell, a Canadian and an ex-district inspector of schools; an excellent fellow and very skilful. The crew decided that the Sergeant wireless operator, a Scotsman, would have to be replaced as he was always drunk and we could never get him sober to go in the aeroplane. (That fellow was later transferred to 622 Squadron. It took him eighteen months to complete a tour and he'd go with anyone that didn't have a wireless operator. Eventually he was awarded the DFM [Distinguished Flying Medal]. The new wireless operator was Frank Watson. We now had a better navigator and a better wireless operator than we would have had after we had the changes. [Frank Watson's wife Brenda a WAAF, who was the daughter of the landlord of the 'Jude's Ferry' at West Row, was called the 'Chop Blonde' because everyone who went out with her got the chop. Frank must have broken the spell]. He was a very nice chap and he had been a 'whiskey traveller', selling drinks around the countryside. Whiskey was his leading sale and eventually that's what killed him, because both he and his wife used to partake of greater quantities. There wasn't an engineer on the Wellington but when we went on to Stirling training at 1651 Heavy Conversion Unit at Wratting Common, Sergeant Bobby Kitchin joined us as the flight engineer. (After Wratting Common we went to 3 LFS (Lancaster Finishing School) at Feltwell). The rear gunner, Sergeant Doug Davis, was very quiet but a very good gunner. He was always awake and sharp. Sergeant Fred Coney was the mid-upper gunner. Once again, very wide awake and keen. Flying Officer Joe Ell, our Canadian bomb aimer, was a wonderful, reliable fellow. Joe always did an excellent job. He never missed.

Flight Sergeant A.M. Halkett DFM (third from right) and his crew pose by the tail of Stirling I N3669 LS-H of 15 Squadron after completing the aircraft's sixty-second operation on 11 October 1942. A month later *H-Harry* had flown sixty-seven operations, which is believed to be a record for Stirlings. *H-Harry* was exhibited outside St Paul's Cathedral during the Wings for Victory week of February 1943. (IWM)

Squadron Leader Smithers and his crew of Stirling W7455 OJ-B of 149 Squadron at Mildenhall on 15 January 1942. That night, 15/16 January, ninety-six aircraft set off to bomb Hamburg for the second night running. Three Wellingtons and one Hampden were lost, and eight additional aircraft crashed in England. This Stirling later passed to 1657 HCU and was written off in September 1943 after being attacked by a Messerschmitt 410 intruder over Suffolk. (*Flight*)

A 15 Squadron Stirling observer at his desk. (IWM)

Pilot Officer R. Brown (seated far left) and his crew during interrogation at Mildenhall, following their return from the raid on Berlin on 22/23 November 1943. Seated next to Brown is Sergeant W. Brodie, flight engineer and then Flight Sergeant P. Harewood, bomb aimer and Sergeant F. Tidmas, navigator. (IWM)

We arrived at Mildenhall in December 1943 and continued training on the Lancaster until our first operation, to Stuttgart, on 15/16 March after I had flown my second dickie trip with another crew to experience the flak and terror of a raid. Stuttgart wasn't a good 'prang' as we called it. '*A-Apple*' and a total of thirty-seven aircraft were lost. Our next two trips were to Frankfurt when over the target we encountered a FW 190 followed by a direct hit by flak. On return to base we found forty countable holes. On 26 March we did our first trip to the Ruhr when the target was Essen. On all my trips I carried my small Webley 6.35mm automatic pistol in the large pocket of my battle dress in the event of me having to bale out and try to escape. I purchased the gun, which was manufactured in 1909, in London in December 1943.

Between raids we did training with our own fighters on mock attacks and also formation flying and cross country. Also, we did practice bombing, mainly in daylight, as all our raids on Germany at this time were at night. Mildenhall was an old base so we had comfortable quarters and very nice brick buildings with mess halls and bars. As long as you weren't listed you were free. We would know by about 10 o'clock whether we were operating or we had to go and test our aeroplane. The ground crew was waiting to test to make sure that everything was satisfactory so you'd be ready for the next day. We had a very close relationship with our ground crew. They were wonderful chaps. They waved us off and they waited for us to return. Between the period when we landed to the time we were ready to do our next test, which would probably be a day and a half, quite often they'd work flat out, day and night to get it done. They were very important and we were so dependent on them that we got very close to them. Quite often they didn't sleep at all during busy operating periods. Quite often we'd have to take another aeroplane because they hadn't finished the inspection. Our individual aircraft was '*K-King*' [ED395] and because my second name is Hercules, we put '*Hercules K-King*' on it. We'd do a test flight before in the morning before the next trip the following night. You'd test everything ready for the next run. You could never be sure whether they'd found all the problems that were involved.

Unless it was a special trip of some kind we went to the briefing straight after lunch. It might have alternatives, which you went to your briefing earlier. The different members of the crew had already completed their briefing. The navigator set up his route. The wireless operator would be getting useful information from the wireless mob. The gunners would be checking their information about fighters and so forth. Then you all come together into the main briefing. It told you the targets, whether you were backup crew or third across the target or something like that. The Met gave details of what they presumed the weather was going to be like. They'd never be sure, but they had a fair idea. It could change very easily; especially when we went to a place like Friedrichshafen when three and a half hours was the time to the target. We did a lot of trips to the Ruhr. Industry and the people that operated the machinery were in the same category. Blood flowed fast if it was the Ruhr because it was a terrible area. The flak concentration was terrific. If we were on backup, then we'd be first into the target for the attack, which was better than being last. The risk of fighters was the same the whole way though. In most cases the planners would try to keep us away from flak areas on our route so that you didn't get a lot of flak other than when you crossed the coast. The target area was the risky part. You held your breath until the bombs were gone because we had to wait until the flash would turn up and indicated where his bombs fell and we could clear out and get cracking on the way home.

The briefing lasted about an hour and the navigators had to be there early because they had a lot of work to do. Sometimes the radio fellow was there with him to get his information. We depended on the navigator to tell us what speed, height, direction and so forth were required. If you varied your speed, it upset the navigator. It was very exciting being told the target and everyone took a big sigh of relief. We were on edge from the time we got all the information till the time that we got back. The station CO wished you goodbye. After the briefing we went straight over to our aeroplane, normally in a small van driven by one of the WAAFs. We'd have all our parachutes and stuff and the navigator would have all his gear. Once in the aircraft we checked that everything was correct, that the switches for the bombs were all OK and that the radio was operating satisfactorily. Then we waited for start up time. The crew would be checking their equipment. The gunners would be setting themselves down; putting their electric plugs in and making sure their heating was working. The engineer who was sitting beside you would be checking all these gauges and making e sure they had the correct amount of fuel and temperatures and everything was right. You would start up when you were about due for takeoff. Then you lined up on the taxi track, come round to the takeoff point and get a green light for takeoff. You'd get a green light that told you were the next and away you'd go.

There was always tension on takeoff. You had a terrific load to lift off the runway. Everyone was holding their breath and hoping that nothing went wrong until we were in the air. The aeroplane was very heavy with fuel and bombs, which varied according to the distance we were going. At full power the loading on the aircraft was horrific and it probably took the full length of the runway to get the wheels off the ground. I'd whip the wheels up as soon as possible to get maximum speed. This was the dangerous point, because if you crashed with the load you had on, you would finish. This happened sometimes. Testing the aeroplane beforehand was the big thing that made it satisfactory. The Lancaster behaved very well under fully loaded conditions really but if one of your motors lost power for some reason or another, that was enough. You were in need of full power and full speed to get that load off the ground. So everyone was tensed up until they saw the trees clearing under them.

We flew straight off and up to a point on the coast and across the sea. We set out for Stuttgart one night and we were only just over the water after leaving Britain when an aeroplane suddenly appeared underneath us. We were so close that we could see his instrument panel. At 18,000ft it was heavy cloud and stormy and we were struggling to keep the aeroplane in the air because it was heavy with ice. We didn't have any de-icing of any kind at all. The only solution was to go down to about 15,000ft to warmer air, get rid of it and climb again. Many didn't do that. They stayed up there and the icing would increase until it got to a stage that the aeroplane crashed. We lost a terrific number of aeroplanes that night, simply because of the icing.

We couldn't climb much higher than 20,000ft with a bomb load. We'd try and get to 20 because this was a reasonable height to get away from as much of the flak as possible. Some got brave and dropped down to 12,000ft over the target but it didn't help because we were in a mass of aeroplanes. If you got out of that stream, the radar got you straight away and the fighters would be vectored onto you so the great advantage was to stay in the stream. We were routed over the lightest covered flak points but it was usually pretty heavy flak run along the enemy coast. You soon know when you were passing over enemy territory.

Inside the aircraft there was plenty of noise but not much vibration. The Lancaster was quite comfortable. The only talking was to make sure the gunners were awake and checking every now and again that everyone was satisfied and awake in their positions. You quite often got air bumps from the aircraft ahead. Sometimes you didn't even have an indication of whether you were on the right track or in a stream. You simply paid attention to the navigator and timing. We were supposed to go over the target within a ten-minute period, so we had to be fairly accurate on our timing so that a mass of aeroplanes went over at the same time. The bomb aimer was normally preparing himself for the bombing run. The flight engineer was pretty busy all the time on the instruments, monitoring the petrol consumption, checking temperatures and the oil and calculating what you've got to get to the target and home again. The wireless operator was listening out the whole time for any coded emergency signals from home to warn of a change of route or overcast conditions.

Approaching the target, everyone tensed up and hoped that the bomb aimer would get his job done quickly. Flak passed you all the time. All you saw was the spot where it went off and then it came slowly and then *pssht* past. You hope it didn't stop on you. Big explosions in the air were pretty frightening. It was a bit of a shock to a young fellow, and mostly young fellows we were. There'd be terrific flak. In the middle of all this there should be some Target Indicators dropping. If there wasn't it was up to you to find the aiming point. Over the intercom the bomb aimer would be saying, 'Left, left, steady' and, 'right, right, steady'. If there were wind you would drift to one side. Then the bomb aimer pressed his button, which automatically dropped the photoflash. The flash meant he'd taken his photograph of the aiming point and he'd tell me to clear out.

A straight and steady approach was the final breathtaking section of the trip. You're in the middle of all the flak and other aeroplanes and you're moving your aeroplane about to get on the same track as everybody else so you're likely to collide with other aeroplanes in the process. It was certainly a great relief when you felt the aeroplane leap and you knew the bombs had gone. We had a set point to turn on, probably 45° first and then another 45 so that you didn't make a quick turn away. Then we'd get onto our home run route. That's when we had to be very careful because the fighters, who normally didn't attack over the flak infested target, wanted to get into our track so that they could shoot us down. You turned your aeroplane continually to check they were not underneath. If the gunners spotted a fighter aircraft they had to straight away tell you, 'Aircraft starboard go'. You would dive straight away towards that side, whether left or right, so that they could not fire their guns at you. They didn't have to manoeuvre at all except to get under the aeroplane. If you weren't seen they just pulled the trigger and blew your tanks to pieces. They might get the bombs at the same time. These were not normally live until after they left the aeroplane when the spinners on the front activated the bomb. If there was a fire onboard the aircraft everyone would grab their nearest extinguisher and try to extinguish it and the engineer would decide whether to evacuate or not. The rear gunner would simply swing his rear turret right round and fall out backwards. He had to put his parachute on first though, because he didn't have it on at that stage. The mid-upper gunner and all the other crew would have to go down and out through the bottom. The pilot would stay in his seat as long as possible to hold the aeroplane level. He was last in the queue. If there was an explosion everyone got out where they could. As long as it wasn't fire in the petrol tanks, there was a reasonable amount of time to get out.

As far as searchlights were concerned it was a matter of diving and increasing your speed, getting away from the lights if it were possible. They were pretty good. Particularly if there was a mass of them coming onto you together, then you had absolutely blinded by the power of light that was onto you. That was the big way, dive and get down away from them. Increase your speed you that you'd get away. As soon as the light got you, then all the flak was concentrated on the one aeroplane. My mate Evan Chitty, an Australian pilot with whom I had toured around England in an old car when we were training, didn't have a chance. His navigator got him off track and he went over Le Havre where they were caught in a mass of searchlights. He would have been completely blinded and wouldn't have known which was up and which was down. They just blew him out of the sky.

On the way home we got to watch that we weren't too relaxed because enemy fighters could be following you, even over Britain, to shoot us down around the home aerodrome. If you had engines out you had priority to land. Otherwise you just took your turn. If you got a red light, we had to go round again. We normally had plenty of fuel to spare unless there'd been a loss of fuel. We would report this and get priority to land if necessary. If we'd lost an engine, that got landing priority too.

It was a big relief to be home. The ground crew would be there to welcome you back and take over the aeroplane and check if there was anything wrong. They always carried out a very careful inspection because you didn't know what flak you'd collected on the way. It could have gone through a cable and left it hanging. We went straight over to debriefing and took our turn. We'd get a ration of rum if we wanted it and we'd pour it into Joe Ell our bomb aimer. He got really high on the rum. The briefing officers asked if we'd had flak on the way across, whether we'd had any attacks, what your calculated point of the bombing was and whether you reckoned that you were at an aiming point or not. If you were on backup they wanted to know how the master bomber was, whether you got the right instructions and if you saw any aircraft shot down. Quite often there'd be plenty of them, but we wouldn't know who they were. We were pretty weary by this time but they were quite quick in getting you through. Then we went and had a meal and off to bed. We'd be absolutely 'plonked' out by this time.

Bomber Command's Battle of Berlin was halted on 24/25 March 1944 when the 'Big City' was visited for the last time by 811 aircraft and the offensive was switched to attacks on German communications and defences in preparation for the Normandy invasion. On the night of 27/28 April 1944, twenty-two-year-old Flight Lieutenant Leonard 'Len' Miller of 15 Squadron took off from Mildenhall at the controls of Lancaster II LL801. It was his thirty-second operation. Len Miller had been born in London's East End and considered himself a 'born survivor'. Following a period at 1651 Conversion Unit at Waterbeach, where the crew converted to Stirlings, Sergeant Len 'Dusty' Miller and his crew had been posted to 15 Squadron at Mildenhall on 19 October 1943. Miller's crew flew three operations on Stirlings before the squadron converted to Avro Lancaster bombers during December. On 14 December, Len was commissioned Pilot Officer. Life was good at Mildenhall. A 1934 MG which he had purchased in 1939 was kept topped up with regular 'donations' of petrol that he 'pinched' from fuel bowsers that were used to refuel the aircraft. There was a drain cock on the tanker and he would crawl underneath with a 'Jerry' can and fill it up. Being quite fit he had no trouble carrying it and no one ever asked. He and his crew furnishing their shared quarters with furniture stolen from the squadron leader's offices and they supplemented their rationed coal by raids on the coal dump. Miller led his crew with camouflage nets over their heads to the coal dump with kit bags. Had they been caught, they would probably have been looking at seven days in the guard house or a severe reprimand, but as Miller said, 'When you stuck your necks out as far as we did, who gave a damn?'

On 27/28 January 1944, his flight engineer, Sergeant Alf Pybus, was killed in action during a raid on Berlin when his aircraft was attacked by two German nightfighters and raked with cannon and machine-gun fire. The following month, Len was awarded a Distinguished Flying Cross and on 1 March he was promoted to Flight Lieutenant.

On 27/28 April, the target for 322 Lancasters of 1, 3 and 6 Groups was Friedrichshafen. Thirty-one Bf 110 nightfighters and three *Luftbeobachter* (air situation observer) Ju 88s were successfully guided into the bomber stream via radio beacon *Christa* and they wreaked havoc. In all, the Friedrichshafen force lost eighteen Lancasters. One of them was the one flown by Flight Lieutenant Len Miller, whose attacker was Oberleutnant Martin 'Tino' Becker of 2./NJG 6. Miller recalled:

> We were coming up for our bomb run when we were hit hard. I untangled my cords from the flight controls and the bomb-aimer and engineer [Sergeant A. Beazley-Long and Flight Sergeant G. Mead] got out the front hatch. I went to check on the rest and they were slumped over their equipment so I made my way to the hatch and dived through. All the while we were still taking fire from night fighters and the port fuel tanks were on fire. We were at 22,500ft at the time and my chute must have caught the top of the hatch because when I came round it was flapping on its retaining swaps and I had to pull it down to pull the rip cord. It didn't work, so I was falling, head first and pulling my chute out of its pack, hoping it would open. I remember the moon above revolving as I fell.

Len Miller must have been blown out of the aircraft when it exploded, killing four of his crew.[23] His chute must have opened no higher than 1,500ft because almost as soon as it had, the RAF pilot was on the ground, or more precisely, hanging upside down in a tree with one leg stuck in the harness of his parachute!

> I remember laughing because I was holding the tree so hard not wanting to release the chute or harness in case I fell and broke my neck. So I slid down the tree slowly hanging onto the trunk; it's as black as the ace of spades out in the forest, and I was only about 2ft off the ground. When I stood up I did see the other two members of my crew come down, so that was good.

He never saw his two crew again until after the war, as they were taken prisoner. Miller recalls:

> I found a stream nearby and walked down that in case there were dogs about. Then I had a drink and found a big holly bush. I used to play cowboys and Indians as a youngster and we'd chase each other through the bushes. Holly bushes are hollow in the middle and when the leaves fall and dry they are very hard and make a lot of noise. Very useful thing, holly bushes, if you know about them.

Left: Lancaster Is of 15 Squadron in formation with LL890 LS-T in spring 1944. LL890 was one of four Lancasters lost on 5/6 July 1944 when 542 aircraft of 3, 4, 6 and 8 Groups attacked two V-1 launching sites and two storage areas in Northern France. Flying Officer M.M. Golob RCAF and his crew were all killed. (IWM)

Below: A B-17 Flying Fortress crew in the 96th Bomb Group at Snetterton Heath, Norfolk with a Lancaster crew in 622 Squadron at Mildenhall in spring 1944. Note the unpainted, Window chute beneath the nose of *F for Freddie*. (IWM)

Miller was wearing a pair of overalls over his flight gear. His mother had sewn pockets inside the overalls where he kept chocolate, and pepper to use against dogs, and other items. The overalls also allowed him to blend into the local population more readily than a RAF flight suit because they made him look like a plumber or an electrician. After a short nap in the holly bush and a meal of chocolate and energising malt tablets, Miller made his way south toward Switzerland. Upon approaching a town, he noticed a German soldier on a bicycle, waited while the soldier went into a building before putting his roguish ways to good use. Miller stole the bicycle and sped off hoping he could find an aerodrome and steal an aircraft and get home. He did not find an aerodrome but made it all the way to eastern France and finally reached the Swiss border. He recalls:

> It was a terrific barbed wire fence about 9ft high and about 13ft wide with sloping banks and patrolling guards. Lucky for me a young tree had grown up through the wire so while a guard went by I lay in the shadow of the tree with my face covered with dirt. As soon as he'd gone, I climbed the tree and stood on one of the posts and dived into the other side and Switzerland.

A Swiss guard apprehended Miller and he was eventually interned. He was placed in a big hotel with a Swiss officer in charge. The inmates were allowed to take lessons or other educational pursuits. Miller took piano lessons and when the old lady who taught him gave him the bill every week, he added a couple of extra noughts on the end, and the bill was sent to the British Embassy, who gave money to pay the bills. Miller pocketed the extra and had some saved up for when he decided to leave the country after the invasion of France. Miller and an Australian named Colin took a train to the French border and hiked through the countryside to avoid border patrols. Colin got terribly blistered feet and could hardly walk, so Miller carried him for about twenty miles when they encountered two young boys and asked them where the French Resistance was. They left, and later two men with Sten guns arrived and took them to a farmhouse. They looked after them for a couple days and gave them two bicycles which they later used to get to Bourg. During their time with various resistance groups, Miller and Colin went on several raids, blowing up railway lines and attacking troops on the tracks. They soon got used to the idea of blowing up trains and found it was 'quite good fun'. After about six months Miller and his friend had to leave. A 75,000-franc reward had been placed on their heads and finally they were flown out in an aircraft that re-supplied the resistance. When he got back to London, Miller was given a month of leave to see his family, who had since moved in with his cousin's family because of the bombings in London. He was sent to RAF Warboys, where he transitioned onto Mosquitoes and flew two final operations, both over Berlin and one on Hitler's birthday. 'He was doing a big broadcast when we went over and all the sirens went off and we shot down all the radio stations, so he didn't get his big radio broadcast,' Miller said with a note of satisfaction. After the war he spent two years in the Royal Auxiliary Air Force flying Spitfires. Every year since the war Miller, Beazley-Long and Mead met under the station clock at Charing Cross on the anniversary of their escape, and in 1979 they travelled together to visit the graves of the other four crew members at Schoneau. During the late 1980s to the early '90s, Len Miller met and became firm friends with Martin Becker, the former Luftwaffe officer responsible for the deaths of four of Len's crew. It was only the exceedingly poor health that both men later suffered and eventually Len's passing, that brought that friendship, and many others, to an end.

Operations in support of the D-Day build up continued throughout May. On 1/2 May, 120 aircraft of 3 and 8 Groups, of which ninety-six were Lancasters, attacked Chambly, the main railway stores and repair depot for the Northern French system. About 500 HE bombs fell inside the railway depot area and serious damage was caused to all departments. The depot was completely out of action for ten days. On 7/8 May, ninety-three Lancasters and six Mosquitoes of 3 and 8 Groups bombed the airfield at Nantes in France, for the loss of one Lancaster. The following night, thirty Lancasters of 3 Group and eight PFF Mosquitoes located the gun positions at Cap Griz Nez but no hits were scored. Further raids were made on 9/10 May on coastal batteries in France and rail targets on 10/11 May. On the night of 11/12 May, 105 Lancasters and five Mosquitoes of 3 and 8 Groups attacked the railway yards at Louvain. Four Lancasters were lost. On the night of 19/20 May, 112 Lancasters and four Mosquitoes of 3 and 8 Groups attacked rail yards at Le Mans and caused serious damage. Two 7 Squadron Lancasters, carrying the Master Bomber and the other carrying his deputy, were lost in a collision over the target. On the night of 21/22 May, 510 Lancasters and twenty-two Mosquitoes of 1, 3, 5 and 8 Groups carried out an attack on Duisburg with the loss of twenty-nine Lancasters, 5.5 per cent of the force. The night following, 361 Lancasters and fourteen Mosquitoes of 1, 3, 6 and 78 Groups raided Dortmund and eighteen Lancasters failed to return. Further raids were flown against rail yards at Aachen (twice) and Angers and Trappes.

The operation to Angers went ahead on the night of 28/29 May 1944, when 118 Lancasters and 8 Mosquitoes of 3 and 8 Groups attacked the railway yards and junction. Frank Dengate recalls:

> We did the usual air test in daylight then attacked Angers [with] 1,780 gallons of fuel and 10,885lbs of bombs. This was a strange trip. We flew across England at 1,000ft from Cambridge to Lands End. It was wonderful sight seeing all road traffic stopped below and people waving – the noise of a few hundred Lancasters must have been deafening on the ground. Then out we went to sea and east towards France. As we got closer we climbed to 19,999ft, the idea being to avoid early radar warning by the Germans. It was a very good prang. No flak. No fighters.

Only one aircraft was lost – Lancaster I LM108 of 622 Squadron was piloted by Flight Sergeant T.R. Teague RNZAF. Five crew were taken prisoner and two evaded capture.

On 3/4 June, 127 Lancasters and eight Mosquitoes of 1, 3 and 8 Groups continued with deception raids on coastal batteries at Calais and Wimereux. On the night of 4/5 June, a gun site at Boulogne was to have been the target for ten Lancasters of 15 Squadron but half an hour before briefing the operation was cancelled. Bad weather affected the night's operations against two of the three coastal batteries in the Pas de Calais and they could only be bombed through cloud. Massive Lancaster support was given before dawn on 6 June 1944 to the Normandy landings. On the night of 5/6 June, the D-Day invasion, postponed by twenty-four hours because of bad weather, finally began with thousands of ships and aircraft setting out for five beach landing areas on the Normandy coast.[24] Most everyone had known for several weeks that the invasion was imminent but only the chiefs of staff knew when and where. It was almost daylight when thirty-five Lancasters from RAF Mildenhall attacked gun sites on the French coast, north of Caen and west of Le Havre between 5 and 5.13 a.m, just before the Allied landings. Red and green TIs were dropped by the PFF and spread for about 600 yards along the beach. The reds were believed to be in the right place but the greens were very scattered. 15 Squadron dropped 305, 500 pounders and 622 Squadron dropped 288 of the same. All aircraft returned safely. Frank Dengate of 15 Squadron recalls:

> On D-Day we operated twice in the one day. Once at dawn and another later on in the day, to Lisieux – a good prang. We did the job. They were only 1,000yds ahead of our boys and so it was very accurate bombing. Once again the pathfinders did the job. They dropped TIs where they wanted us to bomb. You can imagine the mess it made to the armour. I'd reckon half of the fellows would be smashed with the shock just from the bombing, even if it didn't destroy the tanks. Imagine sitting in a tank and getting 1,000-lb bombs dropped on top of you. It'd be a bit of a shock I think. It was very successful. Our boys were able to move forward. We didn't know it was D-Day. Nobody told us. It was kept a complete secret. Even to those operating. We were just told to bomb the defences along the shores of the D-Day landings. As we came back in the dawn, we could see the terrific mass of shipping going towards the French coast, so we realised it was D-Day.

Right: Flight Lieutenant Frank Dengate DFC RAAF of 15 Squadron. (Dengate)

Below: The crew of *K-King* in 15 Squadron 1944 in front of *E-Easy* at Mildenhall. Left to right: Doug Davis, rear gunner; Frank Watson, wireless operator; Frank Dengate RAAF, pilot; Fred Coney, mid-upper gunner; Joe Ell RCAF, bomb aimer; Bobby Kitchin, flight engineer; a replacement navigator. (Fred Coney)

That night, 6/7 June, 1,065 RAF four-engine bombers and Mosquitoes dropped 3,488 tons of bombs on rail and road centres on the lines of communication behind the Normandy battle area for the loss of ten Lancasters and a Halifax. At Mildenhall, 15 Squadron contributed sixteen Lancasters and 622 Squadron seventeen Lancasters for the operation to Lisieux, an important road and rail junction. Crews found a well-marked target with bombs criss-crossing the markers. There was no flak over the target and all the crews returned safely. 15 Squadron dropped 305, 500 pounders on the primary and 622 Squadron's Lancasters, another 288, 500 pounders. The next raid followed on the night of 7/8 June when 337 aircraft were despatched to bomb railway targets at Achères, Juvisy, Massy-Palaiseau and Versailles. At Mildenhall, seventeen Lancasters of 15 Squadron and eight of 622 Squadron took off to attack the important rail and road junction at Massy-Palaiseau, about fourteen miles south of Paris. The target was very well marked with red and green TIs and bomb bursts were concentrated amongst them. The railway track could be seen in the light of the explosions. Crews bombed from only 6,000ft and at this altitude they encountered intense light flak on the leg into the target. They also met considerable fighter opposition. Seventeen Lancasters and eleven Halifaxes were lost. A 15 Squadron Lancaster, flown by Flight Lieutenant W.J. Bell DFC, was badly shot up by a Messerschmitt 410 nightfighter and his navigator, Sergeant C.W. Kirk was killed by a cannon shell. Bell crash-landed at Friston airfield near Beachy Head and the aircraft immediately burst into flames but all the crew escaped with minor injuries. Three other 15 Squadron crews failed to return. Squadron leader P.J. Lamason DFC RNZAF, 'A' Flight Commander, and his crew of LM575 *H-Harry*, were very experienced with an average of forty operational sorties between them. Lamason and one of his crew were taken prisoner while three others evaded and two were killed. The other two crew were Flying Officer C.D. Woodley RCAF in LM534 *A-Apple* and Flight Lieutenant W.E. Palmer in LL945 *M-Mother*. There were no survivors from either crew. 622 Squadron lost two Lancasters. Pilot Officer J.E. Hall in LM491 *E-Easy* and Flight Lieutenant R.G. Godfrey RAAF in ND765 *C-Charlie* both failed to return. There were no survivors from either crew.

Raids on the communication targets continued on 8/9 June when 483 aircraft attacked rail targets at Alençon, Fougères, Mayenne, Pontabault and Rennes, to prevent German reinforcements from the south reaching the Normandy battle area. Three Lancasters and a Mosquito failed to return. On the night of 10/11 June, 432 aircraft attacked rail targets at Achères, Dreux, Orléans and Versailles. Frank Dengate's crew was one of those who attacked Dreux [in PB112] and he reported cloud 'all the way then clear – a good prang'. Fifteen Lancasters, including one in 15 Squadron, flown by Flight Lieutenant W. Dobson, an Australian from Geraldton, Western Australia, who had joined the RAF on a short service commission before the war, and three Halifaxes, failed to return. There were no survivors in Dobson's crew. On 11/12 June, 329 aircraft of 1, 3, 4 and 8 Groups attacked railway targets at Evreux, Massy-Palaiseau again, Nantes and Tours, losing three Lancasters and a Halifax. The following night, 12/13 June, 303 aircraft of 1, 3 and 8 Groups attacked Gelsenkirchen, the first raid of the new oil campaign. Seventeen Lancasters were lost. On 15/16 June, 224 aircraft of 3 and 8 Groups attacked railway yards at Lens and Valenciennes. Frank Dengate recalls:

There was cloud almost to Valenciennes but the target was clear. We bombed on the Master Bomber's instructions as he checked the Target Indicators in relation to the true target. We lost five aircraft.' [Another six Lancasters were lost on the Lens raid while another 297 aircraft of 4, 5 and 8 Groups attacked ammunition and fuel dumps without loss]. Two nights later, on 17/18 June, we went to Montdidier to bomb a rail junction to prevent movement of reinforcements to the invasion front line. There was complete cloud cover and the Master Bomber radioed the code word 'Monkey Nuts', which meant 'Do not bomb'. It was important when bombing over France not to bomb if conditions were not favourable to avoid stray bombs killing French civilians. So we returned with our bombs, 8,876-lbs of them. We saw some flying bombs and hoped that they didn't get as far as London.[25]

V-1 flying bombs were now menacing Britain and the launching sites were frequently attacked. On 21 June, 322 aircraft in loose formations and escorted by Spitfires were despatched in daylight to bomb three flying bomb sites in northern France. 15 Squadron's target was Marquise/Mimoyecques but cloud prevented accurate bombing and so the Master Bomber gave the code word 'Buttermilk' and the aircraft returned with their bomb loads intact. Cloud forced the abandonment of two of the raids after only seventeen aircraft had bombed and at the third target, at St-Martin-l'Hortier, the heavies bombed through 10/10ths cloud cover. Because of Allied air superiority over France, daylight raids became increasingly common. Unlike the American Eighth Air Force, RAF Bomber Command operated in a giant gaggle and not usually in formation, thereby cutting losses to flak.

On the night of 23/24 June, when 412 aircraft of 3, 4, 6 and 8 Groups were despatched to bomb four flying bomb sites, fourteen Lancasters from each of the Mildenhall squadrons took part in attacks near l'Hey. All four flying bomb sites were hit. Five Lancasters, including LM138 in 622 Squadron, flown by Flight Sergeant W.H. Cooke RNZAF, were lost on the night's operations. Cooke and one other member of his crew were killed while five survived to be taken prisoner. Frank Dengate's crew had a lucky escape when a trigger-happy gunner in another aircraft fired at their Lancaster. Many operations were flown in direct support of the Allied armies. The Lancasters bombed battlefield targets to assist ground forces and mounted attacks on flying-bomb sites and depots. On 30 June, 266 aircraft of 3, 4 and 8 Groups carried out a daylight raid on a road junction at Villers-Bocage. Tanks of two German Panzer divisions, 2nd *SS Das Reich*, which was in Toulouse, and the 9th Division, were believed to be en route to Normandy and would have to pass through the junction in order to carry out a planned attack on the Allied armies in the battle area. The raid was orchestrated by the Master Bomber, who ordered the bombing force to drop down to 4,000ft in order to be sure of seeing the markers in the smoke and dust of the exploding bombs. Frank Dengate, now an acting squadron leader in charge of 'A' Flight in 15 Squadron, flew on the raid and recalled that it was 'a good prang, 10 miles ahead of our troops. We lost one aircraft to flak over the target (a Halifax was also shot down) and we also had a collision over Mildenhall involving "Z" of 15 Squadron but both aircraft were OK.' In all, 1,100 tons of bombs were dropped with great accuracy on the road junction and the planned German attack was called off.

Mildenhall, meanwhile, continued to receive visitors. The Maharajah of Kashmir and Jammer visited on 17 June and on 5 July HM King George VI, Queen Elizabeth and Princess Elizabeth once again toured the station before holding an investiture. In July, 15 Squadron alone dropped over 1,000 tons of bombs, mighty when compared with the seventy tons dropped by the Luftwaffe on the RAF Mildenhall district during the entire war.

On 2 July, 374 Lancasters and ten Mosquitoes of 1, 3 and 8 Groups attacked three flying bomb sites. 15 Squadron went to Apps Beauvoir, a storage base for V-1s, escorted by Spitfires. Frank Dengate recorded that it was 'a good prang – no losses'. For his navigator, Flying Officer Art Cantrell, it was his last trip and was subsequently posted to the Canadian OTU at Honeybourne. Meanwhile, the land battle in Normandy was heating up and bombing raids were made on rail targets and flying bomb sites. Frank Dengate returned from a six-day leave. On 12 July, he and his crew in *K-King* took part in a daylight operation by 153 Lancasters and six Mosquitoes of 1, 3 and 8 Groups to the railway yards at Vaires on the outskirts of Paris, but the target area was covered by cloud. The Master Bomber sent the code word 'Buttermilk' to abandon the attack after two of the Mosquitoes had marked and twelve of the Lancasters had bombed. Frank Dengate in 15 Squadron, recalls:

> We had to bring our bombs back home again. Flak hit us and wiped out one of our engines. I had to feather it to stop it catching fire. We were going slowly back to base and we were on our own. It was a bit risky. Fortunately my wireless operator got up in the astrodome and with his Aldis lamp sent a message to one of the other aircraft in our squadron to send some escorts. Sure enough, a Spitfire came and escorted us home. The German fighters were always ready to have a

Above: The crew of *K-King* in 15 Squadron 1944. Left to right: Frank Dengate RAAF, pilot; Fred Coney, mid upper gunner; Art Cantrell RCAF, navigator; Frank Watson, wireless operator; Doug Davis, rear gunner; Bobby Kitchin, engineer; Joe Ell RCAF, bomb aimer. (Dengate)

Left: Flight Lieutenant Frank Dengate DFC RAAF's crew in the open doorway of *K-King*. (Fred Coney)

The royal visit to Mildenhall on 5 July 1944. (Fred Coney)

crack at an individual aeroplane and you didn't have much chance. When we got to Mildenhall I found I had no brakes. The line was cut. I hit the deck and we still had the bomb load on board. I feathered the other outer engine and kept the two inner engines for directing the aircraft for taxiing. I was heading for the hangars so I swung the aeroplane left, jumped the slit trenches and went through a fence into a beautiful wheat field ready for harvest at West Row where we spun round in a semi circle. We eventually stopped without damage and the ambulance and fire engines and everyone else followed through and made the wheat field one great flat mass. It worked out all right but the farmer was upset and came out shaking his fist![26]

The crew of *K-King* took part in several more operations in July, including, on 18 July, the big attack by 942 aircraft on five fortified villages in the area east of Caen, in support of Operation *Goodwood*, British Second Army's armoured attack. The Luftwaffe was noticeable for its absence and Frank Dengate reported that it was 'a wonderful prang on target indicators. 5,000 tons of steel – I wouldn't have liked to have been under that lot.' Four of the targets were marked by *Oboe* and at the fifth target, where *Oboe* failed, the Master Bomber, Squadron Leader E.K. Cresswell and other Pathfinder crews employed visual methods. In all, Bomber Command dropped more than 5,000 tons of bombs from 5,000 to 9,000ft for the loss of just five Lancasters and a Halifax, though Frank Dengate recorded that there was 'lots of flak'. The 16th Luftwaffe Field Division and the 21st Panzer Division were badly affected by the bombing.

By way of a change, on 20 July, Frank Dengate and his crew were part of a force of 147 Lancasters and eleven Mosquitoes of 1, 3 and 8 Groups that attacked the oil plant at Homburg. Dengate reported:

Flight Lieutenant Hopper–Cuthbert (third from the right) and his crew of LL806 LS-J on completion of the Lancaster's 100th operation. *J-Jig* was SOC on 5 December 1944 after 134 operations. (via Harry Holmes)

Lancaster I ME844 LS-C, which was delivered to 15 Squadron on 16 June 1944 and had already completed twenty operations by the time this photograph was taken. The aircraft later joined 44 Squadron, and it was SOC in June 1947. (via Harry Holmes)

… plenty of nightfighters and medium flak and heavy fighter attacks on the way home. Twenty Lancasters, including two in 622 Squadron and 'L for Love' in 15 squadron, were lost. Our next operation was on 22 July in PB112 'K' our old aircraft, in daylight to try and knock out the flying bombs and V-2 rockets at Mont-Candon. There were only eight aircraft in pair's formation, one behind the other. We formatted on two Mosquitoes which were on a radio beam from England and when they crossed a second beam they dropped their bombs and so did we. I don't know what the results were, as we were over cloud. There was no flak and no fighters and none of our aircraft were missing.[27]

On the night of 24/25 July, Frank Dengate completed his thirty-first trip when he and his crew returned to Stuttgart, scene of their first operation on 15 March, for the first of three heavy raids on the city in five nights. The force of 461 Lancasters and 153 Halifaxes encountered heavy icing at 14,000ft and they had to drop down to get rid of it before climbing back up to 19,000ft at the target. Many aircraft turned back. Seventeen Lancasters and four Halifaxes were lost but K-King's crew made it back to Mildenhall. Flying Officer Joe Ell had now done twenty-eight trips and Sergeant Fred Coney and Sergeant Doug Davis had completed twenty-nine each, while Bob Kitchin had also flown twenty-eight trips. Dengate recalls:

Cantrell, Ell and myself were awarded the DFC (Distinguished Flying Cross) whereas the other members of our crew got no recognition although they took the same risks. I was asked to stay on as Squadron Leader Flight Command with 15 Squadron but with my crew split up I had had enough for the present. I took fourteen days glorious leave and early in August, I was posted to 29 OTU. Before returning to Australia I was posted to 467 Squadron RAAF at Waddington and Metheringham, where we trained to go to Okinawa to attack Japan but the Yanks dropped the atomic bomb and consequently probably saved my life and the lives of my crew as well as thousands of others.

Meanwhile, by September 1944, the Allied day and night bombing campaign was being directed against oil depots, coking plants and transport targets in Germany. RAF Mildenhall's Lancasters participated in October's bombing assault on the Westkapelle sea wall on Walcheren in the Netherlands, breaching it to flood guns on the islands barring entry to the river Scheldt. Later that month, 3 Group Lancasters fitted with Gee-H blind bombing equipment came into use. About eighty were equipped out of the 200 on strength in the organisation. For safety, operations could now take place above the clouds and bombing accuracy remained good. The ultimate in RAF Mildenhall's wartime operations came on 14 October when its Lancasters bombed Duisburg twice in one day. 15 Squadron despatched forty-two sorties and 622 Squadron another forty. On 16 November 1944, the Commanding Officer of 15 Squadron, Wing Commander W.D.G. Watkins DSO DFC DFM, who was flying Lancaster III PB137, was shot down on the operation to Heinsburg. In all, 182 Lancasters of No.3 Group were asked to bomb three towns near the German lines, which were about to be attacked by the American First and Ninth Armies. Watkins survived and was taken prisoner. The strategic bombing campaign against Germany was resumed at this time and thirty-one aircraft from Mildenhall took part on the night of 27/28 November in a raid on Neuss, an important German supplies centre. This was the first time that Lancasters from Mildenhall had dropped the new 12,000lb Tallboy bomb. Oil and coking plants continued to be attacked, day and night, in 1945.

No.15 Squadron's most famous Lancaster, LL806 J-Jig, which eventually flew 134 sorties making a record for any Lancaster while serving on one squadron, was finally SOC on 5 December 1944. Another famous Lancaster, which usually sat on dispersal approximately where the present passenger and freight terminal stands, was LS-C R5508, which was flown by South African Squadron Leader John Dering Nettleton VC, of 44 Squadron (KM-B), on the daring Augsburg low-level raid of 17 April 1942. It then served with 1660 CU and 38 MU before it joined 15 Squadron. R5508 was finally SOC in January 1947. LL885 GI-J completed 113 operational sorties, all with 622 Squadron and was SOC in March 1947.

Lancasters LS-M and LS-Q (flown by Geoff Claydon's crew) of 15 Squadron in formation in 1944. (Theo Boiten via M.J. Peto)

Lancaster I L7527 begins to taxi for its first flight from Woodford on 31 October 1941. This was the first production Lancaster, which after trials with the A&AEE in 1941–42 was sent to 1654 CU before joining 15 Squadron on March 1944. L7527 and Pilot Officer T.G. Marsh's crew were lost on the raid on Essen on the night of 26/27 March 1944, when the aircraft is thought to have exploded over Aachen. There were no survivors. (via Harry Holmes)

Lancaster I LM110 LS-G of 15 Squadron, which was lost on the night of 12/13 September 1944, when 378 Lancasters and nine Mosquitoes of 1, 3 and 8 Groups attacked Frankfurt in the last major RAF Bomber Command raid on the city during the war. All members of Warrant Officer A.D. MacDougall RAAF's crew were killed. A second 15 Squadron Lancaster flown by Flying Officer N.R. Overend RNZAF also failed to return. Five members of Overend's crew survived and were taken prisoner. In all, seventeen Lancasters were lost, 4.5 per cent of the Lancaster force. (IWM)

Flying Officer Woods RAAF and his crew of Lancaster I HK616 GI-W *Bill The Conk* of 622 Squadron. This aircraft later served with 44 Squadron, and was scrapped in October 1946. (via Harry Holmes)

Lancaster I LM235 GI-B of 622 Squadron taxiing at Mildenhall for the raid on Stuttgart on 19/20 October 1944. This aircraft joined 44 Squadron in August 1945 and went to 15 MU before being SOC in February 1947. (via Harry Holmes)

Lancaster I ME849 LS-L of 15 Squadron taxiing out at Mildenhall on 5 November 1944 for the raid on Solingen. ME849 joined the squadron in June that year and was later transferred to 44 Squadron before being scrapped in 1947. (via Harry Holmes)

Lancaster I NG364 LS-P of 15 Squadron taxiing out at Mildenhall on 5 November 1944 for the raid on Solingen. The rear turrets are turned to the side to prevent accidental fire from the machine-guns hitting the following aircraft. NG364 was SOC in October 1945. (via Harry Holmes)

Lancaster GI-A of 622 Squadron over the target at Heinsburg on 16 November 1944 when 182 Lancasters of No.3 Group were asked to bomb three towns near the German lines, which were about to be attacked by the American First and Ninth Armies. The Commanding Officer of 15 Squadron, Wing Commander W.D.G. Watkins DSO DFC DFM was shot down on the operation. Watkins survived and was taken prisoner. All seven of his crew were killed. (F/O Wade)

No.15 Squadron and 622 Squadron took part in the memorable raids on Dresden and Chemnitz. On 8/9 February, Bomber Command returned to attacks on synthetic oil plants when Pölitz was bombed by 475 Lancasters and seven Mosquitoes. Wanne-Eickel and Krefeld were also attacked. There followed a series of minor operations involving Mosquito bombers mainly, while the Main Force was grounded, 9–12/13 February. Bomber Command though was merely building up for an operation that has since gone down in history as one of the most controversial bombing raids of the war. For most of the participating aircrew, the Dresden raid of 13/14 February was another well-executed and very efficient area bombing attack. Dresden was targeted as part of a series of particularly heavy raids on German cities in Operation Thunderclap, with a view to causing as much destruction, confusion and mayhem as possible.[28]

The campaign was to have started with an American raid on Dresden on 13 February but bad weather over Europe prevented any US involvement until 14 February. Dresden was to be bombed in two RAF assaults, three hours apart – the first by 244 Lancasters of 5 Group and the second by 529 Lancasters of 1, 3, 6 and 8 Groups. As tons of explosives plummeted from the sky, an $800°C$ firestorm tore through the heart of the Saxon capital, burning thousands of Dresdeners alive. In a firestorm similar to that created in Hamburg on 27/28 July 1943, an estimated 50,000 Germans died in Dresden. Later Winston Churchill tried to distance himself from Dresden and declared that 'the destruction of Dresden remains a serious query against the conduct of Allied bombing'. This was the same Winston S. Churchill who, on 22 June 1941, had said, 'We shall bomb Germany by day as well as night in ever-increasing measure, casting upon them month by month a heavier discharge of bombs and making the German people taste and gulp each month a sharper dose of the miseries they have showered upon mankind.' Sergeant Frank W. Tasker, a Lancaster mid-upper gunner in 622 Squadron said:

> The most successful of our nightly operational flights and the ones that I remember so well were those on Dresden and Chemnitz. Since World War II some Germans have complained about those raids having taken place. Have they conveniently forgotten, how for the first two years of the war, the Luftwaffe was bombing London (where I lived) and elsewhere in UK day and night! Have they also forgotten the V-1 flying bombs and V-2 rockets they were still indiscriminately sending to kill innocent women and children in England? Surely they haven't also forgotten about the gas chambers they used!

An important development came in the autumn of 1944 when several of 15 Squadron's Lancasters were fitted with *G-H*, a new blind-bombing radar system. These aircraft were identified by special yellow tail markings and from October 1944 were, with others from No.3 Group, used extensively as formation leaders on massed daylight raids.

February 1945 was an extremely busy month, with 222 sorties flown by 15 Squadron and 229 by 622 Squadron, and March was even busier. Attacks were now being made on tactical targets in preparation for the Allied crossing of the Rhine and on 23 March a Lancaster of 622 Squadron led sixteen aircraft from Mildenhall in an attack on Wesel, the aiming point being 1,500 yards in front of our troops. Very few casualties were incurred in the final crossing of the Rhine, and Field Marshal Montgomery sent a message to the C-in-C Bomber Command expressing his appreciation for the support that he had received.

The European war was now almost over and the Station Commander, Group Captain K.S. Batchelor, was able to fly to Juvincourt on 16 April to be invested with the *Croix de Guerre*. On 14/15 April, 500 Lancasters of 1 and 3 Groups and twelve Mosquitoes of 8 Group took part in an operation against Potsdam just outside Berlin. Although Mosquito bombers of the LNSF had attacked the 'Big City' almost continually, this was the first time the Reich capital had been attacked by heavies since March 1944. One Lancaster was lost to an unidentified nightfighter over the target. The last bombing operation from Mildenhall came on 22 April, when fourteen aircraft from each squadron took part in a daylight raid by 767 aircraft on Bremen.

Lancaster I NG358 LS-H of 15 Squadron in 1945. The two yellow bars on the fins show that this
aircraft is a *G-H* leader and the bulge beneath the fuelage contains the scanner for the *H2S* airborne
radar transmitter. (IWM)

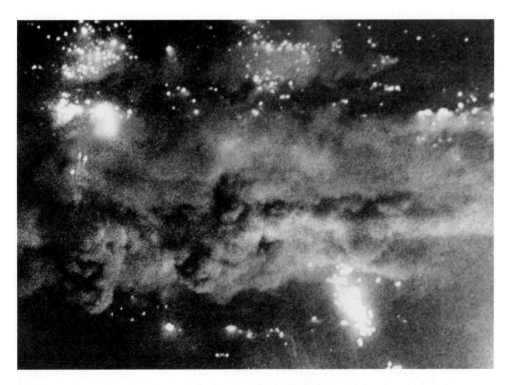

Dresden on fire during the raid on 13/14 February 1945. (IWM)

Dresden after the attack by RAF Bomber
Command in February 1945.

The bomb symbol for the 113th operation
is painted on Lancaster I LL806 LS-J of
15 Squadron after the raid on Kamen on
25 February 1945. *J-Jig* went on to
complete 134 operations. (via Harry
Holmes)

Two Lancasters, including one from 622 Squadron, were lost on this operation. Lancasters of 15 Squadron alone delivered more than 13,000 tons of bombs.

With the Germans at the brink of defeat, thousands of people in the western and north-western provinces of the Netherlands, which were still in German hands, were without food. Parts of the country had been under German blockade and 20,000 men, women and children had died of starvation during a very short period and the survivors were in a desperate plight. From 29 April to 7 May, Lancasters of 1, 3 and 8 Groups flew 2,835 food sorties and PFF Mosquitoes made 124 sorties to 'mark' the dropping zones, and Bomber Command delivered 6,672 tons of food to the starving Dutch people during Operation *Manna*. The US Eighth Air Force began *Chowhound* food dropping missions on 1 May. Many wildly enthusiastic Dutch climbed on to rooftops to wave to the passing Lancasters loaded with sacks of flour, tea, sugar, sweets and supplies of cigarettes. Seven times these aircraft literally flew at rooftop height to drop supplies on open ground near Rotterdam and The Hague. Many sacks burst, so the starving recipients scooped the flour, mixed with soil, into their mouths. RAF Mildenhall's Lancasters alone dropped enough supplies for around 50,000 people. How much had changed since those Wellingtons delivered tiny tea bags. Finally, on 3 May 1945, two aircraft from each squadron took off to lay mines in the Kattegat to try to trap a convoy that had been seen leaving Kiel. Bad weather forced the recall of the planes and this proved to be the last offensive operation of the war to be flown from RAF Mildenhall. Operation *Exodus*, the repatriation of prisoners from Germany was now underway and Mildenhall's Lancasters, each carrying twenty-four prisoners of war, ferried them home from Juvincourt near Rheims to Westcott and Wing between 10 May and 30 June 1945. The two squadrons each sent two aircraft to Bari on the east coast of Italy on 24 May, flying out stocks of spares prior to starting Operation *Dodge*, the repatriation of personnel of the Central Mediterranean Forces. This continued to the end of the year. Rapid return of each load brought incredible scenes, as many, having never been in an aeroplane before and despite their poor health, tumbled from the bombers to kiss home ground.

From May to October, aerial tours of Europe allowed ground crews to see something of the victory that their bombers had wrought. The cost to RAF Mildenhall was high. Over 200 Wellingtons, Stirlings and Lancasters were lost. The station 'Roll of Honour' records the names of over 1,900 officers and men killed on active service, seventy-six of whom are buried in the beautifully kept Military Cemetery at the back of St John's Church in Beck Row. 15 Squadron had dropped 13,124 tons of bombs since changing to Lancasters in December 1943. Its wartime loss was 166 aircraft, including ninety-one Stirlings and forty-five Lancasters on operations, and another thirty-eight Stirlings and eleven Lancasters destroyed in crashes. 622 Squadron, which disbanded on 15 August 1945, had dropped 10,469 tons of bombs on enemy targets since its formation in 1943, losing fifty-one aircraft, including seven Stirlings and forty-four Lancasters.

By the end of the war, no less than 73,741 casualties were sustained by Bomber Command, of which 55,500 aircrew had been KIA or flying accidents, or died on the ground or while prisoners of war. It is a casualty rate that compares with the worst slaughters in the First World War trenches. Operational bomber losses were 8,655 aircraft and another 1,600 were lost in accidents and write-offs. Approximately 125,000 aircrew served in the frontline, OTU and OCUs of the Command and nearly 60 per cent of them became casualties. In addition, almost 9,900 more were shot down and made PoWs to spend one, two or more years in squalid, desolate Oflags and Stalags in Axis held territory. Over 8,000 more were wounded aboard aircraft on operational sorties. Bomber Command flew almost 390,000 sorties, the greatest percentage of them by Avro Lancasters, Handley Page Halifaxes and Wellingtons. Theirs, of course, were the highest casualties.

VE-Day, 8 May 1945, passed quietly at Mildenhall. Both squadrons were busy dropping food to the Dutch and this prevented a general stand down. Nos 622 and 15 Squadrons could boast a Lancaster that had 'topped the century' on missions, a very rare feat when the

The only Lancaster Mk VII to serve with 15 Squadron, NX687 LS-A, runs up its Merlin 24 engines at Mildenhall in July 1945. This aircraft later crashed in France and finished up as a static airframe (6816M) at RAF Halton apprentices school. NX687 was one of 200 Mk VII aircraft built by Austin Motors at Longbridge and were fitted with a Martin top turret with twin 0.5in machine-guns. (via Harry Holmes)

Group Captain Ken S. Batchelor DFC, Mildenhall Station Commander, December 1944–September 1945, escorts a party of Brazilian Air Force officers to inspect a 'Grand Slam' bomb in the bomb bay of a visiting 617 'Dam Busters' Squadron Lancaster. Batchelor had flown on the first of the Wellington operations of the war with 9 Squadron and later commanded 138 Squadron. (via Harry Holmes)

Lancaster I of 622 Squadron at Mildenhall in January 1945. 622 Squadron was disbanded on 15 August 1945. (via Harry Holmes)

average operational life of a bomber in the early days was only forty flying hours. LL885 *J-Jig* of 622 Squadron had completed 113 operation sorties and LL806, also *J-Jig*, of 15 Squadron had completed 134. The latter's record was surpassed by only two other aircraft and in both cases they had been flown by more than one squadron whereas LL806 *J-Jig* completed all its operations with the one squadron.

Bomber Command authorised sightseeing tours to Germany and, from 23 May to mid-October, regular flights were made to fly ground personnel across to view the damage that had been inflicted by the bombers that they had so faithfully supported. Similarly, Operation *Spasm* sorties to Berlin followed during September to November. Training operations also continued and both squadrons participated in periodic *Bullseye* exercises in which live weapons were dropped on Heligoland.

The Commonwealth members of the two squadrons were rapidly de-mobbed and 622 Squadron was disbanded on 15 August 1945, VJ-Day. In the USA, victory over Japan was celebrated on 2 September. 44 (Rhodesia) Squadron, who arrived from RAF Mepal, replaced them later that month. 15 Squadron was reduced to two flights on 24 September. Air Chief Marshal Sir Edgar Ludlow-Hewitt made an informal visit on 25 June and on 10 July an official inspection. The first, since the outbreak of war, was made by Air Vice Marshal R. Harrison, AOC of No.3 Group. During August to December 1945, Mildenhall received official missions from Venezuela, Brazil, Peru and Uruguay, and on 15 September the station was once again opened to the public on the occasion of the anniversary of the Battle of Britain. That summer, 15 Squadron flew the AOC-in-C Bomber Command, ACM Sir Arthur 'Bomber' Harris, on an official visit to Rio de Janeiro in Lancaster B.VII (Far East) NX687 LS-A. The special tropical version left on 23 July and returned to Mildenhall on 6 October. Meanwhile, 15 and 44 Squadrons continued to operate Lancaster B.1s and late in 1945 Mildenhall became a base for inter-related bomber and bombing trials. In October 1945 44 Squadron received three Avro Lincoln bombers for service trials that were to last until May 1946. The Lancaster was unsuitable for long-range service in the Far East and so the Avro Lincoln derivative was designed. The first Lincoln entered service with

Lancaster I NX561 LS-L of 15 Squadron dropping food to the Dutch during Operation *Manna* in May 1945. From 29 April to 7 May, Lancasters of 1, 3 and 8 Groups flew 2,835 food sorties and delivered 6,672 tons of food to the starving Dutch people. RAF Mildenhall's Lancasters alone dropped enough supplies for around 50,000 people. (via Harry Holmes)

Former PoWs wait to board Lancaster I ME455 LS-O of 15 Squadron for the flight home during Operation *Exodus*. Mildenhall's Lancasters, each carrying twenty-four prisoners of war ferried them home from Juvincourt, near Rheims, to Westcott and Wing between 10 May and 30 June 1945. (via Harry Holmes)

57 Squadron at East Kirkby in August 1945, and were about to join 'Tiger Force' to bomb the Japanese mainland when the atomic bombing of Hiroshima and Nagasaki brought the Pacific War to an end. Small numbers of Lincolns were placed in twenty-one squadrons in Bomber Command and three joined 44 Squadron, which had moved to RAF Mildenhall in late August 1945. A conference at RAF Mildenhall on 6 February 1946 discussed in detail the Lincoln's record, and trials ended in May when problems with the engines, undercarriage and turrets had been remedied and the aircraft was ready to enter service.

During six months in 1946, nine Lancaster B.1s (Special), previously operated by 617 'The Dam Busters' Squadron and fitted with enlarged bomb doors to accommodate the 12,000lb *Tallboy* bomb, were used by 15 Squadron to test the deep penetration 'earthquake' bombs. These bombs, which needed to be dropped from as high an altitude as possible to gain sufficient velocity, had been dropped with some success by 617 Squadron during the closing months of the war. During the 1946 trials, cloudy weather often interfered with operations and the project required a blind bombing device, such as TV guidance used by *Blue Boar* before the system could be used operationally by the new generation of jet bombers. A detachment of three B-17G Flying Fortresses was temporarily based at Mildenhall in December 1945 for high-level bombing trials beginning in January 1946. The Fortresses had their armament removed and were modified to carry 4,500lb rocket bombs or a 2,000lb bomb with a special penetration head beneath each wing. Captain Edward Terrell of the Royal Navy had developed the rocket-powered bomb late in the war. It was designed to penetrate 20ft of concrete before exploding. Its weight prevented it being carried in the bomb bay of a B-24 Liberator or B-17, but two of these so-called *Disney* bombs were first used on 10 February 1945 when nine B-17s in the 92nd Bomb Group USAAF dropped eighteen of them on E-Boat pens at Ijmuiden in Holland. One hit was recorded and further trials were ordered, but the Allies sweeping victories in the low countries and the vast distance to suitable targets in Norway brought the *Disney* missions to an end. Prophetically, during the 1946 trials one of the three Fortresses was called *Too Little, Too Late*! On 28 February 1946, the three B-17Gs moved to RAF Marham to join three B-29s to take part in Project *Ruby*, which together with 15 Squadron, were involved in the bombing of former U-Boat pens at Farge on the river Weser, north of Bremen. The huge structure had a concrete roof, 23ft thick. It had almost been ready for use when on 27 March 1945 twenty Lancasters of 617 Squadron had attacked it and penetrated the roof with two 22,000lb *Grand Slam* bombs, which brought down thousands of tons of concrete rubble and rendered the shelter unusable. Three days later over sixty *Disneys* were dropped by the USAAF but only one hit the roof, causing a small crater. It was thought that a target like this could probably withstand a 22,000lb bomb but whether it could withstand repeated hits could only be determined by experiments, and these had to wait until after the war. In February 1946 also, during Operation *Sinkum*, surplus incendiary weapons were jettisoned in Heligoland Bight and Cardigan Bay.

RAF Mildenhall was again open to the public on 25 May 1946 when a wide range of RAF and enemy equipment, including a German V-1 flying bomb and a Japanese Baka suicide plane, was on show. The proceeds were given to St Dunstan's Hostel for the Blind. No.3 Group's Major Servicing Unit was moved to Mildenhall on 8 August 1946 but the station was being run down operationally, the two resident squadrons being posted away to RAF Wyton later that same month. A variety of aircraft flew in for servicing but otherwise there was little activity at the station. The headquarters of No.3 Group however returned from Exning in January 1947 to begin a further twenty-year stay at RAF Mildenhall.

In March 1947, during the disastrous east coast floods, the fens were badly affected and on 16 March, at a time of particular danger, 110 flood victims were picked up by station transport and given shelter at RAF Mildenhall. Mobile searchlights, wood tracking and other supplies were despatched to local danger points and on 21 March an Auster aircraft was made available for civilian experts to view the floods from the air. The next day a party of NCOs and airmen were sent to Lakenheath Lode to assist with heavy flood relief work. On 23 March, another party of twenty-eight volunteers and thirty-six PoWs went to help at Southery Pumping

Lancaster BI (Special) LS-X, which was used by 15 Squadron in February 1946 to take part in Operation *Front Line*, which was a combined exercise with USAF B-29s, dropping 22,000lb Grand Slam and 12,000lb *Tallboy* bombs on U-Boat pens at Farge on the river Weser, north of Bremen. (IWM)

In August–September 1949, 35, 115, 149 and 207 Squadrons at Mildenhall converted to the Avro Lincoln B.II (WD148, one of 281 examples built by Armstrong-Whitworth pictured). However, in February–March 1950 all four squadrons were reduced to a 'number only' basis and many personnel were posted to RAF Marham to convert to the Washington B.1. (Ashley Annis)

Station. The flood danger lessened during April but RAF Mildenhall continued to provide assistance with lighting equipment for night work. The routine of inspections continued but there was little other military activity at Mildenhall. Another Battle of Britain Open Day was held on 20 September 1947 and the next day a contingent from the station attended the Battle of Britain service in Ely Cathedral. They also took part in the march-past, afterwards. In 1948 the Cold War got colder, and on 24 June the Soviets cut off road, rail and barge traffic between Berlin and the Western Occupation zones of Germany. On 26 June 1948, the Berlin Airlift began in response to the Soviet blockade and it kept 2.2 million Berliners alive for nearly a year. The Soviets finally ended the blockade of West Berlin on 12 May 1948 but airlift stockpiling continued for five months. The combined task force comprising United States Air Forces Europe (USAFE) personnel and aircraft, RAF and US Naval flying units, and French and US Army transport units continued until 1 September 1949 and the US component, the 1st Airlift Task Force, was inactivated on 1 October 1949. Another highly significant event that year was the signing, on 4 April, by twelve nations of the North Atlantic Treaty, establishing the North Atlantic Treaty Organisation (NATO).

Meanwhile, at Mildenhall, the Group Major Servicing Unit was disbanded in July 1948 and the station was placed on a reduced establishment basis. The runways and perimeter track were resurfaced and other works were completed in preparation for the planned arrival of 230 OCU (Operational Conversion Unit) from Lindholme. In October, however, it was decided that the close proximity of the B-29s of the 2nd Bombardment Group at Lakenheath made Mildenhall unsuitable for this purpose. Beginning in December 1948, 35, 115, 149 and 207 Squadrons were posted in from RAF Stradishall, which was closing for extensive runway repairs, with the move being completed in three stages, and was completed on 18 February 1949. Once again RAF Mildenhall became an active Bomber Command station, although all four squadrons brought only six Lancasters each to Mildenhall, while detachments were maintained at Shallufa in Egypt. Exercises were carried out and in August–September 1949, 35, 115, 149 and 207 Squadrons converted to the Avro Lincoln B.II. However, in February–March 1950 all four squadrons were reduced to a 'number only' basis. Many personnel were posted to RAF Marham to convert to the B-29 or Washington B.1, the name given by the RAF to seventy (later increased to eighty-eight) Superfortresses, acquired under the American military aid programme, pending re-equipment with an all jet bomber force. 115 Squadron was reformed with Washington's and for fifteen months, beginning in June 1950, 35, 149 and 207 Squadrons similarly re-equipped on the Washington. In all, the Washington equipped eight squadrons in Bomber Command. None of the squadrons returned to Mildenhall, which on 1 April 1950 was placed on a Care and Maintenance basis and only HQ No 3 Group was active. Had it not been for an unexpected turn of events in the Far East in 1950, Mildenhall might well have passed into aviation history.

Notes

1   The Vickers Armstrong Wellington was affectionately known as the 'Wimpy' after the Walt Disney cartoon character 'J. Wellington Wimpy' in *Popeye*.
2   Warren had a close shave flying another *M-Mother*, on 11 February. Returning from an attack on Hannover at 8,000ft they could not land back Mildenhall and went to Digby where they crash landed with the undercarriage up and the second pilot, Sergeant Early, was killed and the rest of the crew injured.
3   *M-Mother* had returned safely from the raid on Bremen but had been jumped by a Ju 88C night intruder flown by Leutnant Rolf Pfeiffer of I/NJG2 from Gilze-Rijn, Holland, as it was coming into land near Beck Row. Sergeant Ronald Warren, the pilot and the five other crew members were killed in the attack. The Wellington took the top off a garage and flattened a row of conifer trees before ploughing into the side of a bungalow demolishing the lounge, kitchen, hall and

bathroom and back bedroom. Ellis Titchmarsh, an insurance agent and his wife, Irene, escaped unhurt as they had taken refuge under their bed when they heard machine-gun fire. Their bedroom was the only room left standing and it took six men to lift the debris of a wall off the bed that saved the occupants' lives. Mr and Mrs Titchmarsh had to take separate lodgings with different people and did not live together again for nearly a year. Pfeiffer was lost on the night of 17/18 August 1941 when his Ju 88C-2 R4+HM of IV/NJG 2 crashed into the North Sea. A Royal Navy vessel found the body of his navigator Gefreiter Otto Schierling in the North Sea on 26 August. Nothing was ever found of Pfeiffer or Unteroffizier Alfred Ranke, the gunner/engineer.

4 Hurricane IV 7225 of 1401 Meteorological Flight at Mildenhall, piloted by Flying Officer Iain Robertson MacDiarmid DFC, had hurtled out of thick cloud towards the formation of four Wellingtons and had torn right through the fuselage of the leading Wellington, R1587, flown by Squadron Leader A.W.J. Clark. The Hurricane impacted upside down on Lark Farm, Soham Fen near Ely, killing MacDiarmid. Clark, Pilot Officer G.H. Cotton, whose twenty-first birthday this was, and Sergeants C E. Bushford, A. Pepper, R.A. Petter and D. George 'Junior' Gray were killed.

5 Pickard and his crew of Wellington IC R3200 LN-O were hit by flak over the area of the Ruhr on the night of 19/20 June 1940 and they were forced to ditch thirty miles off Great Yarmouth. The crew were eventually rescued after thirteen hours in their dinghy, which at one stage drifted into a coastal minefield. Group Captain Pickard DSO DFC lost his life on the legendary attack by Mosquitoes on Amiens prison on 18 February 1944 when his Mosquito was shot down by Feldwebel Wilhelm Mayer of II/JG 26 (KIA 4.1.45) in a Focke Wulf 190.

6 Warrant Officer Tony Gee and two of his crew in 28 OTU at Wymeswold were killed on 7 October 1942 while piloting Wellington IC R1801.

7 Of the 169 aircraft despatched by 1, 3 and 4 Groups, 101 were Wellingtons. Ten Wimpys, nine Whitleys and two Stirlings were lost − 12.4 per cent of those despatched. Only seventy-three aircraft reached the general area of Berlin. After completing twenty-four operations on 149 Squadron, Terence Mansfield went on a bombing leader's course at Manby and when it finished in November 1941 he transferred to 419 Squadron.

8 N3726 OJ-G flown by Pilot Officer Mike Evans.

9 W/C J. 'Moose' Fulton the CO.

10 A Bf 110 of 6./NJG 2 flown by Leutnant Hans-Georg Bötel who was KIA 2/3 July 1942 and had three victories.

11 N6082 was shot down at 2.04 a.m. and crashed in the Ijsselmeer near Wons south of Harlingen. Collins was the only survivor.

12 Flight Sergeant L.A. Hyder, Sergeant Cameron and Sergeant Gough were awarded the DFM. Flying Officer Cameron later joined 635 Squadron and was shot down on 4 August 1944 when he was flying with Acting Squadron Leader Ian Willoughby Bazalgette DFC RAFVR, who was awarded a posthumous VC Cameron survived and evaded capture. Middleton's medal is now on display in the Australian War memorial in Canberra. The RAF Mildenhall Officer's Club was renamed in his honour − Middleton Hall − in 2002.

13 By May 1945, No.3 Group had 330 Lancasters in eleven squadrons on nine airfields.

14 McLeod and five others PoW. 1 KIA.

15 *Oboe* was the most accurate form of high-level blind bombing used in the Second World War and it took its name from a radar pulse, which sounded like a musical instrument. The radar pulses operated on the range from two ground stations ('Cat' and 'Mouse') in England to the target. The signal was heard by both pilot and navigator and used to track the aircraft over the target, If inside the correct line, dots were heard, if outside the line, dashes, a steady note indicated the target was on track. Only the navigator heard this signal. When the release signal, which consisted of five dots and a two-second dash, was heard, the navigator released the markers or bombs.

16 Eighty-six Stirlings were despatched to attack the Heinkel factory near Rostock but a smoke screen concealed this target and bombing was scattered. Eight Stirlings were lost.

17 783 aircraft, including ninety-nine Stirlings, took part in the raid. Thirty-eight aircraft, including two Stirlings, were lost.

18 During the Battle of Hamburg 24/25 July–3 August 1943, 'Window' prevented about 100 −130 potential Bomber Command losses. Over four nights, 3,000 bombers dropped 10,000 tons of

HE and incendiary bombs to totally devastate half of the city and kill an estimated 42,000 of its inhabitants. After the fourth raid on 2/3 August, a million inhabitants fled the city. Albert Speer, Minister of War Production, warned Hitler that Germany would have to surrender after another six of these bombing raids. Paralysed by 'Window', *Nachtjagd* and the *Flakwaffe* were unable to offer any significant resistance. On average, British losses during the Hamburg raids were no more than 2.8 per cent, whereas in the previous twelve months, losses had risen from 3.7 to 4.3 per cent.

19 The 25/26 July raid on Essen caused severe damage to the industrial areas in the eastern parts of the city. The Krupps Works suffered its most damaging raid of the war and fifty-one other industrial buildings were damaged, with another eighty-three heavily damaged. Twenty-six bombers or 3.7 per cent of the force FTR of which, nineteen were destroyed by nightfighters – fifteen of these to crews of NJG 1 and NJG 3, manning the *Himmelbett* nightfighter boxes in Holland and over the Dutch-German border. *Wild Boar* single-engined nightfighters that engaged the bomber stream over the blazing city of Essen claimed the four remaining aircraft losses.

20 *We, Also Were There* by 'Archie' Hall. Dame Laura Knight RA (1877–1970) is considered one of the greatest British painters of the twentieth century.

21 Hudson FK803 MA-N of 161 Squadron took off from Tempsford on the night of 20/21 March 1945 with three Belgian agents for an operation for X Section of SOE called *Benedict/Express/Leader*. Lieutenant G.J.F. Corbishier (*Benedict*) and two W/T operators, Lieutenant J.J.L. Morel and Lieutenant M. de Winter, were to be dropped over Germany and make contact with Belgian forces labourers around Kassel, to organise such sabotage as they could and to pass on any orders they got from the Allied high command. The pilot, Flight Lieutenant T. Helfer, aborted his operation over Erfurt because of bad weather. On entering Luxembourg airspace they received a burst of gunfire from a nightfighter just north of Clervaux, which set the Hudson on fire. Helfer, badly burned and with his parachute on fire, was the only survivor. The Hudson crashed in flames on a hill above Maulesmuhle. Here three of the crew, Flying Officer F.H. Thompson DFM, Ray Escreet and Flying Officer H.S. Johnson are buried together with the three Belgian agents. It is thought that an American nightfighter shot them down.

22 From 18/19 November 1943 to 24/25 March 1944, Berlin was subjected to sixteen major raids, which have gone into history as the Battle of Berlin. During 18/19 November raid, only nine out of 440 Lancaster were lost.

23 Sergeant J.G. Eastman, Flight Sergeant A. Matthews, Flight Sergeant W. Cully and Sergeant R. Watson. The Lancaster crashed at Schoenau, a small village on the west bank of the Rhine and opposite the little German community of Rheinhausen (Oberhausen). Some 16km west-north-west is the French town of Selestat. Those who were killed are buried in Schoenau churchyard. That same night 15 Squadron lost another Lancaster to a nightfighter when Flying Officer S.J.R. Soper RCAF and his crew were killed.

24 1,012 RAF aircraft bombed coastal batteries, 110 aircraft of 100 Group carried out extensive bomber-support operations. Two Halifaxes and one Lancaster were lost. Twenty-four *Airborne Cigar* (*ABC*) -equipped Lancasters of 101 Squadron patrolled all known nightfighter approaches. (two Intruders and 1 *ABC* Lancaster were lost). Fifty-eight aircraft of 3 and 5 Groups flew diversion operations (two Stirlings of 149 Squadron FTR). Thirty-one Mosquitoes bombed Osnabrück without losses. In all, RAF Bomber Command flew 1,211 sorties.

25 317 aircraft of 1, 3, 4 and 8 Groups attacked railway targets at Aulnoye, Montdidier and St-Martin-l'Hortier. One Lancaster was lost on the Montdidier raid. All targets were covered by cloud and the Master Bomber at Aulnoye and Montdidier ordered their forces to stop bombing after only seven and twelve aircraft had bombed respectively.

26 A primed 'Cookie' bomb was on board and the aircraft remained in the field for three days until it was considered safe to work on. PB112 *K-King*, which was repaired, later flew with 195 Squadron and was lost on a day raid on Witten on 12 December 1944.

27 In all, forty-eight Lancasters and twelve Mosquitoes of 8 Group carried out *Oboe leader* bombing of four sites through 10/10ths cloud. No aircraft were lost.

28 The other cities were Berlin, Chemnitz and Leipzig, which like Dresden, were vital communications and supply centers for the Eastern Front. *Thunderclap* had been under consideration for several months and was to be implemented only when the military situation in Germany was critical.

CHAPTER 3

The 'Blackbirds' and the 'Boom Years'

On 25 June 1950, the communist North Korean People's Army crossed the 38th parallel, completely wrong-footing the Republic of Korea (ROK) Army and its American advisors in the south. As war in the 'Land of the Morning Calm' erupted and as Cold War tensions heightened there was uncertainty about the Soviet Union's intentions in Europe. USAF forces in the UK comprised just one B-29 group, at about 75 per cent strength; a photographic-reconnaissance squadron with RB-29s and thirty-three support aircraft, twenty-eight of which were Douglas C-47 Skytrains. It was decided therefore to send deployments of heavy bombers to Britain. On 1 July 1950, Mildenhall was taken off its Care and Maintenance basis and the base was reformed on 12 July, with Group Captain D.L. Thomson as Station Commander, whose principal task was to hand over the station facilities to the United States Air Force, which henceforth would have almost exclusive use of the base. Two days earlier the British Government had approved in cabinet to allow the USAF in the UK to carry atomic bombs. The first elements of the United States Air Force to arrive were commanded by Brigadier General A. Terrill and included the 329th Bomb Squadron, 93rd Bomb Wing, the 4115th Organisational Squadron and the 7511th Air Support Wing commanded by Lieutenant Colonel Anthony J. Perne. The 93rd Bomb Wing, which as the 93rd Bomb Group was stationed at Hardwick in Norfolk with B-24 Liberators during the war years, was equipped with about 45 B-50D Superfortresses, the first seen in Europe. Flying activity was now confined almost exclusively to USAF operations and the RAF handed over the Air Traffic Control Tower on 15 November 1950 (a new tower was built in 1952). The 3rd AAA Brigade of the US Army arrived the following February to take over the station defences from the RAF Regiment. The 16th LAA Squadron and No.2 Wing HQ RAF Regiment then left for RAF Wattisham. On 1 October 1951, the administration of Mildenhall airfield was officially transferred from RAF No.3 Group to the 3910th Air Base Group from Strategic Air Command (SAC). For the first eight years, SAC used the base for the staging of rotational bombers. Except for runway closures in 1954 until 1956, and again in 1958 until 1959, Mildenhall was to serve as a base for SAC bomber, tanker and reconnaissance aircraft until 1959.

Prominent amongst the many distinguished visitors received at the station during 1950 were Marshal of the Royal Air Force Sir John Slessor, the American ambassador to Great Britain, Mr Lewis Douglas and the Chief of the Imperial General Staff Field Marshal Sir William Slim. Visitors the following year included the general of the US Army Omar N. Bradley and the Chairman of the Joint Chiefs of Staff, Lieutenant General Curtis E. LeMay.

During the bombers' stay at Mildenhall there were a few serious incidents. On 10 October 1950 B-50D 49-318, piloted by Lieutenant Robert C. Reagle, crashed on the main runway at Mildenhall. Another incident occurred on 29 August 1951 when, during a low-level pass across the airfield, F-84E Thunderjet 49-2034/A of the 12th Fighter Escort Wing at Manston clipped the tail of B-50D 48-066 parked on its dispersal. The Thunderjet cart-wheeled along St John's Street, Beck Row, setting fire to the village police station and two cottages in a huge sheet of flame 300 yards long, as the tail unit broke off and the fuel tanks exploded. The tail unit narrowly missed a cyclist but incredibly, nobody on the ground was injured. The pilot, Lieutenant Wayne R. Finch, was killed. On 4 November 1953 Canberra B2 WF910 from 231 OCU Bassingbourn climbed away normally after a GCA to RAF Lakenheath. At 1,000ft, both engines failed. The pilot turned the aircraft towards RAF Mildenhall and made a distress call. Unfortunately the aircraft lost altitude rapidly and struck the ground 500 yards short of the runway. The aircraft slewed around and came to rest against a row of cottages. The navigator P/O P.J.C. Smith was seriously injured. The pilot, P/O Harold Roy Saunders (aged twenty-two), was killed.

After the big build up in 1950, the level of American military activity in Europe was lowered and the SAC withdrew many of its bombers from Britain, forming a policy of rotating one group at a time to East Anglian bases. The 509th Bomb Wing replaced the 93rd Bomb Wing at Mildenhall on 7 February 1951 to be replaced in turn by the 2nd Bomb Wing on 5 May, thus beginning a series of wing rotations that was to continue for seven years. Throughout this time the USAF bomber forces remained under SAC control, not being assigned to NATO. In March 1953, the 43rd Bombardment Wing arrived in the UK and used Mildenhall as a maintenance base for its KB-29 tankers. In June 1953, the 306th Wing based its 306th Air Refueling Squadron, with its KC-97E tankers at RAF Mildenhall to support the new B-47 Stratojet's base at RAF Fairford. In January 1954, Reflex Alert was introduced at Mildenhall, which meant that a few B-47s would disperse to the base and remain there on a high alert state. The first B-47s were from the 22nd Bombardment Wing.

In 1951, the main runway was extended at both ends and new taxiways were laid down. The area covered by the base was increased considerably and several roads, including the main Mildenhall to Littleport road, had to be closed or diverted. By the late 1950s the runways were again proving inadequate for the larger aircraft then in use and the base was lost for operational use for almost two years in 1958–59 while further modernisation, including more runway extensions, was carried out. On 17 January 1958, Mildenhall officially became the new home of the Military Air Transport Services (MATS) UK passenger terminal. With this role, came repeated arrivals of a whole range of transport aircraft and DC-6 and DC-7 commercial airliners, bringing cargo and personnel to and from Europe and the US. On 1 January 1959, the first Douglas C-124 Globemaster II appeared at Mildenhall when the 3913th Combat Support Group moved to the base. In April, a regular daily C-118 (DC-6A) service to Frankfurt began. Soon after C-124 and C-133 Cargomaster aircraft began to operate from Mildenhall under the direction of the 1607th ATW (Air Transport Wing).

In June 1959, the B-47 Reflex Alert ended and Mildenhall's origins as a transport base began that summer. On 10 July, the French government refused to grant the US atomic storage rights in France and USAFE was forced to withdraw three tactical fighter-bomber wings from French bases. Redeployment of thee wings to Germany and the UK was called Project *Red Richard*. Because of the *Red Richard* unit relocations, on 1 September 1959 USAFE acquired three SAC bases in the UK at Bruntingthorpe, Chelveston and Mildenhall and on 1 October a fourth base was acquired at RAF Lakenheath. The 7513th Air Base Group, Military Air Transport Service (MATS), was established at Mildenhall on 1 September 1959 to support the new MATS terminal, drawing personnel from the 3913th Combat Support Group that had been deactivated at Mildenhall the previous day. In 1964, the US Naval Air Facility arrived from RAF West Malling. The following year the Silk Purse Control Group and the 7120th ACCS (Airborne Command and Control Squadron) joined them at Mildenhall from Châteauroux in France. The move was brought about after a decision taken in October 1965 to convert the Silk Purse mission aircraft from five Douglas C-118A Liftmasters[1] to three (later five) EC-135As, which needed a suitable runway.

US European Command (USEUCOM) had assigned USAFE the responsibility for stationing, operating and maintaining of the Supreme Allied Command Europe (SACEUR)/USEUCOM airborne command post in August 1961. The command post was originally called 'Bat Boy', but it was renamed 'Silk Purse' in October that year. An initial order for the conversion of five KC-135A tankers to EC-135A flying command posts to serve within the context of the Post-Attack Command Control System as communications relay aircraft between SAC HQ and the commanders of the silo based ICBM forces was placed in 1965. (The EC-135A was followed by thirteen EC-135C airborne command post conversions for SAC's *Looking Glass* Post-Attack Command Control System). The first of the EC-135s arrived at Mildenhall on 1 November 1965 and the first Silk Purse operations, using the new aircraft began on 15 January with one eight-hour mission per day. The move from Châteauroux to Mildenhall was completed by February 1966.

MATS Douglas C-124C Globemaster in May 1958. On 1 January 1959, the first C-124 Globemaster II appeared at Mildenhall when the 3913th Combat Support Group moved to the base. (Tom Trower)

On 7 March 1966, General Charles de Gaulle, the President of France, announced his country's decision to cease participation in NATO, which led to the withdrawal of USAFE forces from nine bases in France within one year. In early July the 513th TCW (Troop Carrier Wing), which had been organised at Evereux-Fauville Air Base on 6 April, moved to Mildenhall as part of Project *Fast Relocation* (FRELOC). It had originally been planned to transfer the 513th TCW to RAF Greenham Common but vocal public opposition there forced the move to be abandoned. At the end of the year the 513th Wing received the Air Force Outstanding Unit Award for its performance in Operation *Pathfinder Express*, the largest joint US-Spanish exercise ever held. After two years in England, the Wing was redesignated the 513th TAW (Tactical Airlift Wing) but with no change in its operational role. There began at this time an extensive reconstruction programme that was to cost $1.3 million.

The last RAF unit at Mildenhall was disbanded at the end of 1967 when headquarters No.3 (Bomber) Group, which had been associated with the station for thirty years, was disbanded with the formation of Strike Command in place of Bomber and Fighter Commands. No.3 Group had been flying Heyford biplanes when it first moved to Mildenhall in 1937 but by the 1960s it was operating Vickers Valiants and Handley Page Victors. No.3 Group had also been responsible for all WS-315A Thor intermediate-range surface-to-surface ballistic missiles (IRBM) based in the southern half of England. The 60ft missile was powered by a 150,000lb thrust Rocketdyne North American Aviation engine, fuelled on liquid oxygen and RP-1 (light-cut petrol) and had a range of 1,500 nautical miles. It was adopted for use by twenty squadrons in the RAF in 1957 as Britain's nuclear deterrent until the entry into service of RAF V-bombers carrying nuclear missiles. Each squadron had three missiles, making a total of sixty deployed at bases throughout East Anglia and Yorkshire. The Thor was phased out of RAF service in August 1963 when the manned V-bombers came on stream and the missile sites were abandoned.

Operations at Mildenhall were curtailed in May 1968 while the runways were extended once more. One thousand foot concrete over-runs were constructed and additional airfield lighting was installed. Mildenhall's large jets operated from RAF Lakenheath until the runway was open again the following February. Events at Mildenhall on 23 May 1969 produced front-page headlines in all the national newspapers. Despite having very little flying experience (a couple of training hours on light aircraft) Technical Sergeant Paul Meyer, a twenty-three-year-old crew chief in the 36th TAS, 316th TAW, stole a C-130E Hercules 63-7789 and took off. He was tracked by radar as he flew towards London and then turned west at Brighton to cross the English Channel to Le Havre. After turning back out to sea and flying for a further five hours, he crashed off Alderney in the Channel Islands. His body was recovered some time later. Dan M. Engle was at work at RAF Lakenheath on the night that Meyer took off:

Avro Lincoln in flight. (via Harry Holmes)

English Electric Lightning F.3 XP737 of 23 Squadron at RAF Leuchars at Mildenhall on 21 May 1966. This aircraft ditched in the Irish Sea off Valley, Wales, on 17 August 1979 after the port undercarriage failed to lower. Flying Officer Raymond T. Knowles of 5 Squadron ejected safely. (Tom Trower)

Douglas R4D-5 17116 of the US Navy at Mildenhall. Many R4D-5s were modified for a variety of special duties, including air–sea warfare training, navigation training, RCM and personnel transport. (via Ray Towler)

Douglas R4D-5 39060 of the US Navy at Mildenhall in May 1966. A total of eighty-one C-47A-DLs were ordered by the USAAF were transferred to the US Navy, which also took delivery of a further 157 C-47A-DK examples. (via Ray Towler)

Douglas R4Ds 50821 and 17171 of the US Navy at Mildenhall in September 1967. (via Ray Towler)

Late in the evening Lakenheath launched about four F-100Ds and it was widely believed that these aircraft shadowed the C-130 during the incident. Some of the American servicemen speculated at the time, that these aircraft also shot down the C-130 into the channel. My opinion is that if Meyer had attempted to turn the aircraft towards either the English or French coasts, then these aircraft certainly would have had little choice but to shoot him down, as he would have been a danger to other aircraft or populated areas. As he crashed about eight hours after he had left Mildenhall, I assume that he had run out of fuel and tried to ditch in the sea.

In the weeks that followed the incident there was a great deal of talk over what had happened before Meyer had taken the aircraft. It was speculated that he intended to use the aircraft to return to the USA (this was outside the aircraft's range) and it is fact that during the flight, Meyer attempted to contact his wife, who lived at Langley AFB, West Virginia.

In August 1969, a top-level conference took place at RAF Mildenhall when President Nixon flew in to meet Prime Minister Harold Wilson. There was a massive security net but a crowd of 10,000 was able to watch the arrival and departure ceremonies.

In February 1970, a C-141A Starlifter made an emergency landing at Mildenhall. The crew feared that poisonous gas was leaking from the rocket engine of a Bullpup air-to-ground missile that the aircraft was carrying. All the emergency services went into action; homes and factories within a 2,000ft radius of the Starlifter were evacuated and roads were cordoned off. It proved to be a false alarm and the 200 evacuees in Mildenhall Town Hall were soon able to return to their homes. Bob Hope, the famous American comedian, started his 1970 Christmas tour of American service units by visiting RAF Mildenhall to open the new service club that was being named in his honour. The film star Ursula Andress and the reigning Miss World, Jennifer Hosten, accompanied him. A large crowd watched the twenty-five-minute ceremony in the course of which Bob Hope shook hands with Harold Williams, a local artist who had painted a portrait of the comedian to hang in the club (Bob Hope and a cast of USO (United Services Organisation) stars visited Mildenhall on 7 May 1990).

The 7120th ACCS was redesignated the 10th ACCS on 1 January 1970 but there was no change in personnel or equipment. Detachment 1 of the 98th Strategic Wing became a new tenant unit during August 1970, and 1971 saw the beginning of another large renovation and expansion programme. New passenger and freight terminals were built and work began on new fuel storage areas and aircraft parking aprons. New buildings included dormitories and a gymnasium. A new chapel was formally opened and dedicated on 4 April 1971.

At 10.55 a.m. on 26 August 1971 F-100D Super Sabre 56-2964 of the 493rd TFS, 48th TFW at Lakenheath, flown by Captain Richard Ames, was on approach to Mildenhall when he crashed. (The 48th TFW had been flying from Mildenhall since March 1971 as runway repairs were being carried out at Lakenheath). Ames' Super Sabre struck the ground some distance short of the runway, bounced into the air again, then struck a cottage at West Row. Fortunately, the cottage was empty and no civilian casualties resulted. After careering 200 yards across a wheat field, the F-100D snapped a telegraph pole in two, demolished part of the perimeter fence and finally came to rest atop a 200,000-gallon fuel dump and burst into flames. The base fire brigade quickly dealt with the burning aircraft. Ames was able to walk from the wreckage with only a back injury and he was taken to Lakenheath base hospital where his condition was reported to have been 'satisfactory'.

During 1971, Mildenhall began large-scale modernisation, with facility renovation and new construction. The new base gymnasium was built, as well as new officer and enlisted dormitories. Military Airlift Command built a new passenger terminal and freight terminal. Other major construction projects included larger fuel pits and additional aircraft parking aprons. On 1 September, General David C. Jones assumed command of USAFE. He believed that the combat readiness of the command could be improved by concentrating operational control of the tactical wings at HQ USAFE. He therefore implemented a sweeping reform of the numbered air force structure and mission, which left the intermediate headquarters with a token management staff to act as field representatives of HQ USAFE in dealing with the

In 1972, when Headquarters Third Air Force moved from South Ruislip to RAF Mildenhall, the staff located to Building 239, which was constructed in 1936 as a RAF Bomber Command Group HQ, and was occupied from 1937 to 1967 by HQ 3 Group RAF. In 1996, the building was named in honour of Major Leon W. Johnson, Medal of Honor recipient and first commander of the Third Air Force in England. General Johnson (pictured here during the award ceremony at Shipdham, Norfolk) was awarded the MoH for leading the 44th Bomb Group on the Ploesti low-level raid on 1 August 1943. (Bill Cameron Collection)

US Navy C-130F of VR-24 at Mildenhall on 12 October 1978. The US Navy moved from West Malling to Mildenhall during January–July 1964 to provide the US Navy with a vital air link between land-based units in the UK and Naval ships at sea. (Lawrie Reid)

tactical units and, in the case of Third and Sixteenth Air Forces, to allow them to carry out their country liaison responsibilities. The result was a reduction of 70 per cent in numbered Air Force manning – Third Air Force went from 234 to sixty-three, Sixteenth from 185 to sixty-two, and Seventeenth from 200 to forty-three. The re-organisation also had an effect on the relocation of HQ Third Air Force. Because of the drastic reduction in the size of the headquarters staff, facilities at RAF Mildenhall could now accommodate Third Air Force and it moved from South Ruislip Air Station to RAF Mildenhall on 30 June.

Meanwhile, negotiations between the United States Defense Department (DoD) and the Ministry of Defence (MoD) in London had been in progress with a view to operating the top secret SR-71A reconnaissance aircraft in the UK on an 'occasional' basis. In 1974 an agreement was reached in principle but the feasibility of such operations still needed to be evaluated. It was decided to send an aircraft to England but the flight was to be staged under the full glare of publicity to disguise the flight's true nature. Major James V. Sullivan and Major Noel F. Widdifield flew the SR-71A (64-17972) that landed at Mildenhall in September 1974 for evaluation his RSO. On 1 September, they had set a new transatlantic record of '1 hour, 54 minutes, 56.4 seconds' over the 3,488-mile course from New York to London, breaking a previous record by three hours. The aircraft's average ground speed was 1,806.96mph and they had slowed to refuel just once from a Boeing KC-135Q Stratotanker. After being put on static display at the Farnborough Air Show, the first time the secret plane had been on public display outside of the US, 64-17972 took off for Mildenhall. After a short sojourn, on 13 September Captain Harold B. Adams and his RSO, Major William Machorek, took off in 64-17972 and raced the sun from London to Los Angeles, California, a distance of 5,645 miles. Though slowed down by refuelling requirements, and having to reduce speed over major US cities, it covered the 5,645 miles in '3 hours 47 minutes and 35.8 seconds', a world speed record. The average ground speed was 1,438mph. On 20 April 1976, the same aircraft arrived at Mildenhall for a ten-day stay and other 'Blackbirds' followed it on short periods of TDY, usually to coincide with NATO exercises.

SR-71A 'Blackbird'

The SR-71A had a top speed of Mach 3.35 at 80,000ft and could survey over 100,000 square miles in one hour from 80,000ft and formate on a tanker to refuel in flight at 600mph. C.L. 'Kelly' Johnson's design (YF-12A) was a result of an advanced interceptor programme won by Lockheed in competition with Boeing, General Dynamics and North American. The winning aircraft had to be able to sustain supersonic cruise faster than Mach 3 and have a sustained altitude capability above 80,00ft. An initial contract for four aircraft was awarded to Lockheed in 1960. The first three were completed as YF-12A prototypes and the fourth was modified to become the SR-71 prototype. Built almost entirely of titanium to withstand external skin temperatures of between 450°F and 1,100°F, the aircraft was also coated with high-emissivity black paint to radiate away stored heat, which gave the aircraft its nickname of 'Blackbird'. This reduced surface temperatures by as much as 50°F. Each degree centigrade rise in temperature resulted in 1 per cent loss in range. Power was provided by two Pratt & Whitney J58 afterburning bleed turbojets; each rated at 32,500lb thrust with afterburner at sea level. At Mach 3.2 the engine only produced 17.6 per cent of the total thrust, the inlet and ejector providing 54 and 28.4 per cent respectively. At maximum speed the SR-71A burned approximately 8,000 US gallons per hour.

The first YF-12A made its maiden flight on 26 April 1962 at a secret location at Indian Springs AFB, Nevada. Three aircraft were built to interceptor standard and the fourth prototype and the first production batch of seventeen were built to SR-71 strategic reconnaissance configuration. A further order for eight aircraft followed in 1961. The SR-71A flew for the first time on 22 December 1964 and test pilot Robert J. Gilliland took the aircraft to Mach 1.5. SR-71 crews wore space-style pressure suits of aluminium coated nylon, capable of withstanding high temperatures. The helmet had a feeding port for in-flight meals taken from bottles or tubes. Deliveries to Strategic Air Command started in January 1966. Nine world and class records for speed and altitude were established by USAF test pilots in two YF-12 prototypes. These included a world absolute speed record of 2,070.102mph on 1 May 1965 set by an YF-12A from Edwards AFB piloted by Colonel Robert L. Stephens and Lieutenant Colonel Daniel Andre. Other records included an absolute sustained altitude (world and class) of 80,257.86ft; 500km closed-course speed (class) of 1,643.042mph and a 1,000km closed-course speed (class) of 1,688.891mph. In April 1971, Lieutenant Colonel Thomas B. Estes and Lieutenant Colonel Dewain C. Vick flew a SR-71A on a ten and a half hour non-stop, refuelled mission of about 15,000 miles. The feat earned them the 1971 MacKay Trophy for 'The most meritorious flight of the year' and the 1972 Harmon International Trophy for 'The most outstanding international achievement in the art/science of aeronautics'. Two SR-71A crews set seven new world speed and altitude records on 27-28 July 1976 near Beale AFB, California. Captain Eldon W. Joersz and Major George T. Morgan Jr in 64-17958 established a new world air Speed record of 2,193.167mph. The SR-71A also set a 1,000km closed circuit course record of 2,092.29mph and an absolute/class altitude in level flight at 85,068.99ft.

The MoD insisted that operations be restricted to a maximum of twenty days in duration and ministerial approval was required for each visit. Initially, SR-71 sorties were rare and generally only lasted a few days. Primarily, the 'Blackbirds' flew over the Baltic Sea to look deep into Poland, East Germany and in the area of Murmansk and Archangel in the Soviet Union, while sub-sonic sorties were flown along the border between East and West Germany. The SR-71 needed several KC-135Q tankers, which carried the special JP7 fuel, unique to the 'Blackbird'. The 17th Bomb Wing operated the KC-135Qs at Beale AFB during 1975 and 1976, until these were reassigned to the 100th ARW (Air Refueling Wing) in September 1976.

The first American Open Day Air Show was held in July 1976, in the year of the Bicentennial Celebrations. A crowd of 100,000 attended, causing traffic chaos for miles around. The BBMF Lancaster flew overhead to rekindle memories of the time when 15 and 622 Squadrons flew from Mildenhall in 1944–45, and the crowd also saw the most modern jet aircraft and witnessed spectacular flying displays by the RAF's *Red Arrows* and by aerobatic teams from other NATO countries. In 1978, the annual Air Fête became a two-day event. First and last appearances have often been highlights of the flying display, which lasted six and a half to seven hours daily. Among a long list of examples are the first displays in Europe by the SR-71A and B-1B or the last anywhere by the English Electric Lightning in RAF service, in contrast to the DH88 Comet *Grosvenor House*, arriving at Air Fête '87 to fly in public for the first time since 1938. Similarly, as befits NATO's largest public event, wider international participation brought the European or British debuts of such as the Royal Netherlands Air Force 'Grasshoppers' and 'Double Dutch' display teams, the Federal German Navy Tornado, French Air Force Mirage 2000 and Epsilon or the Canadian Armed Forces' CF-188.

Fortunately, incidents at the air fête, which was a regular event until 2001, have been few. The 1979 Air Show celebrating NATO was marred by a tragic accident on the second day on 27 May. The Italian *Frecce Tricolori* team was performing before an enthralled crowd when Captain Piergianni Petri, flying one of the team's Fiat G-91R fighters, crashed as he was returning low across country for the final formation of the display. His aircraft hit a tree and burst into flames only 200 yards from a crowded residential caravan site. The remaining seven members of the team landed safely. No announcement was made to the crowd and the flying programme was continued. A trust fund was later established at the base for Captain Petri's eight-month-old daughter.

On 25 May 1986, Meteor T.7 WA669 and Vampire T.11 XH304 of the RAF Vintage Pair Display Team took part in the display, which was to include the Meteor leading the Vampire in a line-astern formation, and a barrel roll to the left. The display went well until the aircraft reached the top of the formation barrel roll when the Vampire was unable to match the Meteor's rate of roll and became displaced down, left and slightly back from the line-astern position. The Vampire then moved forward, passed underneath the Meteor and climbed, turning slightly to the right. The Vampire's starboard rudder, fin and elevator struck the Meteor's port engine nacelle nosing, causing this to separate from the aircraft and fall clear. The Vampire's starboard rudder detached and fell clear. After the collision, the Vampire pitched up and Squadron Leader David Marchant and Sergeant Alan Ball ejected successfully. The Meteor, which was not fitted with ejection seats, struck the ground shortly after the mid-air collision, killing thirty-eight-year-old Flight Lieutenant Andrew Potter and his back seat passenger, twenty-four-year-old Corporal Kevin Turner, an RAF Aircraft Technician. Both aircraft crashed at Worlington, Suffolk, two miles from RAF Mildenhall at about 11.15 a.m. The Vampire crashed in a field between the river Lark and the Mildenhall road. The Meteor, which crashed several seconds earlier, fell in a peat field three quarters a mile away. Potter, a QFI at RAF Scampton, who had been in the RAF for seventeen years, was married with two children. Turner had been in the RAF for eight years and was a single man from Ilkeston, Derbyshire. All four men were from the RAF's Central Flying School at Scampton.

On 3 June 1983 during that year's Air Fête, Beechcraft T-34C Turbo Mentor N2067A demonstrator took off downwind and crashed immediately afterwards. The aircraft was completely destroyed and the pilot and passenger, both Americans who were reported to have been Beech employees, were killed.

Air Fête Feature: Flying the Lancaster

By Flight Lieutenant Andy Sell

It takes about 15 minutes to get all four Merlins going and complete the pre-taxi checks. Taxiing the aircraft is interesting, a combination of brake and small, quick bursts of power being used to bring the aircraft into wind for the power checks. Engines are run up in pairs and magnetos and revs are checked before line-up and take-off. With flaps at 20, zero boost is set and as the brakes are released the captain calls the co-pilot to set either plus 7 or plus 9 boost depending on the runway length. The Lanc tends to slew to the left and this is countered by off-setting the nose slightly and leading with the port outer engine. After a short run, the control column is pushed forward and as the tail lifts off the ground, directional control becomes much easier, until at 90 knots the co-pilot calls rotate and the aircraft gets airborne. The wheels are braked and raised and at 120 knots/150 feet the flaps are brought in. Care must be taken to anticipate this; otherwise a large sink rate is felt. Climb power is plus 4 boost/2,400 rpm and the Lanc climbs at 140 knots to the normal transit altitude of 2,000 feet, where a cruise power of 0 boost/2,000 rpm is set giving a speed of about 1 60 knots. The aircraft is heavy to handle in steep turns, but very stable. Because of the low 'g' limit of 1 5, great care with positioning must be taken to ensure this isn't exceeded.

After breaking into the circuit, the Bomber is climbed to 500 feet and positioned downwind. Zero boost/2,400 rpm is set and as the speed decays below 1 50 knots the flap goes to 20 and the gear comes down. Speed stabilises at 115 knots at the end of the downwind leg. As the continuous finals turn is started, flaps go to 40 and rpm is increased to 2,850, aiming to roll out on the centre line at 105 knots. Speed is then reduced in increments of minus two boost looking for a threshold speed of 90 knots. The Lancaster is then flown level with the runway and as the captain calls the co-pilot to idle the engines, he simultaneously flares the aircraft in for a gentle three pointer. If it works, it is another magnificent landing for the skipper. If it bounces, it is the co-pilot's fault for closing the throttles too quickly/slowly! On clearing the runway the engines are run-up for a final check before taxiing back to the hangar.

Happiness is flying the Lancaster at 100 feet over a group of Bomber Command veterans with four Rolls Royce Merlins purring away. A privilege.

Meanwhile, on 15 August 1976, Strategic Air Command activated the 306th Strategic Air Wing at Ramstein Air Base to assume operational responsibility for SAC operations in Europe as KC-135 tanker operations were moved from Torrejón Air Base, Spain, to RAF Mildenhall. President Gerald Ford paid a brief visit to RAF Mildenhall on 4 August 1976 when his aircraft landed to refuel for the final leg of his journey home after a ten-day diplomatic tour of Europe. Secretary of State Henry Kissinger also passed through in September 1975, as did Secretary of State Cyrus Vance in April 1977. Another distinguished visitor was Anne Armstrong, the first woman to be appointed American ambassador to Britain. She flew into Mildenhall in October 1976 to make a tour of inspection of the Mildenhall and Lakenheath bases.

C-135/KC-135A Stratotanker (Boeing Model 717)

In September 1955 Boeing received its first order from the USAF for the C-135/KC-135A in-flight-refuelling tanker. This followed successful trials with the 'Dash 80' prototype after it had been configured with a Boeing-designed flying boom refuelling system under the rear fuselage. In August 1952 Boeing had announced that it was investing $16 million of its own money in the development of a prototype jet transport (the Dash 80), production models of which were called the Model 707. The Dash 80 first flew on 15 July 1954 and the rest is history. No less than 999 examples were built and they were sold to seventy-four customers.

The USAF required that the cabin should have no windows and that the diameter of the fuselage should be increased by 12in by comparison to that of the 'Dash 80'. This gave the Model 717 a fuselage diameter 4in less than that of the Model 707 civil transport. The whole refuelling package was installed in the lower fuselage. The first flight of a KC-135A took place on 31 August 1956 and it entered service with the 93rd ARS on 28 June 1957. A total of 732 KC-135A has been built. The first 582 aircraft were constructed with a short fin but from the 583rd example onwards; a taller fin (which was then retrofitted to earlier machines) was introduced to make the Stratotanker more stable during take-off. In addition, an early modification saw the addition of strengthening straps around the rear fuselage to dampen jet-induced resonance. Internally, the KC-135A has twenty-two fuel tanks and the main cabin provides a considerable volume for freight, for which a side-loading door is fitted. The cabin can alternatively be fitted with seating for eighty troops. The refuelling boom operator works in a prone position in a fairing under the rear of the fuselage. Fifty-six aircraft were converted to KC-135Q standard with additional navigation and communications equipment to support the SR-71. The KC-135Qs were also modified for the carriage and transfer of the high-flash-point JP-7 fuel used by the SR-71, in addition to the regular JP-4/5 used by the tanker itself. Four KC-135Ds were conversions of RC-135A survey aircraft.

Between 1975 and 1988, Boeing replaced the lower wing skins of all surviving KC-135s to extend their useful lives to a time beyond 2020. Work also began on the re-engining of most surviving aircraft to replace the Pratt & Whitney J57 turbojet engines with quieter, more fuel-economical and less maintenance-intensive turbofan engines. The USAF bought large numbers of surplus Model 707s and stripped off their JT3D-3B (military designation TF33) engines for fitment to the tankers, which then received the revised designation KC-135E. At the same time the airliners' wider-span tailplanes were also fitted to the tankers to maintain stability with the greater thrust of the new engines. More than 160 KC-135As, including the four KG-135Ds, which retain their original designation, were modified.

In 1980, Boeing announced a major upgrade programme for the KC-135 involving the installation of high-bypass-ratio turbofan engines. Under the company designation KC-135RE, the first conversion made its maiden flight on 4 August 1982. Designated in service as the KC-135R the re-engined and upgraded tanker is the mainstay of the USAF's tanker fleet. The engine selected for the KC-135R was the 22,000lb st GFM International GFM56 (military designation F108-CF-100). Using this engine permits the offload of 150 per cent more fuel than the KC-135A at a radius of 2,879 miles. Other changes include fitment of an APU, characterised by intake and exhaust ports on the port side of the rear fuselage, to provide the KC-135R with the ability to undertake autonomous operations from austere locations, and many other systems were also upgraded during the conversion. Delivery of the first KC-135R took place in July 1984 and the 200th aircraft was delivered in April 1990. The KC-135R(RT) designation is applied to a small number of aircraft, most of them trials or ex-special mission machines, fitted with a refuelling receptacle and these aircraft were joined by the surviving KC-135Qs. The latter were fitted with refuelling receptacles, as they underwent the re-engining conversion to emerge as KC-135T tankers with a primary role of supporting F-117 aircraft and other covert programmes. A feasibility study has also been undertaken to fit the KC-135R with underwing refuelling pods for the refuelling of probe-equipped aircraft from other US or foreign services.

The summer of 1979 brought the first deployment of an Air Force Reserve wing to Mildenhall. On 4 August, the 452nd Air Refueling Wing (AFReS) deployed its entire compliment of aircraft and personnel from March AFB, California with a total of twelve KC-135s, fourteen crew and 484 support personnel.

Detachment 4 of the 9th Strategic Reconnaissance Wing was established at Mildenhall on 1 April 1979 to supervise deployments of TR-1A (renamed U-2R in December 1991) and SR-71A aircraft to on TDY deployments to the UK from the home base at Beale AFB, California.[2] On 2 May 1979, SR-71A 64-17979 took off from Mildenhall for the USA and the following day the Labour Government was defeated in the general election and Margaret Thatcher became Prime Minister. The Conservative Government was more amenable towards the US extending the UK SR-71A operation, although initially this was undertaken on a gradual basis. SR-71As continued to make operational sojourns of up to two or three days at a time until in December 1980. Continuous SR-71A operations were begun from Mildenhall. The final deployment of 1979 was by 64-17976, which arrived on 18 October and stayed for twenty-six days. SR-71 operations frequently involved flying reconnaissance missions over the Baltic Sea and around the tip of Norway to monitor nuclear submarines of the Soviet Northern Fleet sailing to and from Murmansk in northern Russia. Approval for the use of a base if an emergency arose was sought and given in principle by the Norwegian government and Bødo Air Base was made available to the US. The first time a SR-71A diverted to Bødo was on 13 August 1981, when 64-17964 suffered an oil malfunction in one of the engines while on a combined mission/delivery to RAF Mildenhall from Beale AFB and it had to divert to the Norwegian base. 64-17972, the first of two SR-71 reconnaissance aircraft was permanently stationed at Mildenhall on 31 March 1982. On 5 April 1982, the Ministry of Defence received Prime Ministerial approval to allow Detachment 4 to operate on a permanent basis with two SR-71As assigned. However, the MoD still retained the final approval of the more sensitive missions. On 19 December 1982, Detachment 4 increased to two SR-71A aircraft, when 64-17971 arrived to join 64-17972. With two 'Blackbirds' stationed in England, the US Air Force began to undertake many more missions and expand its area of interest with more peripheral photography of Eastern Europe and the Middle East.

On 9 July 1983, SR-71A 64-17962 landed at Mildenhall after the long ferry flight from Beale AFB. 64-17962 had previously spent more than two weeks deployed at Mildenhall in September 1976 but the aircraft that landed on 9 July was actually 64-17955, the Palmdale-based test aircraft, which was evaluating the new Loral Advanced Synthetic Aperture Radar System (ASARS-1). It had been re-serialled to conceal the true purpose of the test aircraft flying an operational mission from Mildenhall. 64-17955 completed the evaluation before returning home and reverting to its true identity. The operational evaluation performed as required and the ASARS-1 was subsequently installed for specific missions. On 5 April 1984, Prime Minister Margaret Thatcher publicly announced that a detachment of SR-71As had

US Navy Convair C-131B 41023 of the Mildenhall Naval Facility at the base in 1981.

TR-1A (renamed U-2R in December 1991) at Mildenhall in 1983. TR-1A/U-2 aircraft operations moved from Mildenhall to RAF Alconbury in February 1983.

been formed at Mildenhall. At first, the SR-71As operated from a hangar on the south side but work on a permanent, more suitable pair of barns began in 1985 and was first used when 64-17962 returned from a mission on 8 August that year.

The SR-71As performed invaluable work gathering intelligence of Soviet military dispositions. The 'Blackbirds' were also used to monitor movements of key terrorist leaders as they flew from one airfield to another, following the aftermath of the terrorist attack on the US Marine Barracks in Lebanon. In early March 1979 SR-71A 64-17972 was used to monitor the situation between the Republic of Yemen and Saudi Arabia, when the Yemenis appeared to be on the brink of invading Saudi territory. 64-17972 was flown to Mildenhall and after two cancelled attempts, the 'Blackbird' was airborne before dawn on day three. It completed its tanker rendezvous before streaking into the sunrise across the Mediterranean. Two more mid-air refuelling followed before the aircraft headed for the target area. A malfunction of the automated navigation system resulted in the 'Blackbird' accidentally overflying the planned turn point, as the optical bar camera in the nose and the various individual cameras in the

Above: SR-71A 64-17974 of Detachment 4 of the 9th Strategic Reconnaissance Wing, which operated from Mildenhall during 30 April–13 December 1982 (with a sojourn at Bødo, Norway, 7–9 May) and from 2 August 1983–July 1984.

Opposite above: SR-71A 'Blackbird' 64-17962 of Detachment 4 of the 9th Strategic Reconnaissance Wing cruising at 420 knots at 2,000ft en route to RAF Mildenhall on 2 May 1985. On either side are Jaguars T.2 XX841/S flown by Squadron Leader John Butler and GR.1 XZ119 flown by Squadron Leader (later Group Captain) Steve Griggs AFC, both of 41 Squadron. This unique formation was photographed by Squadron Leader Mike Rondot, Flight Commander, 6 Squadron flying GR.1 XZ359 using an F95 camera in the Jaguar Recce Pod. 64-17962 operated from Mildenhall during 6 September until at least 23 September 1976, 9 July to 30 July 1983 and 19 October 1984 to mid-October 1985. In 2001, SR-71A 64-17962 was dismantled at Palmdale and shipped to England to be put on display at the American Air Museum at the Imperial War Museum, Duxford. The SR-71A arrived on 11 April 2001, and following reassembly was formerly handed over by General Joseph Ralston, the Supreme Allied Commander Europe at a ceremony held on 14 June. (Mike Rondot)

Opposite below: SR-71A 64-17980 of Detachment 4 of the 9th Strategic Reconnaissance Wing. This 'Blackbird' operated from Mildenhall during 5 January–27 April 1982; 7 March–6 September 1983, 19 July 1985–29 October 1986 and 27 July 1987–3 October 1988 (from RAF Lakenheath). After the cessation of SR-71A missions, 64-17980 became one of two Air Force examples that were taken over by NASA at Edwards AFB, which continued to operate the SR-71 until 1999, when the research being conducted was completed. (RAF)

chine bays captured their imagery. The delay in completing the turn produced unexpected results, yielding much valuable additional data. The crew returned the aircraft to Mildenhall after completing a mission lasting ten hours.

American civilians and US military personnel stationed in foreign countries have often faced terrorist attack on or near their bases. In December 1976, a bomb was planted in the officers' club at Rhein-Main AFB, which was, from 1956, the primary arrival and departure point in Europe for US military personnel. Fortunately no one was injured in the blast. In 1985, bombs exploded at bars and restaurants frequented by American personnel near bases in Greece and Madrid and on 8 August terrorists detonated a car bomb near the wing headquarters building, killing two people, injuring sixteen and significantly damaging several buildings. On 24 November a powerful car bomb exploded outside the Frankfurt US Forces shopping centre, injuring twenty-three people and extensively damaging buildings and forty

SR-71A 'Blackbird' in flight.
(USAF)

cars in the immediate area. On 27 December 1985, terrorists attacked the El Al check-in counters at airports in Rome and Vienna, killing fourteen people, including an eleven-year-old American girl and injuring fifty others. The attack was thought to be Libyan backed. America's patience was exhausted.

In August 1981, Colonel Gadaffi, the President of Libya, had established his so-called 'line of death' in the Gulf of Sidra from a point just south of Tripoli across to Benghazi and warned that any American aircraft or surface vessel crossing it would be destroyed.[3] In February 1986, Operation *Prairie Fire* was launched to provoke Libya into a direct military confrontation. Three carrier battle groups crossed the 'line of death' and on 24 March, two SA-5 Gammon missiles were fired at the 6th Fleet but both missed their targets. Later that day, two Tomcats chased off a pair of MiG-25 *Foxbat-A* interceptors, and tension increased as more missiles were fired at the carrier groups. The US Navy retaliated and two Grumman A-6E Intruders sank a Libyan fast-attack craft with AGM-84A Harpoon anti-ship missiles and Rockeye cluster bombs. Vought A-7E Corsairs badly damaged a *Nhore* installation with AGM-88A High Speed Anti-Radiation (HARM) missiles and more A-6Es and A-7Es carried out additional attacks on Libyan targets. A total of four Libyan vessels were destroyed or damaged and one or two SAM sites knocked out.

Regrettably, terrorist action continued on 5 April when a bomb exploded in the LaBelle disco in West Berlin, which was frequented by hundreds of off-duty US personnel – a US Army sergeant and a Turkish woman were killed and 230 people injured, including seventy-nine US servicemen. The Libyan regime clearly backed the attack. More bomb plots were uncovered by intelligence sources aimed at US military targets around the world, with ten planned for Berlin alone. Certainly, swift action was needed to deter the terrorists and their Libyan paymasters. President Ronald Reagan kept a five-year-old promise to the American people to meet terrorism with 'swift and effective retribution' and the decision was taken to bomb terrorist-related targets at Tripoli and Benghazi, using Air Force squadrons on mainland Europe and carrier-borne aircraft of the US Navy in the Mediterranean. NATO countries would not allow US aircraft stationed in its countries to use European bases or overfly their airspace for attacks on Libya. Britain's Prime Minister, Margaret Thatcher, had no such qualms and no restrictions were placed on strike aircraft based in eastern England. This allowed the US planners the option of using F-111F tactical strike bombers based in East Anglia for a retaliatory strike against Tripoli, the Libyan capital, while US Navy A-6E Intruder carrier-borne attack planes bombed Benghazi.

At the time, over 150 F-111E/Fs were based in Britain for NATO duty. The F-111E equipped the 20th TFW at Upper Heyford in Oxfordshire, while the 48th TFW 'The Liberty Wing', based at RAF Lakenheath in Suffolk, was equipped with four squadrons of F-111Fs. The F-111F was equipped with the Ford Aerospace AVQ-26 Pave Tack infrared target acquisition and laser-designating pod mounted under the fuselage centre-line. Armed with laser-guided bombs, the FB-111F could be particularly effective for bombing by night. The WSO ('Wizzo' or Weapons Systems Officer) operated an IR (Infrared) scope in the cockpit to lock the designator pod onto the target. A thin laser beam kept the target 'spotted' for laser-guided Paveway bombs to follow the beam transmission directly onto the target no matter what manoeuvres the pilot puts the bomber through. Despite this incredibly accurate method of bombing, crews were briefed not to launch their bombs unless they also gained positive radar identification. Civilian casualties had to be avoided where possible.

At around 6.15 p.m. on 14 April 1986, Operation *El Dorado Canyon* began when Lakenheath despatched 24 F-111Fs. Earlier, RAF Mildenhall had sent off six KC-135 Stratotankers followed by a KC-135A and two KC-10A Extender tankers, and finally ten more KC-10A Extenders. A further seven KC-10As and two KC-135As left RAF Fairford for Libya. *El Dorado Canyon* marked the first operational use of the Grumman/General Dynamics EF-111A *Raven* ECM aircraft. Five 'Spark Varks' of the 42nd Electronic Combat Squadron in the 20th TFW took off from their home base at Upper Heyford and flew to Fairford to escort the F-111Fs. Off the north-west coast of Spain, the KC-10As took on fuel from other KC-10As. Shortly afterwards, between 8.30 and 9.30 p.m., six F-111Fs acting as spares, returned to Lakenheath and one of the EF-111As also returned to base, leaving the second spare *Raven* to continue to the target area as an airborne reserve. The F-111Fs each carried free-fall and laser-guided bombs, which meant there was no room for external fuel tanks. Three 'silent' in-flight refuelling operations were therefore carried out off Portugal, south of Spain (after passing through the Straits of Gibraltar) and near Sicily.

Meanwhile, the USS *America* and USS *Coral Sea* were at their positions off Libya ready to strike at military targets in Benghazi. Near Tripoli, the three EF-111A *Ravens* began their ECM jamming of Libyan radars at 2354, while the Navy's A-7E Corsair IIs and F/A-18A Hornets blasted the SAM and radar installations around Benghazi with anti-radiation missiles. USAF and US Navy bombing runs started simultaneously at 0001. The eighteen F-111Fs of the 48th TFW roared in 200ft below the Libyan radar sites on the coast and headed for the brightly lit streets of the capital. Nearing the city, the force split into three cells of six aircraft. Two cells headed for the terrorist training camp at Sidi Bilal Naval Base and the barracks at Bab al Aziziya where Gadaffi resided. The third cell flew on to the south before swinging round to bomb the military airport.

Pilots had been briefed to bomb only if they had positive radar and IR scope target acquisition. Four F-111Fs in the Naval base and barracks attack, and one in the attack on Tripoli, did not bomb after experiencing problems with their equipment or failing to obtain the necessary electronic validation of their targets. The eight remaining bombers in the raid on the naval base and barracks made low-level single-pass attacks and each toss-bombed four 200lb laser-guided bombs onto the targets before climbing away to a height of 250ft at 518mph for their rendezvous point over the Mediterranean. The F-111F flown by Captain Fernando L. Ribas-Dominicci and WSO Captain Paul F. Lorence, which had been involved in the attack on the barracks, crashed and exploded as they re-crossed the coast. A long sea search was mounted but no trace of the crew was found.

A KC-135 and four F-11Fs of the 48th TFW re-enact the 14/15 April 1986 *El Dorado Canyon* operation during the May 1986 Mildenhall Air Fête.

The third group of six F-111Fs attacked the military airport with 500lb Mk 82 low-drag retarded bombs, although one bomber was forced to carry its bombs home after a systems malfunction. US Navy A-6E Intruders destroyed at least four MiG-23s, a Fokker F-27 and two Mil Mi-8 helicopters at Benina airfield. Crews began landing back on their carriers while the F-111Fs headed for their tankers and the long flight back to Britain. One F-111F was forced to land at Rota in Spain suffering problems from engine overheating. Despite the limitations of crossing international boundaries and the loss of one fighter-bomber, *El Dorado Canyon* had been relatively successful.

Post-strike photography was carried out by the two Mildenhall-based SR-71s, with both aircraft being airborne simultaneously. This is the only occasion when Det 4 flew both its aircraft together operationally. Air refuelling by seven SAC tankers from Mildenhall was required. This was the first time that KC-10s had been used to refuel the SR-71A in the European Theatre. It was also the first time that photos taken by the 'Blackbird' had been released to the media. A dual mission was flown on 16 April and the two days following, as cloud cover hampered imagery until the third occasion. Images captured on film were taken from the 'Blackbirds' and processed before being loaded aboard C-135C 61-2669, which was assigned to the USAF Chief of Staff, General Charles Gabriel, who accompanied the film to the Pentagon for analysis.

Not all the 'Blackbird' missions went as smoothly. On 6 March 1987, a 64-17964 suffered a technical problem which required the crew to divert to Bødo and remain there for about fourteen days. On 29 June, 64-17964 was forced to land in Norway again but the problem was soon rectified and the errant 'Blackbird' flew back to Mildenhall three days later. On 24 May 1987, the pilot of 64-17973 overstressed his SR-71A while on a mission. The 'Blackbird' recovered safely to Mildenhall, but inspection by technicians subsequently determined that temporary repairs would need to be carried out to enable a flight back to Palmdale for further analysis. The aircraft returned to California on 22 July but it was not repaired, probably because the hugely expensive 'Blackbird' programme was about to be terminated. The aircraft remained at the Lockheed-Palmdale plant before it was placed on display in the Blackbird Air Park. On 1 October 1989 (the first day of fiscal year 1990), the US Air Force issued an order suspending all SR-71 operations, except for proficiency flights, and on 22 November all USAF SR-71 operations ended. Detachment 4 at Mildenhall had ceased flying two days earlier when 64-17967 had flown the last operational sortie

Post-strike reconnaissance by two SR-71As on 16 April 1986, two days after the American bombing of terrorist-related targets in Libya, confirmed that all five targets during Operation *El Dorado Canyon* had been well hit. Targets for the fourteen A-6Es from USS *America* and USS *Coral Sea* in the eastern Mediterranean were the Al Jumahiriya barracks in Benghazi and Benina airport outside the city. The Intruders destroyed at least four MiG-23s, a Fokker F-27 and two Mil Mi-8 helicopters at Benina Airfield (pictured). (USAF)

fitted with an optical bar camera, which was rare at Mildenhall. Detachment 4 flew 894 operational missions, with a further 164 being functional, test, or delivery flights. 64-17960 had performed the most combat missions, completing a total of 342. This aircraft spent fifteen months assigned to Det 4 from late 1985 until early in 1987. Both the SR-71As remained hangared in their barns for the next few weeks while final plans were made for Det 4 (and Det 1 at Kadena, Okinawa) to return the 'Blackbirds' to the 9th Strategic Reconnaissance Wing's HQ at Beale AFB, California, and inactivate. On 16 January 1990, both 'Blackbirds' at Mildenhall flew a functional check flight to ensure all systems were working correctly. Lockheed technicians prepared 64-17964 for the flight home and two days Major Tom McCleary and his RSO Lieutenant Colonel Stan Gudmundson took off and flew a 360° pattern to perform a fast, very low fly-by, before McCleary pointed the nose skyward and headed for Beale AFB. The next day, 64-17967 followed. On 26 January 1990, an SR-71 decommissioning ceremony took place at Beale AFB.[4]

Three days later on 29 January 1990, Secretary of Defense Richard B. Cheney announced plans to close thirty-five domestic bases, reduce forces at more than twenty other US locations and close twelve bases overseas, eight of which were in USAFE. Strategic Air

KC-10A Extender 83-0079 of the 32nd Air Refueling Squadron, 2nd Wing at the Mildenhall Air Fête in May 1990, dwarfing a RAF Nimrod. 83-0079 was one of nineteen Extenders used on 14/15 April 1986 *El Dorado Canyon* operation to refuel the F-111Fs of the 48th Tactical Fighter Wing at RAF Lakenheath en route to Libya. An Air Force requirement for a tanker/transport aircraft had first been identified in 1973 as a result of Operation *Nickel Grass* (the US airlift to Israel during the October War). However, the ATCA (Advanced Tanker/Cargo Aircraft) competition between projected derivatives of the Boeing 747 and the McDonnell Douglas DC-10 was so protracted that it was not until 19 December 1977 that the USAF ordered an initial batch of twenty KC-10As. The first KC-10A Extender (79-0433) flew at Long Beach, California, on 12 July 1980. The sixtieth and last KC-10A for the USAF (97-0124) was flown to McDonnell Douglas's Yuma, Arizona, facility on 29 November 1988, where a British-built Mk 32B hose drum pod was fitted beneath each wing to convert the aircraft into a three-point tanker for probe-equipped aircraft. Extenders took part in 'Desert Shield' and in 1991 forty-six KC-10As were deployed in *Desert Storm* during the war with Iraq.

Command's 11th Strategic Group and its thirteen rotational KC-135 aircraft moved from RAF Fairford to RAF Mildenhall. This move consolidated all KC-135 refuelling aircraft at Mildenhall. On 1 February 1991, HQ USAF implemented an Air Force-wide re-structuring of the Air Force's air refuelling forces. In Europe, the SAC's 306th Strategic Wing inactivated and its aircraft and mission merged with USAFE's 513th Airborne Command and Control Wing at Mildenhall to form the 100th Air Refueling Wing.

RAF Mildenhall is now the 'Gateway to the United Kingdom', the official port of entry for all US forces entering the country. Air Mobility Command, formerly Military Airlift Command (MAC) which was established on 1 June 1992, operates the passenger and freight

On 25 May 1986, Meteor T.7 WA669 and Vampire T.11 XH304 (pictured) of the RAF Vintage Pair
Display Team were taking part in the air display at the Mildenhall Air Fête when they were involved
in a collision. Both crashed at Worlington, Suffolk, two miles from RAF Mildenhall, killing the two
occupants of the Meteor. The two occupants of the Vampire ejected to safety. (MoD)

terminals, which deal with 8,000 passengers and 1,700 tons of freight every month. In January
1985, the first United Kingdom Scheduled Airline Traffic Office opened in the then Military
Airlift Command (MAC) passenger terminal. The base now covers 1,042 acres and has over
500 buildings. The main runway is 9,240ft long and 200ft wide. The base population averages
2,740 US military personnel, 100 departments of the Air Force civilians, 330 British employees
and an estimated total of 4,500 dependents. The number of KC-135 Stratotankers has greatly
increased since the European Tanker Task Force closed its operations in Spain in late 1976 and
during the peak exercise periods, as many as thirty-five can be seen at Mildenhall. Many other
aircraft, including Air Mobility Command's huge C-5A Galaxy, regularly visit the base and an
average of 2,200 aircraft operations are carried out monthly.

The 513th TAW (Tactical Airlift Wing) which was at Mildenhall from 1 July 1967 to 1 November
1988 was the host unit responsible for the operation of the base and provided support for fifteen
assorted tenant organisations, as well as providing maintenance facilities for all the assigned and
transient aircraft. The 513th's only flying arm was the 10th ACCS (Airborne Command and Control
Squadron) which provided the EC-135 aircraft that, in the event of war, would act as alternative
airborne command posts for the US European Command, should its normal headquarters be
destroyed. The battle staff for these vital aircraft was provided by the Silk Purse Control Group and
was drawn from all three branches of the defence forces.

The 1979 Air Show celebrating NATO was marred by a tragic accident on the second day on 27 May. The Italian *Frecce Tricolori* team was performing before an enthralled crowd when Captain Piergianni Petri, flying one of the team's Fiat G-91R fighters, crashed as he was returning low across country for the final formation of the display.

At the 1992 Air Fête the BBMF Lancaster was landed heavily and skidded off the runway onto the grass.

The 313th TAG (Tactical Airlift Group) which was at Mildenhall from September 1978 to 1993, operated C-130 Hercules aircraft and its main role was to provide short-range airlift to Europe and the Middle East. Its Bravo Squadron operated on a rotational basis from bases in the USA. The 313th's major subordinate unit was the 627th MASS (Military Airlift Support Squadron), which operated the busy passenger and freight terminals. Another important subordinate unit was the 5th MAPS (Mobile Aerial Support Squadron), which furnished the European theatre

Fully restored to airworthy condition, DH 88 Comet Racer G-ACSS *Grosvenor House* returned
to Mildenhall for the US Air Fête in May 1987 – fifty-three years after leaving the airfield for the
memorable flight to Australia, since when, after another crash-landing, at Hatfield, it was again rebuilt.

During its final pass at the 1986 Air Fête, SR-71A 64-17960 suffered a momentary double flame out,
resulting in unburnt fuel entering the rear of the engine which then combusted when they were re-lit.
The result was a spectacular 'fireball', which delighted the vast, appreciative crowd. 64-17960 was based
at Mildenhall from 29 October 1985 to 29 January 1987.

with mobile air operations support teams and airlift training teams. One of the major tenant
units at Mildenhall was the 306th Strategic Wing, a unit of the SAC, which operated the KC-
135 Stratotankers that provide in-flight refuelling services for USAF aircraft throughout Europe,
as well as over the Atlantic. During the build up to the Gulf War in 1990, twenty-five USAF
fighter squadrons flew non-stop to the Gulf. Altogether, 256 KC-135s and forty-six KC-10
refuellers were deployed to the area and 4,967 tanker sorties were flown during *Desert Shield*.

Captain Randy Rushworth of the 69th Bomb Squadron, 42nd Bomb Wing at Loring AFB, Maine demonstrating a nose-down take-off at the controls of B-52G-125-BW 59-2585 *Swashbuckler* at the Mildenhall Air Fête in May 1990. The 42nd Bomb Wing was inactivated on 30 September 1990 but 59-2585 completed twenty-two bombing missions in the Gulf War, including one from Diego Garcia to Jeddah on 17 January 1991, when targets were hit en route. 59-2585 was placed in storage at AMARC on 15 April 1993.

The first permanently assigned KC-135R Stratotanker to the 100th Air Refueling Wing opening Air Fête 1992.

Within thirty-five days, the USAF deployed a fighter force that numerically equalled Iraq's fighter capability. Tanker support for fighters and the conventional and stealth bombers during *Desert Storm* was crucial. F-111Fs alone flew 2,500 sorties, and F-117As more than 1,300 sorties, while B-52s completed 1,624 missions. In all, 15,434 KC-135/KC-10 tanker sorties were flown during *Desert Storm*.

The US Naval Air Facility also operates from Mildenhall, providing logistical support to ships throughout northern European waters. Headquarters of the Third Air Force moved to Mildenhall from South Ruislip in June 1972. This key establishment represents all branches of the American forces in the UK in negotiations with the British Government. Other important units at the base are the 2147th Communications Squadron, the 6954th Security Squadron and Detachment 15 of the 31st Weather Squadron.

KC-10A 79-0437 of the 3444th Air Refueling Squadron, 4th Wing AMC from Seymour-Johnson AFB, North Carolina, visiting the Mildenhall Air Fête in May 1992. By this time the blue and white upper livery applied to Extenders had been replaced by olive drab. The 4th Wing is tasked to deploy overseas with the wing's own F-15E Strike Eagles at very short notice.

Rockwell B-1B Lancer *The Reluctant Dragon* of the 9th Bomb Squadron and B-52H-155-BW 60-0052 of the 5th Bomb Wing at Minot AFB at Mildenhall Air Fête May 1994. Deliveries of the Rockwell B-1B Lancer began on 27 July 1985 to Offutt AFB, Nebraska, and the new bomber eventually equipped four bomb wings (three of them B-52 wings). When the B-1A flew for the first time on 23 December 1974, SAC had planned for 250 B-1s to replace its ageing B-52s, but in the end only 100 were completed to B-1B standard. The first B-1Bs were used to equip the 96th Bomb Wing, where they replaced the B-52H during autumn 1984–winter 1985.

The C-130H 84001 (64-0546) of the *Svenska Flygvapnet* (Royal Swedish Air Force), the first European air force to operate the Hercules, landing at Air Fête 1997.

On 1 February 1992, HQ USAF implemented an Air Force-wide restructuring of the Air Force's air refuelling forces. In Europe, the Strategic Air Command's 306th Strategic Wing inactivated and its aircraft and mission merged with USAFE's 513th Airborne Command and Control Wing at Mildenhall, to form the 100th Air Refueling Wing in order to provide air refuelling support in the European Theatre. Other major units serving at RAF Mildenhall include the 488th Intelligence Squadron and the 922nd Reconnaissance Squadron. Both units, under the operational control of the 55th Wing at Offutt AFB, NB perform intelligence data gathering and analysis missions for national agencies. The missions are flown on RC-135 aircraft. The 922nd provides the aircraft and flight crew while the 488th provides the mission crew and technicians for data analysis.

The 100th Air Refueling Wing (ARW) began as a Second World War unit known as the 100th Bomb Group. They flew Boeing B-17G Flying Fortresses from the Norfolk airfield of Thorpe Abbots near Diss. 'The Bloody Hundredth', as it was known, because of its high losses on occasions, saw action in many of the fiercest battles in German airspace, for which it received two Distinguished Unit Citations for participation in seven Second World War campaigns. The group used Thorpe Abbots from June 1943 until December 1945. Today, the restored control tower houses the 100th Bomb Group Memorial Museum. The post-war unit was activated at Pease AFB, New Hampshire as the 100th Bombardment Wing where its mission was strategic bombardment. Then in January 1966, the unit was re-designated the 100th Strategic Reconnaissance Wing and moved to Davis-Monthan AFB, Arizona. Another change of mission in September 1976 brought a new name and location – the 100th Air Refueling Wing at Beale AFB, California. When SAC approved the consolidation of its U-2 reconnaissance forces with the SR-71A forces at Beale AFB, the 100th was chosen to be the lead unit. The U-2 mission was transferred to the 9th Strategic Reconnaissance Wing and the 100th AREFW was activated. Upon arrival at the California base, the 100th AREFW replaced the inactivated 17th Bomb Wing as the host unit at Beale.

The 100th AREFW, while stationed at Beale, provided exclusive air refuelling support to the SR-71A and the U-2R, using assigned KC-135Q Stratotankers. As the only unit equipped with these customised tankers, modified for SR-71A/U-2 refuelling, the unit's effectiveness had a direct impact on SAC's performance of its strategic reconnaissance role. Additionally, the 100th provided airlift support to short notice worldwide deployments of U-2 aircraft. Although the wing operated thirty KC-135Q tankers, up to nine aircraft at any given time were on temporary duty in the Pacific and European Theatres. The unique mission of the 100th Air Refueling Wing gave the unit a rather distinct nature among SAC wings. Due to its worldwide requirements, it had, unlike other SAC units, no alert commitments. Following a merger of the missions of the 9th Strategic Reconnaissance Wing with that of the 100th Air Refueling Wing into a single-wing in March 1983, the 100th was inactivated.

Immediately following its West Coast assignment, the 100th moved to Whiteman AFB, Missouri in June 1990, and assumed its mission as the 100th Air Division. After a six-month inactivation, the unit reactivated as the 100th Air Refueling Wing at RAF Mildenhall. This was the second time that the 100th had an association with RAF Mildenhall. Throughout its existence as a refuelling wing from Beale AFB, the wing had provided fuel for the SR-71As that flew from Mildenhall. At the highpoint of support, six tankers bearing the emblem of the 100th ARW refuelled the 'Blackbirds'. Also the tankers were assigned to support the European Tanker Task Forcem which operated from RAF Fairford and RAF Mildenhall. Aircraft flown by the wing throughout its history have included the B-47 Stratojet bomber, the KC-97 Stratocruiser and later the KC-135 Stratotanker. During its mission as a reconnaissance wing, the 100th flew the U-2, DC-130, CH-3 and assorted drones. Today's 100th Air Refueling Wing flies the KC-135R.

Subordinate refuelling squadrons of the 100th have included the 349th and 350th Air Refueling Squadrons. Today's flying squadron, the 351st Air Refueling Squadron, which was activated in April 1992 at RAF Mildenhall has a direct link with the past. The 351st was one of the four original bombardment squadrons assigned to the 100th Bombardment Group. In the early years the 100th performed a mission of global strategic bombardment, as well as global air refuelling. In 1966, it took on the mission of strategic reconnaissance. Later, following a move to Beale AFB, the 100th provided refuelling support to the SR-71As of the 9th Strategic Reconnaissance Wing with its KC-135Q aircraft. Today's 100th Air Refueling Wing is responsible for the host management of RAF Mildenhall and the entire European Tanker Task Force, providing US, NATO and allied forces with air refuelling support. The 351st is the only air refuelling squadron on permanent assignment in Europe and represents USAFE's vital air refuelling lifeline to military air operations, which involve American, NATO and the allied nations of Europe. In addition, the squadron is the foundation of the European Tanker Task Force. The squadron flies the Boeing KC-135R Stratotanker, each of which proudly displays the 'Square D' of the wartime 100th Bombardment Group.

A force of fifteen to twenty KC-135s on temporary duty from stateside bases supplement the 100th's fleet of nine permanent KC-135s. The rotational force provides the manning and equipment necessary for the employment of the European Tanker Task Force. Together, the 100th ARW and the ETTF have been tasked to aid in various humanitarian missions, such as Operation *Restore Hope* and *Provide Promise* and continued to provide vital air refuelling for Operations *Provide Comfort* and *Deny Flight*. The mission of Operation *Provide Comfort II* was the deployment, equipping and sustaining of forces based in Turkey that provided air protection for the Kurdish refugees that had fled the regime of Iraqi dictator Saddam Hussein.

C-130E 'ETI-187' (63-13187) of '222 Filo' of the *Turk Hava Kuvvetleri* (Turkish Air Force) with a C-17A in the background and a C-5A overhead at Air Fête 1998. 'ETI-187' was delivered under the US Military Assistance Program (MAP) to the Turkish Air Force in October 1964.

In May 1992 C-130K XV292 appeared at the Mildenhall Air Fête with a large '25' on its tail to celebrate twenty-five years of the Hercules in the RAF. It carried these markings, which included the badges of all the squadrons and units on the sides of the fuselage, for two more years.

Share a ride to anywhere!

The United Nations (UN) and NATO established two 'no-fly zones' over major portions of Iraq to further protect the fleeing Kurdish populations. A multi-national rapid deployable air and ground force was sent to Turkey to provide aid if necessary. Actually, two operations, *Provide Comfort II* and *Southern Watch*, provided refugee protection against Iraqi aggression. The US CENTCOM forces, operating from Saudi Arabia, managed the latter, while European Command and NATO provided support to the former. Two no-fly zones were established, with a northern zone above the 36th parallel and a southern zone below the 32nd parallel.

Tankers deployed from the US as part of the Air Mobility Command, refuelled combat-capable aircraft that patrolled the southern sector, while USAFE tankers from the 100th Air Refueling Wing provided air refuelling for the northern sector. The base of operations for *Provide Comfort II* was at Incirlik AB in Turkey while the base of operations for *Southern Watch* was at Jeddah, Saudi Arabia. In support of this mission, the 100th deployed approximately five tankers to Incirlik AB for continuous duty. Aircraft and crews were currently rotated every three to four weeks. This had been continuous mission tasking to the 100th ever since the wing's inception in February 1992. For the first six months of 1993, 778 missions were flown from Turkey in more than 3,000 hours. The deployment used KC-135R aircraft, exclusively. For fiscal 1993 (October 1992 to September 1993) a total of 1,452 missions were accomplished in 6,183 flying hours. Of this total, 277 missions in 1,178 hours were flown by aircraft and crews of the 351st Air Refueling Squadron in the 100th Air Refueling Wing. The European Tanker Task Force rotational assets accomplished the remaining 1,175 missions in 5,005 hours.

Operation *Deny Flight* was the UN mandated enforcement of a no-fly zone over the former Yugoslavia area, now known as Bosnia-Herzegovina. The actual employment of forces,

NASA WB-57F '28' which paid a visit to Mildenhall in October 2005. Twenty RB-57D high-altitude strategic reconnaissance aircraft with increased-span wing, fuselage radome and Pratt & Whitney J57 turbojets were built. The twenty-one RB-57F aircraft were special conversions from B-57B and RB-57D aircraft carried out by General Dynamics for special high-altitude reconnaissance duties. The greatly enlarged wingspan of the RB-57D caused the wings of at least three of the aircraft to break and so the RB-57F, whose wingspan was increased to 122ft, used a new three-spar design, which was further strengthened by the incorporation of honeycomb sandwich wing skins. A new power plant comprised two 18,000lb thrust Pratt & Whitney TF33-P-11 turbofans and two 3,300lb thrust Pratt &B Whitney J60-P-9 turbojets.

aircraft and personnel utilised NATO resources belonging to member nations. The 100th Air Refueling Wing operated two forward locations in support of the flying mission. The wing provided an uninterrupted flow of air refuelling opportunities to military aviation on close air support patrol and no-fly zone enforcement missions. This not only included American and foreign air forces, but US Naval aviation as well. Previously, the 100th had supported *Deny Flight* from locations at NAS Sigonella and Malpenza International Airport. Later, the most current forward locations were at Pisa International Airport, Italy and Istres Air Base, France. Air refuelling of US Navy patrol aircraft was the primary responsibility of the KC-135 tankers that operated from Istres, while US and NATO aircraft refuelled from tankers flying from Pisa. The aircraft assigned to the 100th utilised both in-flight refuelling boom and drogue operations. Most NATO and US Naval aircraft use the drogue method to refuel while the USAF aircraft refuel, via the in flight-refuelling boom.

Operations in support of *Deny Flight* began for the 100th Air Refueling Wing on 9 April 1993, when aircraft and personnel were deployed to NAS Sigonella. On 13 June, additional aircraft and forces were jointly deployed by NATO to enable close-air support operations to commence if necessary. The 100th deployed three additional KC-135 aircraft and approximately seventy personnel to Malpenza IAP in order to staff a second deployment location in support of *Deny Flight*. Later, flight operations moved from Malpenza to Pisa and from Sigonella to Istres. Officially, NATO Operation *Deny Flight* began at noon GMT on Monday 12 April 1993.

The mission of NATO's Operation *Deny Flight* was threefold: 1) To conduct aerial monitoring and enforce compliance with UN Security Council Resolution 816, which

B-52H-170-BW 61-0024 *I'll Be Seeing You!* of the 668th Bomb Squadron, 416th Bomb Wing at
Griffiss AFB, New York, at Mildenhall in 1992. The 416th Bomb Wing disposed of its B-52Hs in 1992
and they were transferred to the 5th Bomb Wing at Minot AFB, North Dakota.

Warning: Restricted Area! Mildenhall Air Fête May 2000.

banned flights by fixed-wing and rotary-wing aircraft in the airspace of Bosnia-Herzegovina; 2) To provide protective air cover (close-air support) at the request of and at the control by the UN Protection Forces, under the provisions of the UN Security Council Resolution 836; 3) To be ready to carry out, in co-ordination with the UN, air strikes on heavy weapons, if they fire from outside (or inside) the 20km exclusion zone into Sarajevo or if they return into the exclusion zone. As of 2 March, almost 13,900 fighter, tanker and NATO Airborne Early Warning No-Fly Zone sorties had been flown, which included more than 7,400 fighter missions. Aircraft available for air-to-ground operations conducted more than 6,650 training missions. On 28 February, NATO airborne early warning aircraft tracked six Galeb/Jastreb aircraft, violating the UN no-fly zone. When the Galeb aircraft refused to heed warnings issued by the NAEW aircraft, NATO fighter engaged them and four Galeb aircraft were shot down.

On 31 March 1993, the UN extended its Security Council Resolution 816 to include banning any flights not authorised by the UNPROFOR and authorised member states to take all necessary measures, in the event of further violations, to ensure compliance with the ban. NATO's enforcement of this expanded ban on flights was approved on 8 April 1993, when NATO notified the UN of their willingness to undertake. More than 4,500 personnel from twelve NATO countries have deployed their troops on this historic mission. The UN did not directly ask NATO to enforce the no-fly zone, but rather asked individual nations or regional grouping of nations for their support of enforcement of the UNSCR 781 and 816. In response, the NATO governing body offered to assist, and that offer was accepted. This marked the first time that NATO as an organisation had moved forward, beyond its borders, with this kind of capability. The implementation of *Deny Flight* showed that NATO's command and control structure developed over the past forty years worked well, to bring together humanitarian and military capabilities of the alliance in responding to world-wide requirements, such as these sponsored by the UN. The historic enforcement officially began on Monday 12 April at 1200 GMT.

As of the close of the first half of 1993, the total support on behalf of the 100th Air Refueling Wing included 549 missions, and over 2,300 flying hours expended. The missions and hours were flown from Sigonella. By the end of 1993, the total amount of support the 100th had contributed included 1,622 missions flown in 7,008 hours.

Air refuelling requirements are accomplished in support of four major Air Force commands, the US Navy and many foreign air forces as well as NATO commitments. Today's mission of the 100th is to conduct air refuelling, force deployments and supporting operations for nuclear and conventional forces anytime, anywhere. The Wing's vision for tomorrow is one of a professional team perfecting the world's most responsive air refuelling and support force on time, every time.

RAF Mildenhall forms a vital part of the NATO defence system and is a key factor within the local economy. The base embarked upon an expansion and rebuilding plan when the decision was taken to move Air Force Special Operations activity from RAF Alconbury to RAF Mildenhall in October 1994. Altogether, more than $40 million in military construction and operations and maintenance funding was approved to renovate buildings, begin new construction and airfield modifications to accommodate the 352nd Special Operations Group. This unit operates its Lockheed MC-130H Combat Talon/MC-130P Combat Shadow aircraft and MH-53M Pave Low III long-range, deep penetration helicopters from Mildenhall.[5]

The Special Operations Command, which was established on 22 May 1990 with HQ at Hurlburt Field, Florida, was created following world events in the 1980s. Following the abortive Iranian Rescue Mission in April 1980 and the subsequent acts of terrorism and hostage taking, the Twenty-third Air Force was activated at Scott AFB, Illinois, on 1 March 1983, consisting of forces trained in air rescue and special operations. In October 1983, the Twenty-third Air Force took part in operations in Grenada. Four years later, US Special Operations Command was set up, with the special forces of each branch of the armed services coming under a central operational control. The Twenty-third Air Force became its USAF component and in August 1987, moved to Hurlburt Field, situated in the vast Eglin AFB complex in north-west Florida. Special Operations personnel have trained there since 1942 when they prepared for the Doolittle raid on Tokyo. Special Operations are just one of the many facets employed in times of crisis and, in particular, the war on terror. From 20 December 1989 to 1 January 1990, the US launched Operation *Just Cause*, the US invasion of Panama. MAC flew 408 missions using C-130, C-141 Starlifter and C-5 Galaxy aircraft to land or airdrop 19,500 troops and 11,700 tons of cargo. Troops from the 82nd Airborne were parachuted onto drop zones at the Madden Dam and the Tocumen/Torrijos International Airport. Twenty-one AC-130 gunships, MC-130E Combat Talons and MH-53E/J Pave Low helicopters of Air Force Special Operations Command (AFSOC), flew over 400 missions during *Just Cause*. AC-130 gunships were among the first in action early on the morning of 20 December, destroying the Panamanian Defence Force's Comandancia HQ with devastating fusillades of cannon and machine-gun fire. The MC-130E Combat Talons and MH-53E Pave Low helicopters were used to infiltrate US Army Rangers and Navy SEALS into Panamanian positions. It was Twenty-third Air Force's final operation before its deactivation. On 22 May 1990, the AFSOC was established at Hurlburt Field with a directive to organise, train, equip and educate Air Force special operations forces.[6]

The 352nd SOG began full operational missions from RAF Mildenhall in March 1995. The MH-53J Pave Low III helicopters are flown by the 21st SOS on medium-range, low-level missions at night and in all weather operations. The helicopter operates as a Pathfinder and has the unique capabilities which permit selective rescue and recovery missions. The MC-130E/H Combat Talon aircraft used by the 7th SOS are extensively modified C-130s with a fifty-two-passenger capacity that are capable of low-level mission to infiltrate or extract Special Operations personnel.[7] Six MC-130E Combat Talon Is were deployed to Saudi Arabia for Operation *Desert Storm* in the Gulf War, which began on 16 January 1991. Combat Talon Is of the 8th SOS, delivered the 15,000lb BLU-82/B 'Big Blue' fuel-air explosive bomb, the largest and heaviest conventional bomb in the USAF inventory. On 15 February 1991, Combat Talons began dropping BLU-82 'daisy cutters' on Iraqi minefields as a prelude to the ground offensive. Combat Talons and HC-130N/P aircraft also dropped 'bombs' containing sixteen million leaflets, with messages telling Iraqi soldiers how to surrender to the ground forces.

MH-53J Pave Low III helicopter of the 21st SOS taking off at Mildenhall with a 52nd Fighter Wing F-16C from Spangdahlem in Germany in the foreground.

Above: MH-53J Pave Low III helicopter of the 21st SOS. MH-53J is used on medium range, low-level missions at night and in all weather operations, and it can operate as a Pathfinder and on selective rescue and recovery missions.

Left: Close up of the frontal area of MH-53J Pave Low III helicopter of the 21st SOS.

MC-130P 'Combat Shadow' tanker, one of five in the 67th SOS, 352nd Special Operations Group
at Mildenhall refuelling a 21st SOS MH-53J Pave Low helicopter. The primary role of MC-130P is
to conduct single-ship or formation in-flight refuelling of special operations forces' helicopters in a
low-threat to selected medium-threat environment. While the refuelling pods for the USAF and the
USMC tankers are basically the same, the aerial refuelling system of the former is integrated into the
aircraft's hydraulic and electrical systems, and the aircraft fuel system is utilised to transfer fuel, while
the latter's is basically self contained within the pod and allows 300gpm flow rate simultaneously from
both pods. The USAF HC-130 and MC-130P offload capacity is limited to 150gpm to one helicopter
at a time.

The BLU-021B 15,000lb 'Big Blue' free-fall bomb (shown without P904 fuze), the 'Mother of all
Bombs' dropped by the 7th and 8th SOS teams of the 1st Special Operations Wing MC-130E Combat
Talon I to clear Iraqi minefields during the Gulf War. Palletised for carriage in the cargo hold, the
bomb was simply jettisoned onto the target.

MC-130H Combat Talon II 88-0193 *Night Rider* in the 7th SOS, 352nd Special Operations Group.

MC-130H Combat Talon II 88-0194 *Dawg Pound* in the 7th SOS, 352nd Special Operations Group. Like 88-0193, this aircraft entered service at the Rickenbacker ANGB in August 1989, transferring to the 6512th FTS, 15th SOS, and finally the 7th SOS in 1993.

The HC-130N/P 'Combat Shadow' operated by the 67th SOS are specially configured C-130, able to air refuel special operations rotary wing aircraft, either in a single ship or formation profiles. They are also used to re-supply multi-national special operations forces.[8]

As a RAF bomber before and during the Second World War, Mildenhall contributed to the preservation and restoration of freedom in Western Europe. As a base for USAF bomber, tanker, airlift and reconnaissance operations since 1950, Mildenhall continues to contribute to the protection of that freedom.

Notes

1   A cargo carrying version of the Douglas DC-6A airliner.
2   U-2 aircraft operations moved from Mildenhall to RAF Alconbury in February 1983.
3   Undeterred, USS *Nimitz* had moved south on 3 August to join up with the *Forrestal* for training exercises which would culminate in a live missile firing in the Gulf of Sidra area. On 18 August two Libyan Sukhoi Su-22 *Fitter-Js* attempted to shoot down two F-14As of VF-41 from the *Nimitz* but the Tomcats promptly dispatched them.
4   Despite the termination of the SR-71 programme in 1990, the Dryden Flight Research Center at Edwards AFB, California, took delivery of 64-17980 and 64-17971. SR-71B 64-17956 also joined NASA in July 1991. These aircraft were only on loan from the Air Force and 64-17971 was returned to the USAF inventory in 1995 when funds were found for a reactivation of the SR-71A programme. Despite requests for the 'Blackbirds' to be reactivated for Operation *Desert Shield* in 1990, the requests were denied. However, continued instability in the Middle East, ethnic cleansing in the Balkans and deteriorating relations between the US and North Korea, Congress appropriated $100 million in the fiscal year 1995 defence budget to reactivate the two SR-71As and the SR-71B for service with the aircraft being assigned to a Detachment of the 9th Reconnaissance Wing. Lockheed Martin was contracted to prepare the two aircraft for operational duty at Kadena AB and RAF Mildenhall on a TDY basis. On 1 January 1997, Detachment 2 at Edwards AFB was declared mission ready with two aircraft, 64-17967 and 64-17971. However, the funding for operations in fiscal year 1998 was not made available and on 15 October 1997. President Clinton imposed a 'Line Item Veto' on SR-71 funding, which effectively killed off the programme.
5   The YHH-53H was a single HH-53B modified as prototype for Pave Low II system for night/all-weather Combat SAR. From 1986 eight surviving MH-53Hs plus 31 HH-53B Super Jolly Green Giant, CH-53C Super Jolly and MH-53C were modified to Pave Low III Enhanced standards with strengthened transmission and extra armour and were re-designated MH-53J. This long-range deep penetration helicopter is adverse weather capable and is equipped for extended operations when air refuelled. Equipped with a nose-mounted FLIR, an integrated digital avionics suite that includes TF/TA radar, Kalman filtered navigation suite (GPS, INS, Doppler), projected map display, secure UHF, VHF, FM, HF communications. PLS, SATCOM, hover coupler, rescue hoist, mission commander's C2 panel, armor plating and an ECM suite with radar and IA missile jammers, flare/chaff dispensers, RWA and missile launch detectors. A service life extension programme (SLEP) upgraded the aircraft's hydraulics, wiring and basic airframe structure for increased gross weight and an automated blade/pylon fold system optimised for shipboard compatibility. All aircraft were modified to support aircrew eye respiratory protection system. From 1999 all surviving front-line machines have been upgraded to MH-53M Pave Low IV standard. Upgrades include the interactive defensive avionics suite/multi-mission advanced tactical terminal capability, which integrates onboard EW systems with off-board, over the horizon, near-real-time intelligence and mission software improvements. Cockpit modifications include three MFDs integrated digital map and mission commander situation in the cabin area. The MH-53M was delivered to the 16th SOW in spring 1999.
6   Apart from the 352nd SOG at Mildenhall, the other units comprise the 16th Special Operations Wing at Hurlburt Field with AC-130H/U gunships, C-41A, C-130, MC-130H and MC-130P

aircraft and MH-53J/M and UH-1N helicopters while the 353rd SOG is based at Kadena AB, Japan and operates MC-130H and MC-130P aircraft.

7 The MC-130H-LM Combat Talon II was designed to supplement and eventually replace the MC-130Es used by the 1st Special Operations Wing for Combat Talon clandestine and special operations. In 1984 the USAF ordered the first of twenty-four C-130Hs (83-1212) for modification to MC-130H Combat Talon II standard, with IBM Federal Systems Division handling systems integration and E-Systems installing the specialised avionics. Electronic and equipment fit included AN/APQ-170 multi-role radar (ground-mapping, navigation, terrain following, and terrain avoidance), INS, high-speed low-level aerial delivery and container release system, and automatic computed air- release point, as well as AN/AAQ-15 IR detection system, AN/AAR-44 launch warning receiver, AN/ALQ-8 ECM pods, AN/ALQ-172 detector/jammer, AN/ALR-69 radar warning receiver, IR jammer, and chaff/flare dispensers. The first MC-130H was delivered to the 8th SOS at Hurlburt Field, Florida, in June 1990. All twenty-four MC-130Hs (83-1212, 84-475/476, 85-011/012, 86-1699, 87-023/024, 87-125/127, 88-191/195, 88-264, 88-1803, 89-280/283 and 90-161/162) were delivered to the USAF by November 1991.

8 Twenty HC-130P-LM combat aircrew recovery aircraft (65-988, 65-991/994 and 66-211/225), designated in 1966 are similar to HC-130H (retaining that type's AN/ARD-17 Cook aerial tracker antenna and the Fulton STAR recovery system) but fitted with underwing drogue pods and associated plumbing for in-flight refuelling of rescue helicopters. The HC-130Ps entered service late in 1966 and they were immediately deployed to South East Asia. 66-214 and 66-218 in the 39th ARRS (Aerospace Rescue and Recovery Squadron) were destroyed by satchel charges at Tuy Hoa, South Vietnam on 29 July 1968. 66-211 was lost when its right wing snapped in severe turbulence at low level 15.5 miles north of Magdalena, New Mexico on 2 April 1986. In 1996, thirteen aircraft (65-991/994, 66-212/213, 66-215/217, 66-219/220, 66-223 and 66-225) were re-designated MC-130P. These currently operate in special operation squadrons. 65-988 currently operates in the 71st RQS and three (66-221/222 and 66-224) operate in SOS squadrons at the time of writing.

CHAPTER 4

The Mildenhall Heritage Trail

Mildenhall has a heritage trail which highlights a varied selection of significant structures throughout the base. The trail consists of a walk through the domestic and industrial areas of the base. Either a wall or pedestal-mounted plaque giving appropriate information regarding the historical significance of the particular structure identifies buildings of interest.

Begin your journey around Mildenhall's Heritage Trail from a starting point across from Gate 2, near Mickie's Tea Bar. 'Building 136' in Dakota Road is the bungalow alongside Mickie's. Proceed towards Washington Square, then around past Third Air Force Headquarters and the Mildenhall Officers Club. Stroll down past the Billeting Office heading back towards Gate 2. Enter the main portion of the base through Gate 2 and proceed down past 562 and 559. In this portion of the tour, many of the buildings are located rather close to each other. The hangars, of course, are near the flight line.

Now walk along the trail past Buildings 554 to 528. Turn toward the AAFES Car Care Center (Buildings 511/512) and proceed towards end of tour. Along the way, watch for Buildings 545 and 546 and be sure not to miss Building 506 (the white dome tucked between other buildings). At the corner, across from the alternate command post bunker (Building 559) turn left and walk towards the gate. The last building to see is 501, just across the street from 562 and just inside Gate 2.

1   **Building 136**. Believed to be the first building to have been associated with the airfield. Most officials believe that the building, originally built as a cottage, actually dates back to 1931. The base civil engineer is said to have used it as his quarters while building the station proper. It was subsequently re-modelled as a warrant officers Married Quarters in 1933, its present day function.

2   **Building 427**. Built in 1931 as an Airmen's Barrack Block to accommodate single airmen assigned to the station, it still continues to quarter airmen, but only those on temporary duty to the base. When built it had four twelve-man communal rooms. A central latrine and a separate room for the corporal who was in charge were located in the centre of the building. This building, as with others, faces onto what is now 'George Washington Square', formerly the station parade ground. The Neo-Georgian style is common among RAF buildings constructed prior to the Second World War. Compare this structure to that of Building 442, another barracks block built four years later.

3   **Building 424**. Another building built in 1931. It functioned as a dormitory for airmen pilots and was originally of single-storey construction. In pre-war expansion, the second floor was added to give a total space accommodation for twenty-six single sergeants. The doorway reflects its Neo-Georgian styling. In the RAF era, residents would have taken their meals in the Sergeants' Mess (Building 425) nearby. Today's visiting resident has only to exit the rear doors to go to the nearest AAFES food facility or cross the nearby public road to taste British fare. Most community services, such as the post office, recreation centre and accounting and finance are all close by in Washington Square. This building is one of the few where the original function still exists. Others, located nearby, have been converted into offices or administrative facilities.

4   **Building 425**. Originally designed as the dining facility for personnel of sergeant rank. During the pre-war expansion the adjacent building (442) was added to extend the space available for the Sergeants' Mess. The small western wing was added in 1939 but proved to be too small to handle the increase in number of customers, thus the acquisition of Building 442. Building 425 is now

the Mildenhall base library. Under the base comprehensive plan, a new addition will be built onto the library without closing it down. The building stands across from what once was the main entrance to the base and also directly across from the very first building at RAF Mildenhall.

5   **Building 442**. Originally built and used as an Airmen's Mess and club complex, this building now is the home to the RAF Mildenhall Community Post Office, sports store and administrative headquarters for the 100th Mission Support Squadron. Constructed in 1931 with a capacity of 343 diners at one time, the facility also hosted a barbershop that remained until renovations in the early 1990s. Pre-war expansion saw the building being requisitioned as an additional Sergeants' Mess, with much larger Airmens' Mess and club facilities moved to Building 436. When the building became the Sergeants' Mess, it and an adjacent one (Building 425) comprised a complex offering meals and recreation to sergeant personnel.

6   **Building 436.** A replacement mess for enlisted personnel was built in 1939 to accommodate yet further increases in personnel. This replaced the original Mess located in 442. Since being built, the basic function has remained the same. While the Enlisted Dining Facility is still here, the upper floor functions a central processing station for military personnel functions. Since 1994, the Dining Facility and its kitchens have been renovated. Where the theatre once was, is an Air Force Recruiting Office and administrative offices for food services.

7   **Building 239**. Constructed in 1936 as a RAF Bomber Command Group Headquarters, this building was occupied from 1937 to 1967 by HQ 3 Group RAF. In 1972, when Headquarters Third Air Force moved from South Ruislip to RAF Mildenhall, the staff located to this building, which in 1996 was named in honour of General Leon Johnson, Medal of Honor recipient and first commander of the Third Air Force in England. Although the original shell still remains unchanged, extensive interior remodelling has taken place, as well as additional office space construction connecting with the building. It is from here that UK-wide negotiation and matters relating to USAF-RAF activities are managed. The front of the building is the only place on the entire Mildenhall complex where the flags of the US and Royal Air Force Ensign are flown. Across the lawn, approaching the headquarters building is Mildenhall's tribute to those who have not returned home – all prisoners of war since the Second World War and most recently, Vietnam.

8   **Building 474 (Base Chapel)**. While not entirely a historic building, a typical Air Force chapel of 'A-frame' design, six unique stained-glass windows telling the story of RAF Mildenhall in symbolic form has been erected to commemorate Mildenhall's history and the personnel who served there. The idea for these windows was originated and developed by Chaplain (Lieutenant Colonel) James E. Somma Jr, USAF, and Dr Colin M. Dring, chairman of the Mildenhall and district museum. Each man spent many hours poring over the history of the station from 1934 to 1982, not only to select significant historical details, but more importantly to highlight the dedication and personal sacrifices made by countless personnel who served at the station. Designed by Ronald E. Page, they are a fine and beautiful tribute. Within the windows has been told the history of the airfield. Contained in them are the badges of Nos 15, 35, 38, 44, 75, 99, 115, 149, 207, 419 and 622 Squadrons, 3 Group RAF, 513th Tactical Airlift Wing (TAW), 306th Reconnaissance Wing, 313th Tactical Airlift Group, Third Air Force and NATO. All the scenes are against a blue background full of movement; varied and yet cohesive. Together these windows are called 'Historic Milestones' and each has its separate name and period.

The early years depicts the period since Mildenhall was opened and also records the time before that and the beginning of aviation. King George V's coat of arms at the top symbolises his connection with Mildenhall and with aviation. Below it is a First World War B.E.2 biplane, which also recalls aviation's long history in the Mildenhall area when army scouts could be seen flying to local battle areas. The next panel shows the winning Comet circling the globe and passing through a rainbow, which, to the delight of onlookers, had appeared over the runway at the start of this historic race.

No.99 Squadron's crest, a puma, occupies the bottom panel with its motto *Quisque tenax* and below, crystallising the spirit of early aviation, the text: 'Your old men shall dream dreams and your young men shall see visions'.

'The Dawn of War' window displays the crest of the Royal Air Force with its encircling motto *Per Ardua ad Astra*. Below is a Gladiator of 1401 (Met.) Flight and in the centre, the massive fly-past led by 99 Squadron at Duxford to commemorate the Silver Jubilee of King George V and Queen Mary. Shortly after the Silver Jubilee, 38 Squadron was reactivated and assigned to RAF Mildenhall, and later 149 Squadron joined them. The insignia of these two night bombing squadrons form the bottom panel, with their mottoes *Ante Lucum* and *Fortis Nocta*. The quotation at the bottom is from Sir Winston Churchill: 'Be master of your own air'.

The third window is called 'The Commonwealth Family'. At the top is the coat of arms of King George V, signifying his interest in the station. Below are Wellingtons of 99 and 149 Squadrons which were the first in the RAF to be equipped with these aircraft and which were in a state of readiness by June 1939. After 9 Squadron had converted to Stirlings, they continued operations over Germany and Italy. A newly formed Canadian squadron arrived, later replaced by 115 Squadron and 75 (New Zealand) Squadron.

The Commonwealth family of a mother and father with two children symbolises unity and commemorates the many Commonwealth airmen who served at Mildenhall. In the third panel flies a Wellington bomber. In the right-hand panel are elements from the crests of 419 Royal Canadian Air Force Squadron – the charging moose – and 75 New Zealand Squadron, the mining hammers in saltire. The quotation from Thomas Paine signifies that critical aspect of the war and the suffering therein: 'These are times that try men's souls'.

'The Fight for Freedom' window shows the intensification of that struggle. At the top of this window is No.3 Group's crest. Below stand three prisoners of war symbolising the freedom for which so many airmen gave their lives, and below them a Stirling coned in enemy searchlights. At the bottom are the insignia of 15 Squadron – the great barn owl, its wings spread, with the motto *Bellamus Noctu* – and 622 Squadron – the winged horse with the motto, 'Aim sure'. The quotation is from Isaiah: 'He has sent me … to proclaim liberty for the captives'.

The Operation *Manna* window, surmounted by the royal arms of Queen Elizabeth II, depicts the station's work in peacetime. It commemorates June 1945 when Mildenhall's two squadrons joined other Bomber Command squadrons in dropping food and supplies to the starving population of the Netherlands and in ferrying home newly-freed prisoners of war from Germany and occupied Europe. Also, the relief work undertaken by the station when the coastal areas of East Anglia were flooded after one of the worst winters on record is remembered. Assembled at the bottom are the insignia of Nos 35, 44 (Rhodesian), 115 and 207 Squadrons. The inscription at the bottom is from the Psalms: 'He rescued me from deep waters. He delivered me from my strong enemy'.

The final window is 'The American Presence'. In the top panel is the crest of the US Air Force. Below it is the dove of peace, in the hope that the combined Air Forces might preserve peace in Europe. A KC-135 flies across the third panel. The insignia of NATO, the Third Air Force 513th Tactical Airlift Wing (TAW), 36th Strategic Wing (SW) and 313th TAG (Tactical Airlift Group) appear in the bottom panel. The quotation is from John F. Kennedy: 'We will pay any price, bear any burden, support any friend … to assure the success of Liberty'.

On 25 October 1982, for the first time since Americans arrived in 1950, a member of the British Royal Family visited the base; HRH Prince of Wales dedicated the six stained glass windows. Inscribed on metal salvaged from Lancaster I ED383 of 15 Squadron, which crashed near Lakenheath on 26 February 1944 following its return from an operation, killing five of its crew, is a dedication plaque. It bears the words: 'To the glory of God, and in memory of the service of the men and women of RAF Mildenhall. Dedicated by HRH, the Prince of Wales, 25 October 1982'. The Prince said during his dedication speech, 'The windows help to remind us of the close co-operation and friendship that existed between the two air forces during World War II and emphasise the relationship that exists today of mutual respect and admiration for each nation's professionalism and sense of duty.' The cost of the windows was £7,150. It is planned to build an additional educational centre for the chapel complex.

9 **Building 464.** The Officers' Mess, which virtually faces Gate 1, was constructed in 1931 with the western wing added in 1939. This was, and continues to be, the social centre for the RAF

Mildenhall officer community. Today's Officers' Club is a multi-functional complex, which offers VIP accommodations, formal dining, and a casual bar and fine china shops. As a centre of Mildenhall's hospitality, the 'O' Club often serves as the focal point and reception centre when important visitors come through. Its formal dining room offers an ambiance of luxury and fine tradition. Each of its dining rooms is equipped with large ornate fireplaces. Nearby buildings offer the visiting officer comfortable accommodation. The building also features a nearby tennis court.

10 **Building 443**. Originally built in 1931 as the station sick quarters, this structure was eventually equipped with a gas-proof annex for use during gas attacks. The gas-proof annex and several additional separate medical wards were added pre-war and during the war respectively. Windows now seen in what used to be the gas-proof annex were added when the building was renovated much later. Today, this building serves as the base civil engineers office and houses the administrative section, real estate functions and offices for the 100th Civil Engineering Squadron. The Defence Works Services also has its offices located in some of the original medical wards. The only modern medical facility of today's Mildenhall is located next door in Building 444, and functions as the Flight Surgeon's Office, while across the street, in a building of more recent construction, the base dental clinic has been established.

11 **Building 562**. Originally the station headquarters, this building, completed in 1933 as an Office and Operations Block, including library and lecture room, sits adjacent to the original main gate. As the 100th Air Refueling Wing's Headquarters, the buildings' central function remains unchanged. Just prior to the Second World War, the nearby earth-bermed building (559) was completed as the Wartime Operations Centre. Its semi-hardened construction provided some measure of protection against enemy attack. It now functions as an alternate command post.

12 **Building 558.** This building was originally built in 1931 as a parachute store. This facility remains unaltered in its function and external appearance to this day. It is here that parachutes are rigged, cleaned and repaired. In 1995 a major renovation to the building began.

13 **Building 554**. Completed in 1933, this structure served as the station armoury. It also housed several functions relating to bombing as well as its store for small arms. Bombardiers used an instructional device within the building to learn the finer points of using the 'Course Setting Bomb Sight'. Two other items of interest the building contained were a Photographic Block and a Gas Respirator test facility. From the 1950s to the '70s it functioned as the meeting place for the American Youth Association. Until recently, this was the headquarters for the 627th Air Mobility squadron. It has been re-modelled as a headquarters for use by one of the Squadrons of the 352nd Special Operations Group, which moved from RAF Alconbury.

14 **Building 545**. First erected in 1931 as the main store and workshops for the newly built RAF station. Today, workshops continue to be located within the building complex, and manufacture, repair and inspect metal panels and parts used on aircraft. In the complex, which includes a section for non-destructive inspections and a fabrication workshop, repairs can be accomplished on such items as aircraft flaps, skin surface panels, and aerospace ground equipment. The building's location was within easy reach of the hangars and aprons of the early airfield. Today, Building 545 is a facility where aircraft survival equipment systems are maintained, repaired and manufactured. These shops are located in close proximity to the flight line and just behind the large hangars that the US Navy and the 352nd Special Operations Group use.

15 **Building 546**. Originally built for use as a crew assembly point and briefing room, it was completed in 1931 as part of a two-building complex. Its twin has long since been demolished to accommodate expansion. During the Second World War, this structure served as the protestant chapel. In the post-war era this was also the base chapel until a new one was built later. The pre-war watch office, nothing more than a bungalow with a bay window, was less than 50m away located between hangars 539 and 550. A second tower, for wartime use, was to the old facilities' front. Additional aircraft handstands have been built in their place since the end of the war.

16 **Building 539**. One of three 'Type C' aircraft hangars constructed at Mildenhall in 1935 during the second phase of hangar construction. These hangars represent a more up-to-date version of

the earlier 'Type A' originally constructed when the base first opened. Hangars of the 'Type C' are of typical pre-war design and remain a common sight on RAF airfields. In 1995 the hangars were modified to accommodate aircraft once again. Now, although no aircraft except for smaller US Navy courier aircraft and CH-53J Pave Low III helicopters of the 352nd SOG use the structures, the hangars still prove useful as warehouses, aerospace equipment maintenance facilities and backshops.

17 **Building 528.** The 'Type A' hangar, first built at RAF Mildenhall in 1933 as part of the first phase of hangar construction. This hangar and one other of the same design were the original hangars built when the airfield activated. The design, unlike hangars 538, 539 and 550 built from 1930 designs, originated during the 1920s. This hangar and the one previously mentioned were used by air race participants in 1934 to work prepare and store their aircraft as well as serving as sleeping quarters for the participants.

18 **Buildings 511/512** provided the station with a motor vehicle complex, better known as the 'motor pool'. Completed in 1931, it was added to during the later wartime expansion phase with additional bays and garages. This building has long been associated with motor vehicles and the maintenance of refuelling vehicles. Although it serves the same purpose of vehicle servicing and repair, customers no longer drive their military vehicles in for repair. The buildings are now home of the Mildenhall Car Care Center, an operation of the Army Air.

19 **Building 506.** Of 1942 vintage, this dome-shaped structure served as the instructional centre for navigators and anti-aircraft gunners receiving training. The dome was originally used by anti-aircraft gunners to practice their craft. A completely different use was to train navigators in astro navigation using celestial triangulation techniques. This strange structure can be seen in modern guise in today's Air Forces as one of the forerunners of current synthetic training. This one building is the best preserved example of its kind of only a small handful that remains intact. The 100th Communication Squadron's secure communications function currently resides within the structure.

20 **Building 501.** The original 'Type G' guard house built in 1931 served for many years as the Station Guardroom. It still welcomes visitors who enter through the station's original Main Gate, now Gate 2. Building 501, the original Provost Marshal's office, was built in 1931 and contained rooms for fire protection items, personal hygiene products and paint storage. The Station Guard doubled as the 'Fire Piquet', sounding the fire alarm. Personnel assembled here prior to being released on '48-hour passes' and were inspected by the 'Eagle-eyed' Station Warrant Officer who maintained an office within the building. He functioned as the station's disciplinarian. A reminder of those early days is still present; the building contains the original guardroom jail cell. The guard house faces what was originally an office and operations block, containing the pre-war station headquarters. That same building now is home to the headquarters for the 100th Air Refueling Wing.

Additional Buildings of Interest

Although these are not included on the Heritage Trail due to their location within the operational parameters of the flight line, they hold particular interest and are indicative of the changes, which have taken place since the ending of the Cold War.

Building 719. Hangars or 'barns' of a modern design, until 1990 these housed the two operational SR-71As, which flew regular missions from Mildenhall. The buildings were designed with doors on both ends so that the 'Blackbird' could roll right into the building. In line with policy in force at the time, the SR-71A remained hangared unless it was on an operational mission. A nearby building provided logistical, administrative and maintenance support.

Building 705. A building related to SR-71A 'Blackbird' support. This building with its peculiar tube-like extensions was used as an engine test cell for the SR-71A. The aircraft was backed into

MC-130H Combat Talon II 88-0194 *Dawg Pound* in the 7th SOS.

the hangar-like building, secured and its engines fired up, exhaust and noise was filtered through the huge tube-shaped protrusions on the rear elevation of the building. Today this building acts as a storage site for large equipment.

Control Tower. After more than fifty years of intensive use, the post-war control tower built in 1952 was decommissioned on 30 May 2004. It was replaced by a more modern structure, the fifth control building to be used at Mildenhall since the airfield opened in 1934. This building, which cost £15 million, came into use on 19 April 2004, while all fixed-wing aircraft were on TDY at Fairford and Lakenheath as the Mildenhall runway was being resurfaced. Included in the new building are a huge fire station, an operations centre and a series of training room – one of which contains a simulator designed to complete the training of new controllers.

Quonset Huts. What military installation would be without these readily-identifiable structures so 'GI' in appearance. While not many survive today in their original configuration, some have become incorporated into new construction, having newer structures built around or onto them. A small variety exist within Mildenhall boundaries, while others have given way to areas set aside for car parks, and modem office complexes.

Army & Air Force Exchange Building. Although the front elevation has been modernised, the core building had withstood major change. A brick addition has been built on the near end and a prefabricated warehouse has been added to the far side. Modern facing has been added to the main entrance as well. This is one of the areas due to receive modernisation in the future. Plans have been made to construct an AAFES Food Court next to the existing exchange. Recent additions with the immediate area have included a facility for the sale of 'American Donuts' and the Bookmark, now managed by AFFES, in the former Stars and Stripes Bookstore. British vendors, located in the Mildenhall Mall, offer a variety of goods and souvenirs.

Mildenhall village with the base in the background in September 2006.

The new Mildenhall consolidated Enlisted Club is to be built on acreage nearby. It will replace existing facilities, which have been severely limited due to a shortage of space. The new club will incorporate facilities for the top four ranks, as well as junior enlisted members.

Some buildings which were at one time RAF officer quarters now function as shops for Civil Engineering Services and the base Ergonometry Cycle Centre. Other buildings, of similar construction are temporary quarters for families when they first arrive at Mildenhall.

Appendix 1

RAF Units Stationed at Mildenhall

Unit	Aircraft	Dates
99 (Madras Presidency) Squadron	Heyford, Wellington	November 1934–March 1941
38 (B) Squadron	Heyford, Hendon	September 1935–May 1937
1401 (Met) Flight		November 1936–October 1941
HQ No.3 (Bomber) Group		January 1937–March 1940
73 (F) Squadron	Fury, Gladiator	March 1937–June 1937
149 (East India) Squadron	Heyford, Wellington, Stirling	April 1937–March 1943
211 (B) Squadron	Audax/Hind	June 1937–September 1937
HQ No.5 (Bomber) Group		September 1937–October 1937
HQ No.4 (Bomber) Group		April 1937–June 1937
218 (Gold Coast) Squadron	Battle, Blenheim	June 1940–July 1940
419 (Moose) Squadron RCAF	Wellington	December 1941–August 1942
115 (B) Squadron	Wellington	September 1942–March 1943
75 (B) Squadron RNZAF	Wellington, Stirling	August 1942–March 1943
1503 BAT Flight		1942–September 1942
1505 BAT Flight		September 1942–December 1942
1403 (Met) Flight		November 1942–December 1942
15 (B) Squadron	Stirling, Lancaster, Lincoln	April 1943–August 1946
622 Squadron	Stirling, Lancaster	August 1943–August 1945
44 (Rhodesia) Squadron	Lincoln	August 1945–August 1946
No.3 Group Major Servicing Unit		August 1946–July 1948
HQ No.3 (Bomber) Group		January 1947–December 1967
35 (Madras Presidency) Squadron	Lancaster, Lincoln	February 1949–February 1950
115 (B) Squadron	Lincoln	February 1949–March 1950
149 (East India) Squadron	Lincoln	February 1949–March 1950
207 (B) Squadron	Lincoln	February 1949–March 1950

Appendix 2

Permanent US Flying Units at Mildenhall

Unit	Aircraft	Dates
93rd Bomb Wing	B-50	July 1950–February 1951
93rd Bomb Wing	B-50	December 1951–February 1952
306th Strategic Wing	KC-135, RC-135	October 1976–1 February 1992
55th Wing	EC-135, RC-135	February 1992–present
313th Tactical Airlift Group	C-130	September 1978–1993
420th Bomb Wing	KB-50	February 1962–March 1964
435th Tactical Airlift Group	C-130	January 1976–September 1978
509th Bomb Wing	B-50, KB-50	February–May 1951
509th Bomb Wing	B-50, KB-50	June–August 1952
513th TAW/ACCW Detachment (Det) 1,	C-130, EC-135	July 1976–1 February 1992
98th Strategic Wing	KG-135	August 1970–October 1976
Det 4, 9th Strategic Recon Wing	SR-71A, U-2R	April 1979–January 1990
Naval Air Facility	C-131, C-12	1964–present
European Tanker Task Force	KC-135	1970–present
100th Air Refueling Wing	KC-135	February 1992–present
352nd Special Operations Group	MC-130, HC-130, MH-53	March 1995–present

Appendix 3

Rotational Units on Temporary Duty to Mildenhall

Unit	Aircraft	Dates
2nd Bomb Wing	B-29	May–August 1951
452nd AFREW (AFRes)	KC-135	August–September 1979
22nd Bomb Wing	KC-97	December 1953–February 1954
43rd Bomb Wing	KC-97	August 1954–December 1954
44th Bomb Wing	KC-97	autumn 1957
53rd Weather Squadron	WB-50	August 1959–March 1960
55th Strategic Recon Wing	RB-50, KB-29, RB-47	April 1953–summer 1956
97th Bomb Wing	RB-50, KB-29	summer 1954
98th Bomb Wing	KC-135	August 1970–October 1976
303rd Bomb Wing	KC-97	March–June 1954
305th Bomb Wing	KC-97	September–December 1953
306th Bomb Wing	KC-97	July–September 1953
380th Bomb Wing	KC-97	April–July 1957
1370th Photo Mapping Group	B-50	June–September 1954
3904th Composite Wing	C-47	autumn 1952

Appendix 4

USAF Host Units at Mildenhall

7511th Air Base Squadron	USAFE	11 July 1950–22 August 1950
7511th Air Base Group	USAFE	22 August 1950–26 September 1950
7511th Air Support Wing	USAFE	26 September 1950–16 May 1951
3910th Air Base Group	SAC	16 May 1951–1954
3913th Air Base Squadron	SAC	1955–1 January 1959
3913th Combat Support Group	SAC	1 January 1959–1 September 1959
7513th Air Base Group	USAFE	1 September 1959–1 June 1965
7513th Tactical Group	USAFE	1 June 1965–1 July 1966
513th Troop Carrier Wing	USAFE	1 July 1966–1 July 1967
513th Tactical Airlift Wing	USAFE	1 July 1967–1 November 1988
513th Airborne Command and Control Wing	USAFE	1 November 1988–1 February 1992
100th Air Refueling Wing	USAFE	1 February 1992–present

Appendix 5

US Units 11 July 1950 to Present

7511 Air Base Squadron (USAFE)	11 July 1950–22 August 1950 (D)
7511 Air Base Group (USAFE)	22 August 1950–26 September 1950 (D)
511 Sup. Squadron	22 August 1950–26 September 1950 (D)
7511 Ma. Squadron	22 August 1950–26 September 1950 (D)
7511 Air Support Wing (USAFE)	26 September 1950–16 May 1951 (D)
7511 Air Base Group (USAFE)	26 September 1950–16 May 1951 (D)
7511 Com. Squadron	26 September 1950–16 May 1951 (D)
7511 Inl Squadron	26 September 1950–16 May 1951 (D)
7511 FSS	26 September 1950–16 May 1951 (D)
7511 APS	26 September 1950–16 May 1951 (D)
7511 Maintenance & Supply Group (USAFE)	26 September 1950–16 May 1951 (D)
7511 FMS	26 September 1950–16 May 1951 (D)
7511 Sup. Squadron	26 September 1950–16 May 1951 (D)
7511 MVS	26 September 1950–16 May 1951 (D)
7511 Med. Squadron	26 September 1950–16 May 1951 (D)
Detachment (Det) of 28 Weather Squadron (MATS) (MAC)	1 August 1950–present
Det of 1963 AACS Squadron (AACS)	c.50–unknown (u/k)
93rd Bombardment Wing (SAC)	15 July 1950–c.October 1950 and c.December 1951– c.March 1952 (M-US) (B-50/KB-29)
329th BS	15 July 1950–c.October 1950 and c.December 1951–c.March 1952 (M-US)
Det of 3 Air Postal Squadron (USAF)	c.July 1950–c.1963 (D)
Det of 7025 Air Postal Group (USAF)	c.1963–c.1967 (D)
Det of European Postal Courier Region (USAF)	c.1967–present
USAF Infirmary (USAFE)	15 February 1951–c.1951 (D)
83rd Smoke Generator Battalion (US Army)	c.May 1951–c.1955 (D)
HQ Battery, 32 AAA Brigade (US Army)	c.May 1951–1 October 1953 (M-Bushy Hall)
6th Chemical Smoke Generator Battalion (US Army)	15 January–25 April 1952 (M-Brize Norton)
34th AAA Operations Det (US Army)	c.May 1951–May 1955 (M-Bushy Hall)
6th Signal Radar Maintenance Unit (US Army)	c.May 1951–November 1952 (M-Cranwich)
82nd Chemical Smoke Generator Battalion (US Army)	c.January 1952–c.June 1957 (M-u/k)
Det of 1979 AACS Squadron (AACS)	c.May 1951–1955 (D)
7702nd Augmentation Det, 32nd AAA Brigade (US Army)	c.May 1951–16 September 1953 (D)
22nd Bombardment Wing (SAC)	c.May 1951–c.1952 (M-US) (B-29)
2nd BS	c.May 1951–c.1952 (M-US)
19th BS	c.May 1951–c.1952 (M-US)
22nd Ma. Squadron	c.May 1951–c.1952 (M-US)
4112 EMS	c.May 1951–c.1952 (M-US)
4112 OMS	c.May 1951–c.1952 (M-US)

726th Augmentation Det, 32nd AAA Brigade (US Army)	c.May 1951–1 October 1953 (M-Bushy Hall)
HQ Det, First Provisional AAA Automatic Weapons Battalion (US Army)	25 July 1952–c.July 1957 (M-u/k)
3910th Air Base Group (SAC)	16 May 1951–c.1954 (M-Lakenheath)
3910th Ops Squadron	16 May 1951–1954 (M-Lakenheath)
3910th Inl Squadron	16 May 1951–c.1954 (M-Lakenheath)
3910th Sup. Squadron	16 May 1951–c.1954 (M-Lakenheath)
3910th Med. Squadron	16 May 1951–c.1954 (M-Lakenheath)
3910th FSS	16 May 1951–c.1954 (M-Lakenheath)
3910th MVS	16 May 1951–c.1954 (M-Lakenheath)
3910th APS	16 May 1951–c.1954 (M-Lakenheath)
3912th Air Base Squadron (SAC)	c.May 1951–c.1954 (M-Lakenheath)
81st Chemical Smoke Generator Company (US Army)	c.1955–c.July 1957 (M-u/k)
U/k Squadron (509th BW) (SAC)	c.1952–c.1952 (M-US) (B-50/KB-29)
Det of 7493 (IG) Special Investigation Wing (u/k)	c.1956–c.1959 (D)
3913th Air Base Squadron (SAC)	c.1955–1 January 1959 (D)
3913th Combat Support Group (SAC)	1 January 1959–1 September 1959 (D)
Det of 8 Aviation Depot Squadron (SAC)	1 June 1958–1 February 1959 (D)
MATS Terminal established	1 March 1959–present
1623rd Support Squadron (MATS)	1 March 1959–c.1961 (D)
310th Bombardment Wing (SAC)	c.1958–c.1958 (M-US) (Units – u/k) (B-29)
19th Aviation Depot Squadron (SAC)	1 February 1954–c.1959 (D)
Det of 7500 Air Base Group (USAFE)	1 March 1959–c.1959 (D)
Det of 6931 Communications Security Squadron (USAFSS)	1 March 1959–1 September 1959 (D)
53rd Weather Squadron (MATS)	c.August 1959–18 March 1960 (D)
Det of 605 Communications Squadron (AFCS)	1 September 1959–c.1961 (D)
6931 Communications Security Squadron (USAFSS)	1 September 1959–c.1961 (D)
7513th Air Base Group (USAFE)	1 September 1959–1 June 1965 (D)
7513th Tactical Group (USAFE)	1 June 1965–1 July 1966
7513th ABS	1 September 1969–c.1961 (D)
7513th Mat. Squadron	1 September 1959–1 June 1965 (D)
7513th CSS	1 June 1965–1 July 1966 (D)
7513th CAMS	1 June 1965–1 July 1966 (D)
7036th Tactical Squadron (USAFE)	1 June 1965–1 July 1965 (D) (T-29/C-47)
Silk Purse Group (USAFE)	15 November 1965–present
7120th Airborne Command Control Squadron (USAFE)	15 November 1965–present (C-118/C-135A/H)
Det of 48 Tactical Hospital (USAFE)	c.1961–c.1965 (D)
Det of 1979 AACS Squadron (AACS)	c.1959–c.1961 (D)
USAFE ATCO Squadron (USAFE)	c.March 1959–c.1966 (D)
APO AMT (u/k)	c.1961–c.1961 (D)
1625 Supply Squadron (USAFE)	c.1961–c.1966 (D)
Det of 7480 Supply Group (u/k)	c.1959–c.1964 (D)
European Exchange System (EES)	c.1964–present
Det of 59 Veterinary Inspection Flight (USAFE)	1 December 1960–1 June 1966 (D)
Redistribution & Marketing Division (USAFE)	c.1964–c.1966 (M-Molesworth)
Det of 7101st Air Base Wing (u/k)	c.1961–c.1965 (D)
Det of 1979 Communications Squadron (AFCS)	c.1961–c.1962 (D)
6931st Communications Security Squadron (USAFS S)	c.1961–c.1961 (D)
Det of 2874 GEEIA Squadron (GEEIA)	c.1961–c.1965 (D)

Det of 6936 Communications Security Squadron (USAFSS)	c.1961–c.1963 (D)
Det of 6936 Communications Security GROUP (USAFSS)	c.1963–c.1965 (D)
1858th Facility Checking Flight (AFCS)	c.August 1962–c.1963 (D)
US Navy activity	c.1962–present
2147th Communications Squadron (AFCS)	c.1962–present
Det of 7500 Air Base Group (USAFE)	c.1965–c.1966 (D)
Det of 100 Air Police Squadron (USAFE)	c.1965–c.1966 (D)
Det of 2nd Aero Medical Evacuation Group (MAC)	c.1965–present
Det of AFCD (u/k)	c.1965–c.1966 (D)
RM USAFE (USAFE)	c.1963–c.1966 (D)
Det of 36th Tactical Fighter Wing (USAFE)	u/k–1 July 1965 (D)
627 Military Airlift Squadron (MAC)	c.1966–present
S Aerial Port Squadron (MAC)	c.1966–present
2 Mobilization Squadron (AFCS)	c.1966–present
Det of USAF Security Service (USAFSS)	c.1966–c.September 1967 (D)
513th Troop Carrier Wing (MAC)	1 July 1966–1 July 1967 (D)
513th Tactical Airlift Wing (MAC)	1 July 1967–1 November 1988 (C-47/C-130)
513th Combat Support Group (MAC)	1 July 1966–present
7441st TCS(P)	20 July 1966–1 April 1967
7412th TCS(P)	20 July 1966–1 June 1967
Alpha Squadron	c.June 1967–present
Bravo Squadron	c.June 1967–present
513th CES	1 July 1966–present
513th Sup. Squadron	1 July 1966–present
513th APS	1 July 1966–1 May 1967 (D)
513th SPS	1 May 1967–present
513th CMS	1 July 1966–present
513th TRS	1 July 1966–present
Det of 322 Air Division (MAC)	c.July 1966–present
Det of 7260 Supply Group (USAFE)	c.1966–present
7260 ATCO (USAFE)	c.1966–c.1967 (D)
513th Airborne Command and Control Wing USAFE	1 November 1988–1 February 1992
100th Air Refueling Wing USAFE	1 February 1992–present
Mildenhall (TACAN Annex), Weston Ditch, Suffolk. Used by USAF at RAF Mildenhall	u/k–present

Index

RAF GROUPS

1 Group, 73, 76, 78, 81, 88, 91, 94

2 Group, 25, 27

3 Group, 20, 25, 27, 29, 34–35, 39, 44, 48, 58, 73, 75–76, 78–79, 81, 83, 87–88, 91, 93–95, 97, 101, 103, 107, 140–141

3 Group Servicing Unit, 58

4 Group, 21, 27, 78–79

5 Group, 21, 27, 76

6 RCAF Group, 51, 73, 79, 88

8 Group, 75–76, 78–79, 81, 88, 91, 94

RAF SQUADRONS

6 Squadron, 112–113

7 Squadron, 76

9 Squadron, 27–29, 33, 39, 139

15 Squadron, 59, 64, 66–69, 72–74, 76, 78–79, 83, 88–94, 94–96, 140–141

23 Squadron, 102

35 Squadron, 96–97, 140–141

37 Squadron, 27, 29

38 Squadron, 20, 23, 27, 29–30, 140–141

40 (B) Squadron, 21

44 (Rhodesia) Squadron, 93, 95, 140–141

57 Squadron, 93

73 (F) Squadron, 21

75 NZ Squadron, 55–56, 58–59, 140–141

90 Squadron, 59

99 (Madras Presidency) Squadron, 18, 20–22, 24–25, 28, 30, 34–35, 39, 140

115 Squadron, 27–28, 56, 59, 96–97, 140–141

148 Squadron, 25

149 'East India' Squadron, 21, 27–36, 38–45, 48–52, 54–55, 57–59, 96–97, 140–141

207 Squadron, 96–97, 140–141

211 (B) Squadron, 22

214 Squadron, 27, 59

215 Squadron, 27

218 (Gold Coast) Squadron, 34, 59

419 Squadron RCAF, 33, 44, 49–50, 53, 140–141

425 'Alouette' Squadron, 50

464 RAAF Squadron, 51

487 RNZAF Squadron, 51

617 Dam Busters Squadron, 92, 95

622 Squadron, 67, 76, 78–79, 88, 91, 93, 140

MISCELLANEOUS RAF UNITS

No.1 RNZAF Unit, 27

No.3 Blind Approach Training Flight, 35

15 OTU, 27

29 OTU, 83

230 OCU, 97

231 OCU   99

401 Flight, 32

1503 BAT Flight, 51, 58

1505 BAT Flt, 51

1651 HCU, 67, 73

1657 HCU, 68

1403 Met Flt, 32, 58

AMERICAN UNITS

2nd Bombardment Group USAAF, 97

2nd Bomb Wing, 102

5th Bomb Wing, 125, 131

17th Bomb Wing, 109, 127

23rd Air Force, 132–133

42nd Bomb Wing, 124

43rd Bomb Wing, 100

48th TFW, 115–117

93rd Bomb Wing, 99–100, 101–102

96th Bomb Group USAAF, 74

96th Bomb Wing, 125

100th Bomb Group, 124–125

100th ARW, 124–128, 132

306th SAW, 108

316th TAW, 103

339th Bomb Squadron, 5

352nd SOG, 132–136, 142, 144

416th Bomb Wing, 131

509th Bomb Wing, 100, 102

513th TAW, 101, 103, 121, 140–141

GERMAN UNITS

JG 1, 29

2./NJG 6, 73

10./NJG 1, 59

2nd *SS Das Reich* Panzer Division, 79
9th Panzer Division, 79

GENERAL INDEX
Aachen, 33, 76
Aalborg, 33
Acheres, 78
Admiral von Scheer, 28
Advanced Air Striking Force, 27
Alexander, Squadron Leader G.W., 50–51
Allahabad, 14
America, USS, 117, 119
Ames, Captain Richard, 106
Andress, Ursula, 106
Andrews, Squadron Leader L.V., 34
Angers, 76
Apps Beauvoir, 79
Bab al Aziziya, 117
Baines, J.K.C., 16
Baldwin, Stanley, 17
Baldwin, Air Vice-Marshal J.E.A. 'Jackie', 29, 48
Barton Bendish, 27
Barton Mills, 30, 38
Bassingbourn, RAF, 99, 101
Batavia, 39
Batchelor, Group Captain Kenneth. S., 88, 92
Beale, AFB, 109, 112, 119, 127
Beck Row, 9–10, 58
Becker, Oberleutnant Martin 'Tino', 73, 75
Bedford, Duchess of, 21
Bell, Mrs Annie, 10, 17
Benghazi, 116–117, 119
Benina Airport, 118–119
Berlin Blockade, 97
Berlin, 42–44, 69, 72–73, 88, 116
Bertil, Prince, 51
Billancourt, 48
Billington, Sergeant, 42
Bircham Newton, RAF, 32
Black, Tom Campbell, 11, 15–17
Black Magic, DH 88, 14, 16
Blinkers, Sergeant, 51
Boulogne, 34, 76
Bourn, 59
Bremen, 30, 34–35, 39, 45, 50, 88–89
Bremerhaven, 44
Brest, 35, 38–39, 44
Briden, Flight Officer M.F., 30
Broad, Captain Hubert, 11
Brown, Pilot Officer R., 69
Brunsbüttel, 28
Brunswick, 67
Buckle, Squadron Leader R.S., AFC, 35
Caen, 81
Calais, 76

Cambridge, 76
Cap Griz Nez, 76
Cardigan Bay, 95
Cathcart-Jones, Owen, 11
Cavenham, 35
Chamberlain, Neville, 21, 25, 27
Channel Islands, 34
Chemnitz, 88
Cheney, Richard B., 117
Cherbourg, 67
Chowhound, Operation, 91
Churchill, Winston S., 34, 49, 88, 141
Clacton, 34
Clark, Squadron Leader Anthony W.J., 38
Clarkson, Flight Lieutenant Christopher, 11
Cobb, John, 37
Cochran, Jacqueline, 14
Collins, Warrant Officer Len, RAAF, 47, 50
Cologne, 36, 39, 49–50, 63
Coltishall, RAF, 30
Coman, Sergeant Jim, 43, 48
Coney, Sergeant Fred, 67–68, 77, 80
Cookson, Squadron Leader Sawry DSO DFC, 36–37
Coral Sea, USS, 117, 119
Coryat, Pilot Officer, 45
Cresswell, Squadron Leader E.K., 81
Cromer Knoll, 30
Cuxhaven, 29
Cymbalist, Sergeant, 37, 46
D-Day, 76
Debden, RAF, 21
De Gaulle, General Charles, 103
Dengate, Frank Hercules 'Herks', 67–68, 70–72, 76–81, 83
Denmark, 33–34
Deny Flight, Operation, 127, 129–130, 132
Desert Shield, Operation, 120, 124, 137
Desert Storm, Operation, 120, 124, 133
Diamond, Sergeant Frank, 59–61, 64, 66
Dishforth, RAF, 50
Disney operations, 95
Dodge, Operation, 91
Dortmund, 59, 76
Dortmund-Ems Canal, 56
Dresden, 88–90
Dreux, 78
Duguid, Flight Lieutenant A.G., 29
Duisburg, 42, 83
Dunkirk, 33
Düsseldorf, 35, 62
Duxford, RAF, 18, 32
East Coast floods, 95
East Kirkby, RAF, 95
East Wretham, RAF, 55–56, 58

Edwards AFB, 109, 115, 137
Edwards, Mr A.O., 11
Edwards, Air Vice-Marshal, RCAF, 48
El Dorado Canyon, Operation, 117–120
Ely Cathedral, 97
Emden, 34
Empire Day Air Show, 20
Engle, Dan M., 103, 106
Escreet, Flight Lieutenant Ray F. DFM, 66–67
Essen, 49–50, 56, 59, 64
Euston, 36
Evans, Pilot Officer Mike, 43
Exning, 39
Exodus, Operation, 91
Fairford, RAF, 102, 117, 120, 127, 144
Farge, 95
Farnborough Air Show, 108
Fast Relocation, Project, 101
Feltwell, RAF, 27, 29–30, 51
Field, Flight Officer L.R., 30
Field, Group Captain R.M., 34
Flemington racecourse, 16
Ford, President Gerald, 111
Forman, Pilot Officer, 39
Fox, Duggie, 43
Frankfurt, 70, 102, 115
Franks, Pilot Officer J.H., 33, 39
Frecce Tricolori, 109, 122
Friedrichshafen, 70, 73
Friesian Islands, 48, 51, 67
Friston, RAF, 78
Fulton, Wing Commander J. 'Moose' DSO DFC
    AFC, 47, 49–51, 53
Gabriel, General Charles, 118
Gadaffi, Colonel, 116–117
Gee, Sergeant D.A. Tony, 42
Gelsenkirchen, 35
Genoa, 34, 43
Gibraltar, 58
Gilman, Flight Officer H.D., 16
Gneisenau, 28, 39, 42, 44
Goad, Sergeant Jack, 30
Golob, Flight Officer M.M., 74
Gomorrah, Operation, 64
Goodwood, Operation, 81
Gotha, 34
Gough, Sergeant Harold, 56–57
Grant, Peter, 29
Grantham, RAF, 21
Gray, Sergeant George, 36, 38–39, 45–46
Great Snare Hill, 9
Great Yarmouth, 21
Greenham Common, RAF, 103
Gregory, Pilot Officer, 42
Grosvenor House Hotel, 11

Grosvenor House, DH 88, 13, 109, 123
Gulf War, 123–124, 133, 135
Guthrie, Squadron Leader Archibald, 29
Halkett, Flight Sergeant A.M., DFM, 68
Hall, 'Archie', WAAF, 66
Hamburg, 30, 34, 35, 40, 47, 51, 58, 63–64, 88
Hampton, Trevor A. 'Happy', 36–37, 45–46
Hanlon, Sergeant, 39
Hanover, 28, 35
Hardwick, 99
Harraton House, 39
Harris, Sir Arthur T., 20–21, 44, 48–49, 63–64, 93
Harris, Squadron Leader Paul, 28–30
Harrison, Air Vice-Marshal R., 93
Harwell, RAF, 27
Hatfield, 11, 17, 123
Haylock, Bill, 13, 16
Heinsburg, 87
Heligoland Bight, 28, 95
Hendon, RAF, 18, 21
Hiroshima, 95
Homburg, 81, 83
Honington, RAF, 27
Hope, Bob, 106
Hosten, Jennifer, 106
Hurlburt Field, 132–133, 137–138
Hyder, Flight Sergeant Leslie, 56–57
Ilfracombe, 39
Isle de Groix, 48
Istres, 130
Johnson, Major General Leon W., MoH, 107, 140
Jones, General David C., 106
Jordan, Mr W.J., 51, 54
Just Cause, Operation, 133
Juvincourt, 91
Juvisy, 78
KC-135 Stratotanker, 111–112
Kellett, Wing Commander Richard, AFC, 28–30
Kent, Duke of, 53
Keyes, Sir Roger, 35
Kiel, 39, 42, 45, 47
King's Lynn, 29
Kingsley, Wood Sir, 18
Kissinger, Henry, 111
Knight, Dame Laura, 66–67
Korean War, 99
Krefeld, 88
L'Hey, 79
Lakenheath Lode, 97
Lakenheath, RAF, 39, 44, 48–49, 58–59, 97, 99,
    101–103, 111, 115, 117, 120, 141, 144
Lakenheath Warren, 9
Lamason, Squadron Leader P.J. DFC, RNZAF, 78
Lands End, 76
Langley AFB, 106

Le Creusot, 63
Le Havre, 76
Le Mans, 76
Lemon, Flight Officer 'Cheese', 30
Leonard, Mr, 13
Lindholme, RAF, 97
Lingen, 56
Linton-on-Ouse, RAF, 21
Lion Has Wings, The, 28
Lorence, Captain Paul F., 117
Lorient, 48
Loring AFB, Maine, 124
Lossiemouth, RAF, 28, 44
Louvain, 76
Ludlow-Hewitt, Sir Edgar, 21, 93
Malpenza, 130
Malta, 35
Manna, Operation, 91, 94, 141
Mannheim, 39
Mansfield, The Right Honourable Terence,
    42–43, 49–50
Manston, RAF, 99, 101
Marham, RAF, 27, 30, 51, 96
Marseilles, 34
Martlesham Heath, RAF, 43
Massey, The Honourable Vincent, 51, 53
Massy-Palaiseau, 78
McLeod, Sergeant W.M., RNZAF, 59
Melbourne Centenary Air Race, 10–17
Mepal, RAF, 93
Metheringham, RAF, 83
Methwold, RAF, 27
Meyer, Sergeant Paul, 103, 106
Middleton St George, RAF, 51
Middleton, Flight Sergeant Rawdon Hume VC,
    RAAF, 51–52, 55–56
Midgley, Flight Lieutenant D. DFC, 66
Milan, 34
Milch, General Erhard, 21
Mildenhall Met Flight, 32
Miller, Flight Lieutenant Len, 72–73, 75
Moll, J.J., 16
Mollinson (née Johnson), Amy, 11, 14, 16
Mollinson, Jim, 11, 14, 16
Monheim, 33
Mons Wood, 10, 45
Montgomery, Field Marshal, 88
Morhen, Sergeant G.J.P., 39
Morrison, Sergeant D.R., 50
Munich, 21, 59
Münster, 39
Mussolini, Benito, 33
Nagasaki, 95
Nantes, 75
NATO, formation of, 97

Neuss, 83
Newmarket Heath, RAF, 27, 29–30, 35, 39, 55–56
Norway, 30, 33
Nuremberg, 43, 51, 64
Oakington, RAF, 34
Oberon, Merle, 28
Oboe system, 62–63
Oiled, Operation, 44
Ostend, 34, 44
Padua Airfield, 35
Palmdale, 112, 115, 118
Panama, 133
Pangborn Clyde, 13, 16
Paris, 25, 48
Parish, Pilot Officer C.W., 34
Parmentier, K.D., 16
Pathfinder Express, Operation, 103
Pattison, Flight Lieutenant, 49
Peenemünde, 65–66
Petri, Captain Piergianni, 109, 122
Petter, Sergeant R.A., 45–46
Pfeiffer, Unteroffizier Karl-Georg, 59
Phillips, Eric, 64
Pickard, Percy C., 42
Politz, 88
Potsdam, 88
Powell Group Captain J.A. OBE DSO, 35, 45
Powell, Mr Ernie, 10
Prairie Fire, Operation, 116
Prinz Eugen, 44
Provide Comfort, Operation, 127
Provide Comfort II, Operation, 127, 129
Provide Promise, Operation, 127
Pybus, Sergeant Alf, 73
Razzle, 34
Reagan, President Ronald, 116
Red Richard, Project, 100, 102
Restore Hope, Operation, 127
Rhein-Main AFB, 115
Ribas-Dominicci, Captain Fernando L., 117
Richardson, Ralph, 28
Riddlesworth, Flight Officer A.F., 30
Robertson, Sir MacPherson, 10, 17
Rostock, 49, 62
Rota, 118
Rotterdam, 37, 43, 91
Rowley Mile, 27
Royal Jubilee, Review of the RAF, 17–20
Rubin, Bernard, 11
Ruby, Project, 95
Salon, 34
Savard, Flight Lieutenant Logan, 50
'Scatter' plan, 27
Scharnhorst, 28, 39, 42, 44
Scott, Charles W.A., 11, 15–17

Scott, Flight Officer E.G., 30
Sell, Flight Lieutenant Andy, 110
Shiells, Pilot Officer J.L. DFM, 59
Shuttleworth Trust, 17
Sidi Bilal Naval Base, 117
Sigonella, NAS, 130, 132
Sinkum, Operation, 95
Skipper, Henry, 13, 17–18
Smith, Captain Ross, 11
Smithers, Squadron Leader, 68
South Ruislip, 107–108, 124, 140
Southern Watch, Operation, 129
Spasm, Operation, 93
Spiers, Flight Officer J.H.C., 30
SR-71A 'Blackbird', 108–109, 112–113, 115–116,
   118–119, 127, 137, 143
St Pierre, Squadron Leader Joe, 50
St John's Church, Beck Row, 91
Stewart, Flight Lieutenant J.B., 29
Stradishall, RAF, 21, 25, 39, 64, 97
Sylt, 29, 33
Target For Tonight, 42
Tasker, Sergeant Frank W., 88
Teague, Flight Sergeant T.R., RNZAF, 76
Thatcher, Margaret, 112, 117
Thor missile, 103
Thorpe Abbots, 126
Thunderclap, Operation, 88
'Tiger Force', 95
Tirpitz, 44
Toulouse, 79
Trappes, 76
Tripoli, 116–117
Turin, 34–35, 51, 55
Turner, Colonel Roscoe, 13, 16
Turner, Flight Officer F.W.S., 30

Turtle, Flight Lieutenant R.W.A., 44
Upper Heyford, RAF, 51, 58, 117
Valley, RAF, 104
VE Day, 91
Venice, 35
Versailles, 78
Villers-Bocage, 79
Vintage Pair Display Team, 109–110, 121
Waalhaven, 33
Waddington, RAF, 83
Waller, Kenneth, 11, 14
Wanne-Eickel, 88
Warboys, RAF, 75
Warren, Sergeant Ronald, 37–38
Waterbeach, RAF, 39, 73
Watkins, Wing Commander W.D.G., DSO DFC
   DFM, 83, 87
Watts, Harry, 42
Wesel, 88
West Berlin, 116
West Malling, RAF, 102, 107
West Row, 9–10, 58
Westcott, RAF, 91
Weston Zoyland, RAF, 44
Wilhelmshaven, 27–30, 33
Wilkie, Sergeant High 'Wendell', 59–61, 64
'Window', 64
Wilson, Harold, 106
Wimereaux, 76
Wing, RAF, 91
Woburn, 21
Wolfe, Squadron Leader, 50
Wratting Common, RAF, 67
Wright, John H., 13–14
Wyton, RAF, 28